AMERICAN ANTEBELLUM FIDDLING

American Made Music Series

ADVISORY BOARD

David Evans, General Editor
Barry Jean Ancelet
Edward A. Berlin
Joyce J. Bolden
Rob Bowman
Susan C. Cook
Curtis Ellison
William Ferris
John Edward Hasse
Kip Lornell
Bill Malone
Eddie S. Meadows
Manuel H. Peña
Wayne D. Shirley
Robert Walser

AMERICAN ANTEBELLUM FIDDLING

Chris Goertzen

University Press of Mississippi • Jackson

The University Press of Mississippi is the scholarly publishing agency of
the Mississippi Institutions of Higher Learning: Alcorn State University,
Delta State University, Jackson State University, Mississippi State University,
Mississippi University for Women, Mississippi Valley State University,
University of Mississippi, and University of Southern Mississippi.

www.upress.state.ms.us

The University Press of Mississippi is a member of the Association of University Presses.

Copyright © 2020 by University Press of Mississippi
All rights reserved
Manufactured in the United States of America

First printing 2020

∞

Library of Congress Cataloging-in-Publication Data

Names: Goertzen, Chris, author.
Title: American antebellum fiddling / Chris Goertzen.
Other titles: American made music series.
Description: Jackson : University Press of Mississippi, 2020. | Series: American made music series | Includes bibliographical references and index. | Identifiers: LCCN 2019031021 (print) | LCCN 2019031022 (ebook) | ISBN 9781496827272 (hardback) | ISBN 9781496827289 (trade paperback) | ISBN 9781496827296 (epub) | ISBN 9781496827302 (epub) | ISBN 9781496827319 (pdf) | ISBN 9781496827326 (pdf)
Subjects: LCSH: Fiddle tunes—United States—19th century—History and criticism. | Fiddlers—United States. | Fiddle tunes—United States—19th century. | BISAC: MUSIC / Genres & Styles / Folk & Traditional
Classification: LCC ML3551.4 .G64 2929 (print) | LCC ML3551.4 (ebook) | DDC 787.20973/09034—dc23
LC record available at https://lccn.loc.gov/2019031021
LC ebook record available at https://lccn.loc.gov/2019031022

British Library Cataloging-in-Publication Data available

CONTENTS

ACKNOWLEDGMENTS
- VII -

INTRODUCTION
- IX -

PART ONE

Fiddle Tunes in Music Commonplace Books
Young Musicians Illustrate American Taste at the Beginning of the Nineteenth Century
- 1 -

PART TWO

Charles Morris Cobb, William Sidney Mount, and
Their Large Manuscript Music Collections from the 1840s to the 1850s
- 61 -

PART THREE

Fiddlers Moving South, and West, and away from Notation
- 139 -

NOTES
- 217 -

BIBLIOGRAPHY
- 219 -

INDEX
- 225 -

ACKNOWLEDGMENTS

My thanks for the friendship, encouragement, and expert aid of Paul F. Wells, Steve Green, Harry Bolick, Andy Kuntz, and dozens of other fine fiddlers interested in the history of fiddling. Teams of librarians and archivists at these institutions gave unstinting aid: Library of Congress, Music Division; New York Public Library at Lincoln Center, Music Division; Leahy Library, Vermont Historical Society; George J. Mitchell Department of Special Collections and Archives, Hawthorne-Melville Library, Bowdoin College; The Long Island Museum of American Art, History and Carriages Collection; Music and Performing Arts Library, University of Illinois; Frank Melville Jr. Memorial Library, State University of New York at Stony Brook; and Dutchess County Historical Society. And again, I'm grateful for the peaceful writing environment of the Brahmshaus in Baden-Baden, Germany. My wife, Brahms scholar Valerie Goertzen, got us invited to stay there a third time in summer 2018, and parts of the third section of this book took shape there. My most fervent thanks go to Valerie, who has traveled with me to innumerable research destinations, helped corral endless parades of books (and manuscripts, and helpful people), and then served as patient sounding board and meticulous reader. And finally, thanks again to Craig Gill and his helpers at the University Press of Mississippi; they made the final stages of putting this book together as painless as possible.

INTRODUCTION

This book concerns American fiddling from about 1805 to the start of the Civil War. This period is the first for which we have generous amounts of contemporary testimony about fiddlers and fiddling. We also are lucky enough to have inherited generous helpings of fiddle tunes written down in ways that give us a good degree of confidence that we can imagine how they sounded in performance. Some readers will be especially interested in musing about the changing nature of fiddling and in the details of the historical evidence that allow this speculation, while others will simply want to play the music. In order to serve both constituencies, I have split the pages fairly evenly between prose and transcribed or photographed melodies.

Today, we recognize fiddling when we see and hear performances. There are sizeable repertoires of fiddle tunes, mostly two-strain lively melodies in types that fit the general characters and tempos historically associated with certain dance genres. These tunes are performed mostly by fiddlers—musicians holding violins, but employing fiddle performance techniques and producing timbres and accentual patterns somewhat distinct from those characteristic of art music, though covering a wide span in every way; fiddling is less standardized in repertoire and techniques than is art violin playing.

In the antebellum period, the word "violin" was normally used, not "fiddle." When we conceive of fiddling as the meeting of the inherited physical violin with oral traditions of repertoire and technique, we must keep in mind that this was not a single encounter: the complex of fiddle traditions has frequently been invigorated by fresh interactions with all aspects of the art violin. It is very lucky for those of us interested in the history of fiddling that the vernacular and more cultivated approaches to making music on the violin have common ground, and have overlapped in various ways for centuries. Many living fiddlers read music to some extent, as quite a few fiddlers of past generations did. Many fiddle tunes, while flourishing primarily in oral tradition, have also been written down and even published repeatedly. It is this rich body of cultural materials shared between oral and written traditions that allowed this book to be researched.

How can we best ferret out oral tradition from written evidence? There's plenty that we will never be able to know, but a worthwhile amount that we can know, or surmise, or guess, or just enjoy speculating about. The basic materials that allow us to extract evidence of oral tradition from written tradition are these:

INTRODUCTION

testimony (letters, narratives), variation between notated versions of given tunes, mixed competence in the use of notation, and even having skilled transcribers of the past notate specific ways that given fiddlers performed given tunes.

This book falls into three sections. The first part focuses on young fiddlers/violinists who copied down tunes from published collections during the first decades of the nineteenth century. Early printed collections of tunes available to American fiddlers were either imported from Great Britain, or if published in this country, still closely resembled the British models. However, a few tunes with American names and of American composition turn up in even the first substantial American published compilations of instrumental tunes. These collections were not issued in large runs, and were apt to be rare in the countryside, meaning most of the young United States. Aspiring instrumentalists who did not own given published collections would often borrow copies of those collections from their neighbors, and write out the tunes they intended to learn. Their selections regularly included handfuls of tunes that seem to have been in oral as well as printed tradition. These young instrumentalists thus offered windows on their individual tastes and personal repertoires, which, taken together, constitute our first picture of American musical taste and provide information about early American fiddling.

In the 1840s and later, music publishing became easier and markets grew. As printed general collections of tunes for instrumentalists became both much larger and more affordable, the practice of keeping music commonplace books faded. However, two men whose lives are easy to trace compiled large manuscript collections of tunes that they played on the fiddle/violin. Charles M. Cobb, of Woodstock, Vermont, wrote out thousands of melodies in a book that he labeled *The Universal Musician*. His aim was comprehensiveness, and his manuscript is a crowded mess full of information about music in his time and place. How the contents of his book changed during the years he wrote in it illustrate how the fiddle yielded to bands in terms of primacy in increasingly crowded New England, yet didn't entirely lose its place in musical life.

At the same time, portraitist and genre painter William Sidney Mount of Stony Brook, New York, also fiddled, and was a member of a circle of similarly literate and skilled fiddlers. He enjoyed making music and didn't mind earning money from what never quite became a second profession. In these two musicians' collective story, we see fiddling becoming more cultivated and self-conscious, tilting in the direction of art music. Nevertheless, Cobb's and Mount's transcribed music included old fiddle tunes played in at least partly traditional ways, along with tunes edging in the direction of art composition and requiring considerable technique (i.e., position work and specified articulations).

The final section of this decidedly heterogeneous book follows fiddling on the antebellum segment of a long journey that would deemphasize genteel cultivation, fiddling as it survived and developed in the hands of musicians moving south and west, and "traveling" in any case away from the use of notation. The evidence here is the most pertinent to fiddling as distinct from violin playing, but

INTRODUCTION

consequently the hardest to make coalesce into musical sound. This section will itself fall into three parts. First comes a brief but careful look at the first published collection of southern fiddle tunes, George Knauff's *Virginia Reels* (most parts of which were initially published in 1839). Here I condense many of the thoughts expressed in my book on this topic (Goertzen 2017), add supplementary evidence, and finally offer a performing edition of the tunes. Second, I explore what one can do with contemporary prose testimony—letters and other narratives. I will take bits of testimony including tune names and descriptions—as my sample, an anecdote describing fiddling at an 1835 picnic by garrulous Texas pioneer Gideon Lincecum—and see how far a few words describing fiddling can be pushed in the direction of replicable musical sound. In the last part of this final section, the main source of notation will be a problematic collection on deposit at the Library of Congress, a set of transcriptions of tunes as played by a long-lived fiddler who formed his repertoire in western Virginia before the Civil War. The transcriptions were made by his fiddler grandson, a man of great energy but with mixed abilities in the craft of transcription. This is the playing of David Hamblen as remembered by his grandson, Armeanous Porter Hamblen.

PART ONE

Fiddle Tunes in Music Commonplace Books

Young Musicians Illustrate American Taste at the Beginning of the Nineteenth Century

In the early 1800s, even though the United States had achieved political independence from Great Britain, the new country remained a sparsely populated British province in terms of culture. Nearly all of the few music professionals had been born and trained in England (apart from a smaller contingent of German immigrants). The sheet music and tune anthologies these men issued were of British music plus a few new songs and marches following British practice but titled to respond to local patriotism (e.g., "Washington's March"). The dissemination of this published music faced obstacles that are now helpful for diagnosing an emerging local element. Books were expensive then, and personal libraries tiny. Since stocks of even the most popular tune compilations were slender, many of the teenagers who wished to play violin, flute, and other treble instruments copied tunes from music books that they did not own, books they encountered in their neighbors' libraries. They also might acquire such tunes at a level or two removed from the published forms, if they copied out attractive melodies from the personal handwritten tune books maintained by their friends. Either way, they wrote out their selections in their own pre-bound manuscript books.

"Commonplace books" are what we call individuals' compilations of memorabilia (proverbs, poems, recipes, or on occasion pieces of music) recorded by hand in blank books. Instrumentalists and singers in many English- and German-speaking areas maintained melody-filled commonplace books during the late eighteenth and early nineteenth centuries. This was the heyday of the practice, the era when laboriously copying melodies was possible and practical, a reasonable thing to do. The first truly American element in secular American music (apart from the obvious one of enjoying patriotic compositions in pan-British style) was the complex process of selection, of Americans making choices among British musical items. The young musicians were gathering up tunes that they intended to learn, and thus were documenting their collective musical taste, and, if they followed through and did learn the tunes, their actual musical practice. Their music commonplace books included song airs, marches, and dances, generally entered in no particular order, though tunes in given genres sometimes were copied in clusters. The tunes are almost always notated in unhesitant hands in instrumental (beamed) notation, reflecting the fact that the compilers were not transcribing from live performances, but rather working directly from their friends' or neighbors' published or handwritten collections.

ARTHUR McARTHUR, BEFORE HE BECAME A PROMINENT LAWYER

Some compilers of these manuscripts signed them or can be identified in some other way. A few left enough traces in the historical record that we can get to know them. The first music commonplace I ever saw (during my graduate years at the University of Illinois) was conveniently signed "Philander Seward's Musical Deposit." Seward was a fairly common name, but *Philander*—I could track him down! Decades later, during a visit to the New York Public Library, I encountered a splendid collection with the name Arthur McArthur appearing on the flyleaf; the inside of the cover bears a bookplate identifying the book as from McArthur's library in Limington, a small town in Maine. A number of the tunes in it go below the compass of the flute, that is, onto the G string of the violin: this qualified this commonplace book as fodder for this study. McArthur turned out to be unusually easy to research, and his music commonplace book is much larger than the Seward collection; we will look at it first.

McArthur wrote these words at the start of the manuscript: Fryeburg Academy, Dec. 25th, 1805; it must have been a Christmas present. On the facing page he wrote Bowdoin College, August 28th, 1808, the date he matriculated there (he would be part of the school's second graduating class, in 1810). Bowdoin's special collections library houses the "McArthur Family Papers" (n.d.), in which Arthur McArthur figures prominently. Indeed, this rich evidence survives largely because he would grow up to be a respected lawyer with a substantial career and rich family life. But professional success and social prominence were far in the future when he wrote tunes in his music commonplace book. He was a high-spirited—indeed, unruly—boy. He grew up on a large farm in the thinly populated countryside and, as noted in the opening pages of his music commonplace book, attended a nearby boarding school and then college. He maintained this manuscript during his school years and for a few years after that. A few other musicians added entries a generation later, but contrasting handwriting makes clear who recorded what.

The McArthur family papers center on three generations of this clan. The most prominent member of the middle generation—and our subject—Arthur McArthur Sr. was born January 14, 1790. He was the ninth of eleven children of John McArthur (1745–1816), a native of Scotland and the third settler of the town of Limington, and Mary Miller McArthur (1753–1835). In 1767, when he was seventeen, John McArthur moved from Perth (north of Edinburgh—a busy crossroads then and now) to Cape Elizabeth, on the coast of Maine south of Portland. In 1775, he and his growing family shifted about forty miles inland to the banks of the Little Ossipee River, about three miles south of the future town of Limington. John worked with lumber, then became a farmer, and served several civic functions in time, including that of deputy sheriff (Ring 1991, 11–14).

John McArthur's son Arthur was rambunctious. In an early letter written home from the Fryeburg Academy on April 17, 1804, he described a schoolyard fight with outward disapproval but inward relish: the loser "got his ass kicked very seriously." Arthur kept a handwriting copybook that year, and, doubtless under the orders of a teacher, wrote a full page of each of two cautionary maxims: "Sobriety is Commendable" and "Quit Vicious Companions." His sister Mary urged him to "be pious" (letter, Apr. 4, 1807). In a description of Bowdoin campus life, he wrote to his family on November 11, 1808 (toward the end of his first semester there), he went into detail in laying out his choices among friends: "Here you [can] choose the sober and steady friend, the light and airy, the pleasant and humorous, the dissipated and riotous." He vowed to dodge the "quicksand" that had engulfed so many of his "unfortunate fellow students." A bit later, he told his brother that he tried to "avoid the Scylla of a wine cask and the Charybdis of a brandy bottle" (letter, May 3, 1809). His success in that endeavor seems to have been mixed; family biographer Elizabeth Ring notes that he was suspended several times from Bowdoin (1991, 40). Nevertheless, he displayed considerable intellectual breadth and energy while there. I am especially impressed by elaborate diagrams he made of advanced problems in geometry; he displayed a formidable capacity for working hard when he chose to do so.

McArthur grew up, settled down, and became a community leader. His later business cards read "Arthur McArthur, Counsellor at Law, Limington, York County, Maine. Practicing Before Court of Claims, Washington, D. C." Although he worked away from home quite often, he was an attentive and compassionate family man and energetic contributor to the health of the community. A majority of adult males served in the military in some capacity in his day—he was a major and later lieutenant colonel in the local militia. He was a freemason, a school board member and trustee of Limerick Academy (a boys' school he helped found), and owned pews in his church. Parallel to his love for melodies—many of which were traditional—he pursued an antiquarian bent with a local focus: he gathered materials for a history of Limington and environs, though he would die before this project could be completed. He supported concerts, tried to assemble subscribers for a dancing school, and negotiated and took part in the purchase of an organ for his church (one with seven stops, a sturdy case, and a reasonable price).

In a book celebrating Bowdoin College, institutional historian Nehemiah Cleaveland summarized that while McArthur's "college course was of doubtful promise, his subsequent career has made all right" (1882, 162). In 1829, Arthur married Sarah Prince Miltimore (1805–1881), daughter of the Rev. William Miltimore of Falmouth, Maine. Several of the McArthurs' six children moved west.

In this family's share of a nationwide tragedy, sons fought on both sides in the Civil War. Arthur Jr. (1830–1862; Bowdoin 1850) taught school in the Midwest and South, putting down roots in Sabine Parish, Louisiana, as a teacher and lawyer in 1859. He joined the Confederate army as a major in the Sixth Louisiana regiment, and was killed in battle at Winchester, Virginia, on May 25, 1862. William (1832–1917; Bowdoin 1853) served with the Eighth Maine and rose to the rank of brevet brigadier general. He inherited his father's responsibilities operating the family farm and in various civic functions. Catherine (1834–1864), the only daughter and the most avid musician among the children, graduated from Mount Holyoke Seminary in 1853 and taught school in Maine and in Flint, Michigan (1860–1863). In sum, Arthur McArthur Sr. was from a respectable and prosperous family, was successful in his profession, and lived a full and apparently largely happy life. He died on November 29, 1874.

McArthur said nothing about his musical activities in his letters. However, his sister Mary wrote to him soon after he first left home to go to boarding school: "I am at present in a perfect state of health, but cannot spend my time so [enjoy]able as if you were here to play us a fine tune on your flute" (letter, Jan. 1, 1803). Many years later, his daughter Catherine noted in her diary that she and a friend had visited him in his office of an evening, and enjoyed hearing him play the flute. Much earlier, in a diary he kept briefly while at boarding school, he noted on many dates that he attended singing school. How he learned violin and flute remains unclear, though that he learned to play more than one instrument was not the least bit unusual.

The two letters mentioning his flute playing for female family members are not matched by anecdotes describing his fiddling, perhaps partly because we have no letter or other testimony about him accompanying dances. However, the family papers include a music commonplace book written in a hand other than McArthur's, and signed at the end "Thomas W. Shannon, Esq., Master Musician in the District of Maine." One tune, "Durand's [Durang's] Hornpipe," dips below the flute and fife range to the violin's g string. Shannon's book includes just nineteen tunes and the start of another, and just one of these tunes also appears in McArthur's own commonplace book. One plausible explanation for the small size of this overlap would be that Shannon was among McArthur's teachers, and that the little book Shannon signed was made as a teaching tool and always owned by McArthur. If that was the case, there would have been no need for McArthur to record those tunes in his own book. Also, the range of this version of "Durang's Hornpipe" offers some additional modest evidence that McArthur fiddled.

ARTHUR MCARTHUR'S MUSIC COMMONPLACE BOOK

McArthur's own music book is unusually large and diverse. Most such manuscripts contain entries representing many different musical genres, but concentrate on one or a few, usually secular tunes for a solo instrument. Some other compilers emphasized songs, or pieces for keyboard. McArthur's manuscript is not quite a grab bag, but it is striking in that it encompasses very different substantial sections, and so offers us a chance to get acquainted with a broad expanse of music heard in the United States during the early 1800s. It includes opening instructional portions for his instruments, songs, marches, a group of tunes miscellaneous in genre for a solo instrument, religious tunes, pieces for keyboard, trios, and a few novelty items. I will lay out the book first—both in summary and with a full table of contents—then look closely at a few representative tunes.

The early parts of the book may trace a natural progression in terms of psychology. First we have what McArthur felt he ought to learn. The first dozen pages are meticulously copied directions for playing his instruments, first the violin, then the flute. Next come just a few hymns, the brevity of this section perhaps signaling boyish impatience with obligatory good behavior. He then recorded a handful of songs, in most cases writing out the melody with the first verse of text underlaid, then adding the rest of the lyrics below. Interspersed in this section are two texts without melodies, and a few songs where the lyrics are not given. This section gradually becomes more heterogeneous, then ends with a handful of songs laid out as were the first ones to round out the first fifty pages of the commonplace book.

The collection then loosens up a little, with a novelty tune, the intriguing "Riney [Ranz] des Vaches" (the famous Swiss herdman's song said to have inspired deadly nostalgia among Swiss mercenaries), followed by a handful of miscellanea before a short section of "Lessons" the purpose of which is unclear. Then we enter the book's longest section, of trios (two parts in treble clef, and one in bass clef). Over half of the tunes in this section of the book are marches.

Next, a short series of hymns (also in three-part settings) precedes a similarly short section of what is clearly a much later filling in of empty space by a music teacher—we leap from pieces dated 1814 to 1826. Then we return to McArthur's handwriting, and finally encounter the material that we as students of the fiddle have been waiting for, thirty-eight tunes on just eleven pages of single-line instrumental melodies, many of which remain familiar to fiddlers today. It is as if a short, relatively conventional music commonplace book compiled by an instrumentalist expecting to play alone has been sandwiched among contrasting ingredients. Finally, following a song on a grand staff comes a big surprise, a march for five instruments. This takes up the top three-fifths of several pages; some single-line melodies are fit in below to use up the space.

After this comes the last major part of the book. We jump ahead in time to 1826, to an extended series of pieces for piano, many of them with detailed fingerings; Arthur McArthur's daughter Catherine seems to be at work here. In the midst of this section, a music teacher recorded many tunes. At the end of the book, two blank pages precede an index composed in the style of the time, ordering by first letter but not worrying about the following letters. Many pieces are dated, and the dates tend to start over when new categories of tunes enter the picture. This evidence suggests that McArthur originally intended to group all of the entries by genre, though the later incremental filling in of nearly all blank space by him and by others confused the issue.

In Figure 1, I list all of the contents of this big music commonplace book and give some additional information, starting with the page range for a given section (referencing page numbers as written in by McArthur). Categories of tunes (named by me) are in bold print; a contrasting fancy font and underlining marks the names of items that I later present in photographs and discuss.

Now I will look more closely at a very few entries in the commonplace book, the ones listed in an elaborate font within the above chart.

The first page of McArthur's book illustrates very compact "Instructions for the Violin." The top paragraph reads:

> The violin must be held with the left hand, and resting between the nob of the thumb and the first finger, leaning the body of the instrument against the collarbone with the elbow immediately underneath, that the fingers may more easily touch the strings. The bow must be held between the thumb and fingers of the right hand, just above the nut, the hair being turned inward against the outside of the thumb and the fingers placed at the distance from each other upon the wood, so as to command the whole length of the bow.

These directions leave a great deal up to the student to decide. For instance, the instruction reading "leaning the body [of the instrument] against the collarbone" is vague. If the violin rested *above* the collarbone, it could be gripped between the collarbone and the player's chin, giving enough support that the left hand would be relatively free of that function, and could move around like that of an art violinist, but if the collarbone was not assigned that job, the left hand would be less free to shift out of first position. Also, the description of the grip of the left hand doesn't specify whether or not the palm of that hand touches the neck (as is often the case for fiddlers) or is held free to allow vibrato and, again, facilitate shifts. Thus, these directions don't push the instrumentalist firmly in the direction of either violin or of fiddle technique.

The rest of this page and most of the remainder of the pages of advice on "violin" performance concern where to put the left-hand fingers to get given pitches (including specifying how upper positions worked, but again only in terms of finding pitches). These meager remarks actually constitute a more generous serving of technical directions than many contemporary published violin methods/collections contained! Most violinists/fiddlers in the young United States learned face-to-face—sometimes from European-trained immigrant musicians, but more often from other fiddlers/violinists of minimal formal training. In sum, the conveying of technique from one instrumentalist to another remained almost entirely in oral tradition. Aspiring violinists/fiddlers had little or no choice in the matter, particularly if they grew up in rural areas, as did most young musicians, even if they were scions of prosperous and influential families like Arthur McArthur.

FIGURE 1. CONTENTS OF ARTHUR McARTHUR'S MUSIC COMMONPLACE BOOK	
Pages 1–18	**Section 1. Teaching materials**: 4 pages about the violin, the **FIRST PAGE** photographed; pp. 5–18 are for the flute. For both instruments, most of the prose and diagrams help the player locate pitches rather than going into detail about technique.
19–20	**Section 2. Religious**: Alpha (a4), Portugal (a3) and Winter (single line), all 1806.
21–28	**Section 3. Songs**: The Mason's Daughter (lyrics only); the rest are melodies underlaid with the first verse of text, with the other verses given in blocks; all tunes are dated 1806: Masonic Hymn, Bonny Jean of Aberdeen, Nae Luck About the House, Life Let Us Cherish, and **SAVOURNA DELISH**. Pages 29–36 are missing.
37–46	**Section 4. Misc.**: (often songs, even if not texted here): Few Happy Matches, by Watts (text only, 1809), Low Down in the Broom (vocal notation; no text), Mary's Dream (song), Blue Bells of Scotland (no text, instrumental notation), Exile of Erin (vocal notation, no text), The Streamlet that Flow'd round her Cot (same), Roslin Castle (just one line, in D Minor; still 1809, notation now instrumental), Roslin Castle (whole piece, in usual key of E Minor, marked Feb. 1812), Glasgow Lasses (June 1811), Quibilano (Feb. 1812), Masonic Air (June 10, 1812), Silver Star, Horse Races (vocal notation, Feb. 10, 1813, Baltimore (Feb. 11, 1813), Humours of Glenn (grand staff, 1809), Hob or Nob (1810), Jackson's Bottle of Claret, The Kiss
47–52	**Section 5. Songs** (melody with first verse of text underlaid, other verses given): Sterne's Maria (1810, as are next few), Ye Lads of True Spirit, Leander, The Galley Slave (not texted), Owen (texted), For England When with Favoring Gale (no text)
52	**Section 6. Single piece**: Riney [Ranz] des Vaches, "the famous air by which the Swiss are said to be so powerfully reminded of their country" (grand staff, 1810)
53–56	**Section 7. Mostly sung**: Oscar's Ghost (return to single staff), There's Three Good Fellows Down in Yon Glens, Megan Oh! Oh Megan Ee (grand staff, plus text), Irish (three lines, top two with treble clefs, top texted), Bangor Castle, Anthem (texted melody, 1807), Anthem (single line in vocal notation, but no text, 1807)
57–82	**Section 8. Trios, mostly marches**: two treble lines and one bass (unless otherwise marked): Pleyel's Hymn (1808), One Two and Begin by Herrick, Duetto by Olmstead (a2, both treble clefs), Fresh and Strong (same), Belknap's March (single line), Lessons 1, 2, 3, 4, and 5 (staffs a3, but not completely filled out—hard to tell what points are being made; 1806 for this and following ones), Adam and Eve (a3, two treble and one bass, as are remainder in this section), Vice President's March, God Save America, Reed's March, Major Minor, Dirge by Herrick, Litchfield March, Pepperell March, Oxford Camp, March in the Blue Beard, Rise Columbia, Bonaparte's Grand March (bass line left blank), Pauvre Madelon, Massachusetts, March, French Air, O Dear Mama, Southegan Bridge by Herrick, Health to All Sweet Lasses, No. 51 March #2 (only part of top treble line filled in), Lord Barnett's March (1807, as are following), Grovenor's March, Dorsetshire March, Prince Eugene's March, **SWISS GUARD'S MARCH** (with this piece, we shift to 1808), Lesson by Morelli, Handel's Clarionett
83–90	**Section 9. More hymns**: Arlington (Dr. Arne; these are a3 and texted; 1810), Arundel (marked Williams College), Bridgewater, Christmas, **PORTUGUESE HYMN** (Dixon's College), Justice (Dixon's College), Holy (Sacchini), Newell (Dr. Arne; Mar. 1814), Wareham (Dr. Arne)
91–95	**Section 10. Inserted later**: In the margin of an entry of a tune presented a3, Cathleen McChree, was written: "Arranged for the flute, violin, and Violincello by J. Plimpton, Professor of Music, Limington, Oct. 22, 1826." Other pieces here—each a3—are Waltz and The King of Prussia's March

96–107	Section 11. Single-line instrumental tunes. This is the section most like the majority of other music commonplace books of the day, and the section of most interest in the studying of fiddling. Boyn[e] Water (1806, as are all until further notice), Young Widow, Haunted Tavern, O'er the Hills and Far Away, Humours of Boston, College Hornpipe, Chester Castle, The Bells [Belles?] of New York, Appollo Turn'd Shepherd, The Seasons, Highland Reel, Saw Ye My Father, Fisher's Hornpipe, Lord McDonald's Reel, Money Musk, Nong Tong Paw, Chorus Jigg, Money in Both Pockets, Four Times Over, Irish Wash[er]woman, Jenny Nettles, Sweet Ellen, The Indian Philosopher (1808, this tune and following), **LOGAN WATER, LANGOLEE, VICAR AND MOSES, ROSE TREE,** [untitled], Pantheon Cotillion, Mulberry Tree, French Tune (1809), Ricket's Ride (1807), McDonald's Reel (1808), Chargoggagoagomanchagogg (1809, this tune and following), La Belle Catherine (a2, both treble), Hark Away, High Pretty Martin Toploc, When the Hollow Drum, Silver Moon.
107–113	**Section 12. Ensemble tunes, with single-line tunes fitted beneath**: Harlington (grand staff, texted), Gen. MacDonald's March by H. Knowlton (this area likely penned by Knowlton, all on the entered date of Jan. 14, 1814. This piece a5: primo, secundo, 1st horn, 2nd horn, bassoon. This piece takes up the top three-fifths or so of several pages, so that the remainder of tunes in this section are single lines fit into the remaining space). Doct. Swazey's Fancy, Tink a Tink (Nov. 16, 1816), Morepang (same date), Spirit of Ireland, Hurra, or the Swiss Battle Song (false start; see below)
114–154	**Section 13. Piano pieces**, all on grand staff, most with fingerings written in meticulously; the hand could well be McArthur's in early parts of the section, but yields to another hand later (probably Mr. Plimpton). French Air (Oct. 31, 1825), Foots Minuet, Turkish Quick Step, Shawl Dance, Den Ant de las Silas, Mozart's Favorite Waltz, Limington March, Heyden's March, Paddy O'Rafferty (single line, but with advice to play d as a drone), Serenade (flute, violin, 'cello; see fragment on right of photo of preceding), Waltz (a3, "Composed by J. Plimpton. N.B. This Waltz was arranged/written in Bb for the Kent Bugle obligato. For Master George Frederic Handel. Plimpton transposed to D for flute obligato. Oct. 4, 1826"), Grand March in Pizzaro (a3), Minuetto (a3), Hurra, or the Swiss Battle Song (grand staff, with treble texted), Blue-Eyed Mary (as previous), Ere Around the Huge Oak (as previous), Trumpet March (not texted), Katharine Ogre (melody, texted; Aug. 7, 1828), Auld Robin Gray (as previous), Willis Grand March (return to grand staff), Willis Quick Step, Waltz by Beethoven (grand staff, with fingerings written in here and following), Andante. The Surprise, by Haydn (not just fingerings, but also dynamics for just this and the next two pieces), Quick Step [by] Haydn, Austrian Waltz by Haydn, The Nightengale by Haydn, Courland Quadrille by Haydn, Danish Waltz, la Grande Entré, Sta Cecilia, Fancy by Ignace Pleyel, Marquis of Pombal's March, Austria Grand Imperial March; two blank pages, then:
The rest	**Index** (organized by the first letter of each entry, but not alphabetized within the sections defined by that first letter; this was normal practice at the time).

Figure 1. Contents of Arthur McArthur's music commonplace book

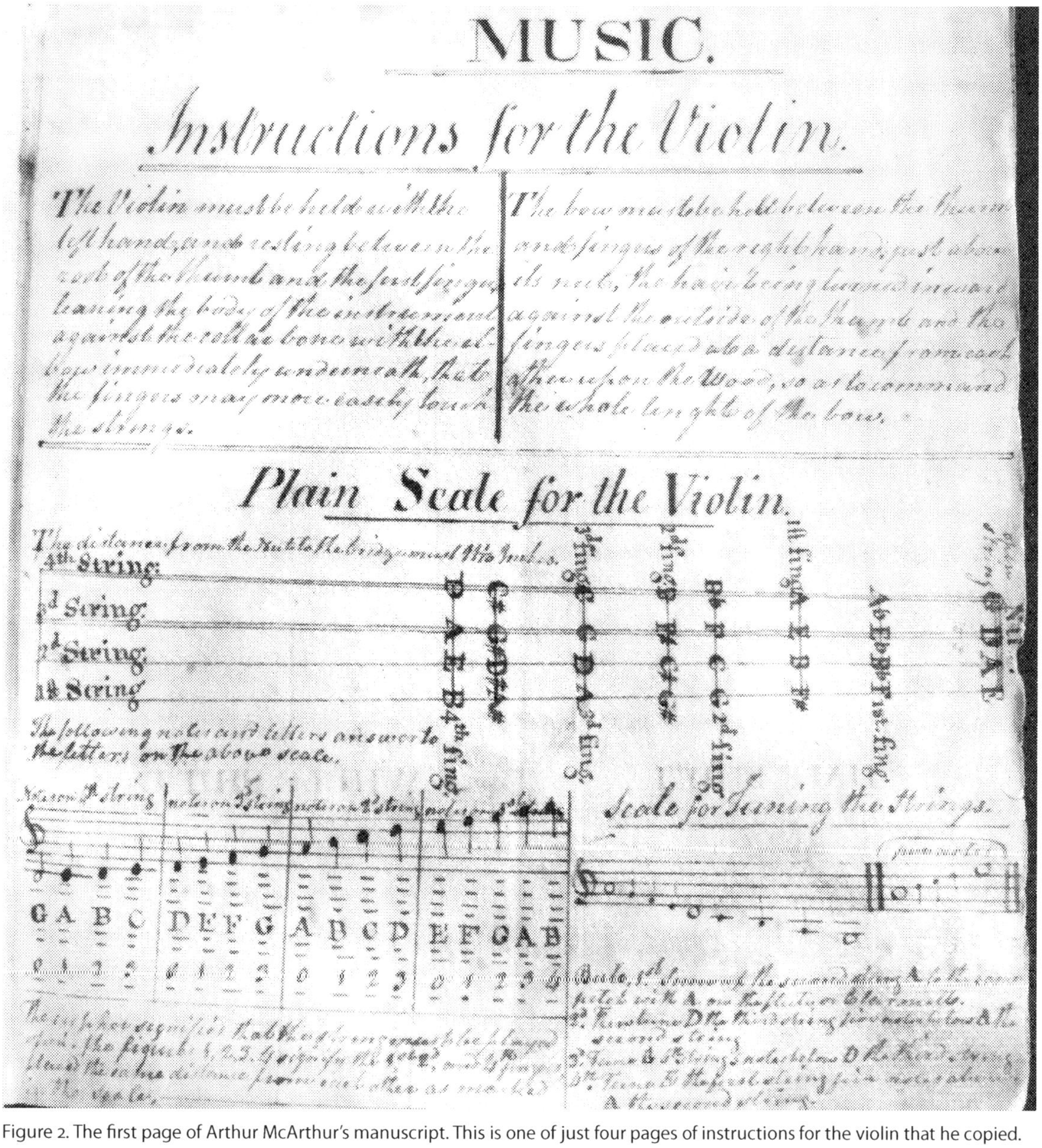

Figure 2. The first page of Arthur McArthur's manuscript. This is one of just four pages of instructions for the violin that he copied.

The directions for playing the flute that follow delve a little more deeply into performance practice, including, for instance, brief discussion of ornamentation. But McArthur followed this instructional section with many pages of vocal music, perhaps because he had been to numerous "singing schools" as a young boy. He first essayed three hymns that he could have learned in that environment ("Alpha," "Portugal," and "Winter") on pages 19–20 of the commonplace book. (All three are dated 1806 by him; he habitually noted the dates he entered tunes in the book.) But his beginning his personal anthology with sacred music was a false start. He jumped from the paltry two pages of hymns to the lyrics (only) of "The Mason's Daughter" (the gist: a freemason's daughter can yield to the charms only of a youth whose fine character will naturally lead to him becoming a freemason). Then a long section emphasizing songs follows. In the first pages of this section (pp. 22–26), he entered songs using a common format. The melody, presented in vocal notation (in which most of the notes are separate rather than beamed together), has the first verse of the text underlaid; all of the remaining verses of lyrics then follow below.

I chose to look closely at the last song in this section, "Savourna Delish." I selected it partly because it had enough contrast in tone that it would reproduce adequately in a photograph. Also, the history of the tune exemplified a common pattern of usage, the theme of the lyrics was pertinent, and the mode of the tune exemplified how many songs and fiddle tunes dodged being in a conventional form of major, instead employing a partially gapped scale (in which the fourth degree, here *f*, was skipped over in the lower octave).

"Savourna Delish," like "The Rose Tree," was an old tune retexted and re-popularized in the ballad opera *Poor Soldier*. Most of the eighteen airs in that much-performed work were adapted from oral tradition; these two were also retexted (differently from that in *The Poor Soldier*) and published in Thomas Moore's *Irish Melodies*, editions of which were known all over the English-speaking world in the 1810s–1820s (see Wells 2003b, 496–503). This was a common cycle: tunes in oral tradition were borrowed for use within large publicly performed and then published ballad operas and/or distributed in printed collections of songs. Then these newly "pop" tunes reentered oral tradition. More precisely, such melodies had never evaporated from general traditional usage, but had their strength in oral tradition boosted by their sojourns in the commercial world.

The lyrics of "Savourna Delish" narrate a tragedy with real-life echoes. The young narrator/singer believes that he must seek his fortune as a soldier across the sea, leaving his sweetheart disconsolate. He is successful in battle and in gathering riches. However, when he seeks out his love on his return home he finds her grave instead. This sad drama narrates a gamble many young men of the time felt they had to accept. In both Ireland (where this song originated) and Scotland (also an early home of "Savourna Delish"), young men who were not the eldest son had little financial future. Primogeniture was not just a custom or a systematic means to concentrate power among the rich, but also an absolute necessity among the majority of peasant farmers, whose properties were so small that subdividing them would leave no heir with a viable income. Ambitious second and subsequent sons in poor families needed to leave home, often to become sailors or mercenaries. They would probably be unable to communicate home during their year(s) spent finding their fortune, and could well come home to find their former sweethearts married (think of the Child ballad "House Carpenter") or dead, as in this song.

Alternatively, lovers might not be reunited because the young traveler chose not to return. Who knows what Arthur McArthur's father, John, intended when he sailed to America from Perth, Scotland, as a teenager? This story certainly suits the American cultural theme of dislocation and its emotional consequences, and the song became popular here for many decades. It graced the theater stage, which helped it remain popular enough to enter personal collections. Both the Lester S. Levy Sheet Music Collection (now at Johns Hopkins University) and the parallel collection of the Library of Congress have several copies of individual settings of this song labeled "as performed by" this or that singer, with some editions being from early in the nineteenth century and some from the middle.

Was it the sad and timely theme of the lyrics that drew McArthur to this song? That reasoning probably holds for others who recorded the melody, but turns out to be unlikely here, or at least not the main cause. Most of the songs preceding this one in McArthur's music commonplace book have cheerful themes, and most of these songs were originally Scottish. This one started its life in Ireland, and was spread throughout British culture due to its being employed as an air in the very popular ballad opera *Poor Soldier* (performed many times in the United States, and said to have been a favorite of George Washington). But it was also popular in Scotland independent of theatrical use. Niel Gow, the most famous Scottish fiddler of all time, anthologized it in the fourth volume of his *Complete Repository*, although noting that the tune was Irish (1800, 10). This wasn't a unique characteristic: the Gows and their contemporaries in the flowering of Scottish fiddling in the late eighteenth and early nineteenth centuries anthologized several dozen originally Irish tunes, and often marked them as being so.

Since this Irish tune became also a Scottish one in practice, and since quite a few of the other songs that Arthur McArthur wrote down were also Scottish, an alternative reason for its being in the collection solidifies. John McArthur encouraged his son to learn music, and he is bound to have concentrated on tunes that were his own favorites, many of which would have been from his original home in Scotland. The father's affection for these tunes, fueled by a psychological partnership of familiarity and nostalgia, was deeded naturally to the son.

Modal tints make the melody sound "old," and thus both meriting nostalgia and foreshadowing the importance of Celtic elements in American fiddling. Most of the English tunes and thus early American tunes recorded in commonplace books are firmly in major. We have two approaches to this tune in terms of rhythmic texture represented in Figures 3a and 3b, and the sparse and dense approaches also offer contrasting views of mode. McArthur's version of "Savourna Delish" is in a gapped scale in its lower register, and more modal in that particular way in the first strain than in the second. A fair number of Scottish fiddle tunes are like that, that is, neither firmly in major nor consistently gapped, but leaning perceptibly in the gapped direction—a matter of a flavor rather than outright modal allegiance. Further, first strains are more likely to be modal in this way than second strains.

Interestingly, the top two versions in Figure 3b exhibit a fillip of mode in a different way, an inclined seventh degree of the scale. That is, while both versions are firmly in the key of D Major, the seventh degree, which leans upward most of the time, on occasion is lower (in short ornaments of the note *b*). Last, it is hard to know what mode to diagnose for the third version of the tune in Figure 3b.

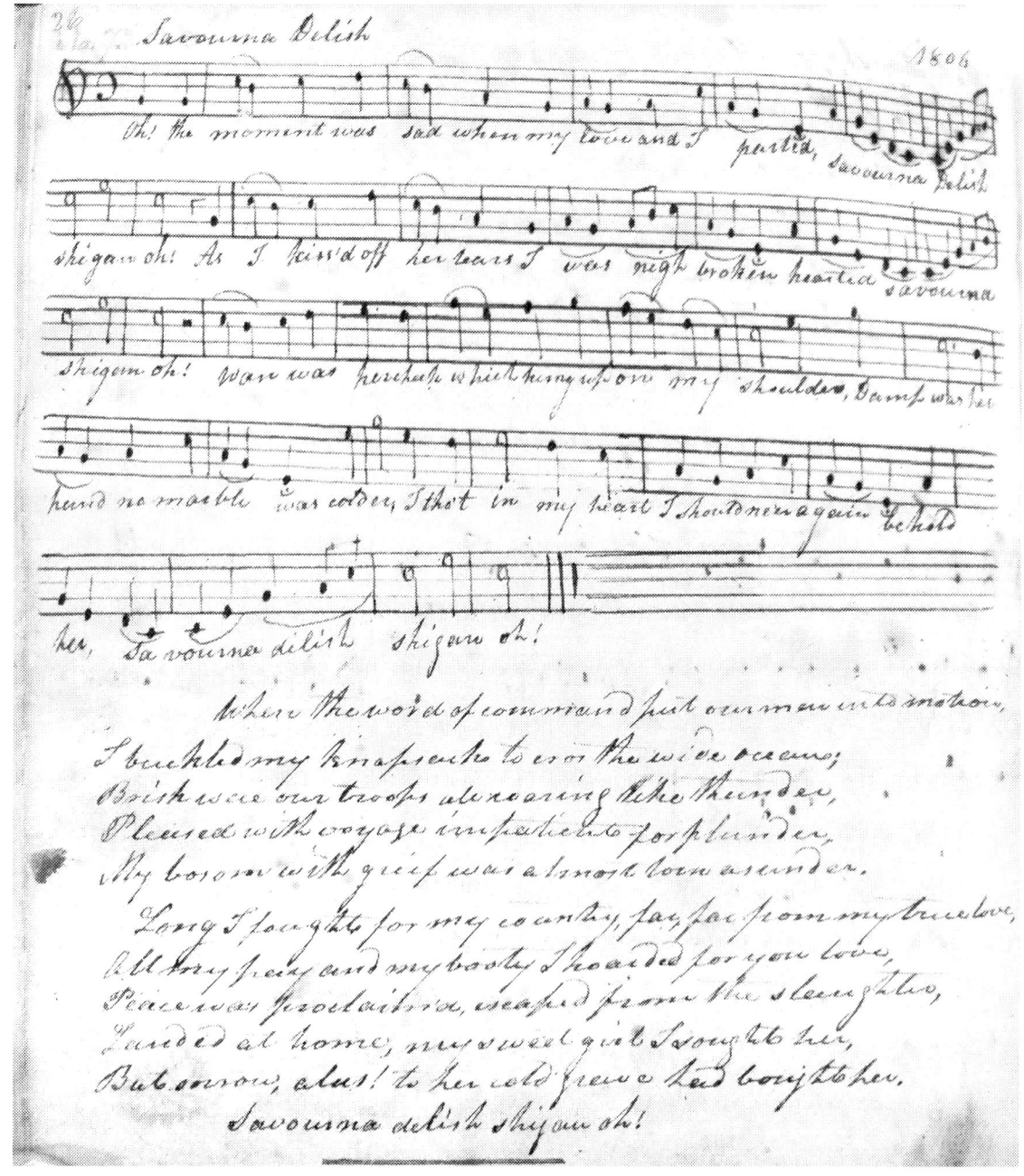

Figure 3a. "Savourna Delish," an Irish (and Scottish) song in Arthur McArthur's manuscript.

FIDDLE TUNES IN MUSIC COMMONPLACE BOOKS

Savourna Deligh   A Favorite Irish Air

(Gow [1800], 10; bass line omitted)

Savourna Delish

(Clark, 1820-30, 8-9)

(not texted, but largely in vocal notation in this American manuscript)

Savourna Delish

(Merrow 1806, 54)

(probably would welcome a key signature of two sharps)

Figure 3b. Three other versions of "Savourna Delish," one from a Scottish fiddle publication and two from American music commonplace books.

Perhaps the anthologizer, American J. M. Merrow, really intended a D Dorian version. More likely, he simply forgot to put in the key signature of two sharps, which would have brought the tune to its most frequent home more or less in D Major. But the lack of sharps offers another tantalizing possibility: If this written example was of a version meant to be in D Major, but lacking the key signature through error, what if this notated version entered a chain of transmission? An instrumentalist learning from this written form could then pass on what was now a Dorian tune—in a version of the forget-then-fill-in process characteristic of oral tradition, but here with the collusion of ink. The sum of all this: the tune is attractive in an "old" way partly due to some degree of modal tinting.

It is also very much worth noting that Gow's version is fiddled rather than sung, and the other two versions of "Savourna Delish" in Figure 3b also lack texts (though, as I note at the bottom of the middle version—which was taken from the Clark manuscript—that version was originally in vocal notation). Both Scottish and Irish fiddle tunes of the eighteenth and early nineteenth centuries had a habit of gaining or losing texts. "Savourna Delish" is certainly not the only song that might well be performed as a fiddle tune. Indeed, what is most interesting about what I have labeled as section 4 of this music commonplace book is how mixed it is in terms of vocal versus instrumental notation, despite the fact that the tunes were all in their primary identities songs, whether or not they are texted in this particular manuscript. Why was this? Just as near the start of the book McArthur's jump from instrumental instruction to songs might have been because he had more experience singing than playing (due to the singing schools he had attended), in this section written a few years later he is moving away from choosing singing to showing that he preferred to play tunes on his fiddle and/or flute, whether or not these tunes had histories of being sung.

There is less to say about McArthur's marches, nearly all of which are in the ensemble section of the book. They are presented there a3, on two treble clefs and a bass clef (an additional handful of marches in the commonplace book come after this ensemble section, but none is in McArthur's hand). I'm fairly sure that he meant for the top line to be played by the flute, the middle part by the violin, and the bottom part perhaps by a bassoon or low string (or horn). The marches are remarkably similar to each other, and each one is very stable from version to version: there is little possibility of posting interestingly contrasting versions here! I give a photograph of McArthur's "Swiss Guard's March" as Figure 4. The "Swiss Guards" in question must have been the Pope's bodyguards; I don't know if we are to think of their original march from Switzerland to Rome in 1505 or if we are simply meant to picture the gaudy uniforms and grand setting of their day-to-day activities at a later time. I should also note that marches, though of martial/patriotic origin, could also appear in concerts, or could serve at a dance. A description of a dance held at a Virginia plantation in 1773 proceeded as follows: "About seven the Ladies and Gentlemen began to dance in the Ball-Room, first Minuets one round; Second Giggs; third Reels; and last of all Country-Dances; tho' they struck several marches occasionally" (Fithian 1957, 76).

Figure 4. McArthur entered "Swiss Guards March" in his manuscript in a version for two treble instruments and one bass instrument. This is how he arranged most marches.

This is a typical march; I chose it to reproduce because I enjoyed the images conjured by the title and because it illustrates the hazards of copying. McArthur omitted the third beat in measure 5 (which ought to contain a quarter note on *f*—it is easy to leave out one in a series of notes on the same pitch), and he may have gotten temporarily confused by the first and second endings of the first strain. In the third measure of the third brace, he employed dotted rhythms that I don't find in that measure in other versions. That is as big a difference from other versions as these marches typically display, apart from the occasional transposition (this march is usually in D Major, but occasionally in C, and tends toward flat keys in versions for piano). Versions set a2 include the melody and either other part, normally without modification of either line.

What might McArthur's opinion of these marches have been? He certainly wrote plenty of them down. I can only speculate that he arranged almost all of them as trios at least partly because the melodies were unexciting—the volume and timbral variety of an ensemble were sorely needed. Despite their lack of melodic interest, they were important tunes to know, since expressing patriotism with an explicit martial edge was expected. Nearly every American music commonplace book primarily for solo instrument was well stocked with marches, a fair number of which had America-referencing titles, though the majority remained British in both composition and title.

Sacred pieces might or might not take up a substantial part of an early nineteenth-century music commonplace book. McArthur, always a religious boy (whether or not this ameliorated his behavior), wrote down three hymns as the very first pieces of music in his book (in 1806), then recorded seven more four years later, and finally posted a last pair four years after that (pp. 19–20, 83–88, and 89–90, respectively). I give one of the hymns he wrote down in 1810 in Figure 5. The melody (in the middle line) will be familiar to many readers through its long association with the text "Adeste Fideles," translated and often performed as "Come All Ye Faithful." But in this case, the music is simply called "The Portuguese Hymn" ("Portuguese" due to a long-term widely held belief that it was written by a musical king of Portugal). McArthur inserted further information to the right of that title: L.M. (long meter: 4 lines of 4 poetic feet each) and "Dixon Coll.," suggesting that Bowdoin College owned (and McArthur copied from) William Dixon's gathering of hymns bearing this long and informative title: *Psalmodia Christiana. A Collection of Sacred Music in Four Parts Designed for Public Worship. Containing 200 Plain Psalm Tunes, 50 Fugues, & a Few Pieces in the Hymn Stile for the Three Great Festivals, Christmas Day, Easter Day, and Whit-Sunday* ([ca. 1790]).

At that time, any text shaped in a given "meter" might well be sung to any hymn tune accommodating the appropriate number of syllables per line. Here, McArthur underlaid the text of one of Isaac Watts's many reworkings of psalms (Watts carefully transformed them into appropriately scanning hymn lyrics). McArthur copied out the first verse of Watts's take on the end of Psalm 92:

Figure 5. One of a handful of hymns that McArthur copied into his music commonplace book.

Lord, 'tis a pleasure there to stand in gardens planted by thine hand.
Let me within thy courts be seen, like a young cedar, fresh and green.

I wonder if this particular text appealed to young Arthur McArthur because of the botanical imagery. For the first hymn tune he recorded, coincidentally entitled "Portugal," he wrote out a text that he noted was from James Harvey's *Meditations and Contemplations*, which was published many times, including in Philadelphia in 1784–1785. Harvey wrote religious texts that were quite melodramatic—a trait worshipers then welcomed—and both literally and figuratively flowery, that is, both wordy and packed with verdant images. McArthur praised country life repeatedly in his letters, and perhaps was combining that orientation with piety here.

He wrote out "Portugal" in a four-part arrangement, doubtless as in his source. The second hymn he transcribed as a duet, the third as a single line. He seems to have been experimenting. Hymn tunes, like fiddle tunes, will sometimes be performed with one or another kind of accompaniment, but sometimes will be written down as solos; McArthur was figuring out how he preferred his religious music performed, and apparently decided that trio arrangements were his favorite. Hymns as solo lines work like march tunes: they are quite stable. However, contrary to how marches are usually treated, the arrangements in which these stable hymn tunes can become embedded are remade often. Also, these arrangements give the impression that a four-part hymn was then the product of successive composition just as early Renaissance polyphonic works had been. In this scenario, the composer wrote the tune first, then he or someone else added the line below designed so that the resultant two-part tune constituted a satisfactory completed composition. Then the alto line came along with the same requirement of a finished effect, and finally the top line; the melody was now in the tenor position. In his three-line hymn transcriptions McArthur left out the last step. The same "Portuguese Hymn" appeared in other commonplace books right about this time occasionally a2 (as in "Carolyn Bowen's Music Book") and certainly a4 (as in the commonplace book beginning with the tune "Quito S. M."; both manuscripts are offered digitally through the project *American Vernacular Music Manuscripts ca. 1730–1910*: popmusic.mtsu.edu/manuscriptmusic/).

The portion of McArthur's unusually varied music commonplace book that looks the most like the meat-and-potatoes parts of the average music commonplace book of his time and place is pages 96–107, on which he recorded forty-one single-line tunes and one treble duet. We must keep in mind that most instrumental tunes were arranged in such a way that all of the common treble instruments could perform them, including the flute and fife, for which the lowest available note was *d*, the same pitch to which to the third string on the violin is typically tuned. All of the melodies in this section were readily *available* to violinists/fiddlers, while only one ("Lango Lee") required the player's left hand to go into positions up the neck, and then only to third position, the simplest shift. And a handful of melodies in this section could not be played on the treble winds, because they went below *d*, that is, went down onto the fiddle's *g* string: "College Hornpipe," "Lord McDonald's Reel" (twice!), "Four Times Over," and "Hark Away." These could have functioned as fiddle tunes exclusively, while the other melodies in this section remained less idiomatic and thus more versatile.

Figure 6a is a picture of a full page from the McArthur manuscript, a page containing four melodies. The tunes on it present variety in several spheres. Facing Figure 6a is Figure 6b, transcriptions of alternative versions of these four tunes, each from manuscripts dating from about the same time. These tunes include common ones (the first and last) and rare ones, and ones that could be performed as reels or hornpipes (again, the first and last) plus a pair of jigs. In all four cases, the two versions of a tune differ in small ways throughout their lengths, but retain stability in general contour and in harmonic implications. Although written down, and probably copied from published sources (first- or second-hand, but ultimately from print), they show in their patterns of variation that they are in oral tradition. McArthur could have played most of the melodies in this section of his commonplace book on his flute, but absolutely all fit nicely on his violin. With most of his training as an instrumentalist seemingly ad hoc and face-to-face, his technique cannot have been very sophisticated. He played the violin informally, performing many tunes then in oral tradition, many of which we know also had long histories in tradition: he was fiddling.

PHILANDER SEWARD, BEFORE HE BECAME A PROMINENT FARMER

The second music commonplace book I'll look at, owned by the University of Illinois, is the first one I ever encountered, and one I've written about before (albeit more briefly than here). On one opening, the compiler wrote out a proposed title: *Philander Seward's Musical Deposit*. I found the name Philander Seward just once in appropriate census records (that is, records that fit his being a teenager early in the nineteenth century). Once I was reasonably sure who Seward was and where he lived, it was easy to learn more about him.

Philander Seward was born in 1791 in Greenwich Township, Fairfield County, Connecticut. His parents, William Seward III and Thankfull Parmalee Seward, moved their family to Fishkill, Dutchess County, New York, when he was very young. This area, on the east side of the Hudson River some seventy miles north of New York City, had a longer history of colonization than had McArthur's Maine, but remained rural. Dutchess County stretches from a mountainous south to a hilly north. Parts can be farmed; apple orchards have long been important there. In 1682, the Wappinger tribe of Native Americans relinquished a large tract of land including the future county for a measure of gunpowder, lead, sundries, and money. Only a half-dozen white settlers had arrived by 1713 (Smith 1877, 177). Families bearing a mixture of Dutch and English last names slowly gathered. At the time of the revolution, Fishkill (from the Dutch *Vis kil*, or fish stream) was the largest settlement in the county, with some fifty buildings—an academy (a

Figure 6a. A typical page from the part of the McArthur manuscript devoted to single-line melodies for treble instruments. These melodies suit a beginning violinist because they do not require the performer to shift out of first position, and they work on the flute too, since they do not go below the note d that was then the lowest pitch available on both flute and fife.

Logan Water
(Stiles 1816, [33])

Lango Lee
(Merrow 1806, 61)

The Vicar and Moses
(Williams 1799, [56])

Rose Tree
("French National March" [1810s?], [2])

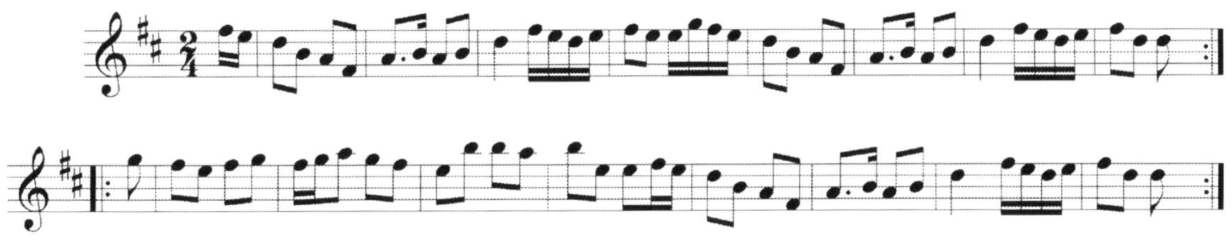

Figure 6b. Alternative versions of the melodies penned in Figure 6a. These versions were all written down in American music commonplace books at about the same time as McArthur penned his version; all were accessed through the website American Vernacular Music Manuscripts ca. 1730–1910.

school for boys), two churches, a hotel, even a printing press. The town had a valuable geographical feature: just a single narrow mountain pass allowed approach by land from the south. As a result of Fishkill's strategic location—easy to defend, near the fortifications that would soon become West Point and not very far north of New York City—it was used during the Revolution as a deposit for military stores, a holding point for prisoners of war, a destination for refugees, and a camp for part of the American army (Smith 1877, 185–88).

Seward's wife's family, the Montforts, arrived in 1740, then the Sewards came in the mid-1790s, right after the town had settled back into its modest skin after the Revolution. They purchased an already developed pair of parcels of land about eight miles north of the Fishkill town center, one parcel of 252 acres and the other of 70 acres in what would become New Hackensack (with small bits of their land carved out for already present residents and for a church; *Eighteenth Century Records of the Original Town of Fishkill*, 116 and 202). This Reformed Dutch Church, originally built in 1725, retained "in the upper story ... port holes for defense against the Indians." For a postwar renovation—perhaps while the Sewards were moving onto the abutting land—"the congregation turned out in full-force with horses, oxen, carts, and negro slaves" (Smith 1877, 195).

As the only son (he had three elder sisters), Philander Seward would inherit this large farm and the family pews in the church. In the 1850 census, his household consisted of Seward himself ("farmer," aged fifty-nine), his wife Susan (aged forty-seven), sons Philander G. and Mausie (aged twenty-one and nineteen, also listed as farmers), younger sons James A. and Ogden S. (aged fourteen and twelve), a woman named Catherine Brainard (aged twenty-five) and an Irish immigrant girl named Phebe L. Adkins (aged thirteen), probably both domestic help. A tutor lived in a neighboring household (Buck and Buck [n.d.] 153). Seward did quite well; apart from a pair of rich retirees, he and a half-dozen other farmers stood high above the rest of the county in terms of wealth (Buck and Buck [n.d.] throughout). As in the case of Arthur McArthur's family, several of Seward's children moved west, two to Illinois, while son William (like an additional daughter, apparently not yet in the picture at the time of the above census) "was drowned in Texas in early manhood" (*Commemorative Biographical Record of Dutchess County* 1897, 347).

"PHILANDER SEWARD'S MUSICAL DEPOSIT"

The treasure trove of family papers that helped me understand the life and musical activities of Arthur McArthur wasn't paralleled for Philander Seward. All I know about Seward's musical activities—or, for that matter, about his personal qualities—is from the contents of his music commonplace book. This handwritten book contains seventy-seven items: sixty-two titled but not texted tunes notated on single staves with treble clefs (a few are duets), ten accompaniment lines notated in bass clef, plus three song texts and an epigram. Several of the tunes were first published in 1807, so Seward could not have completed

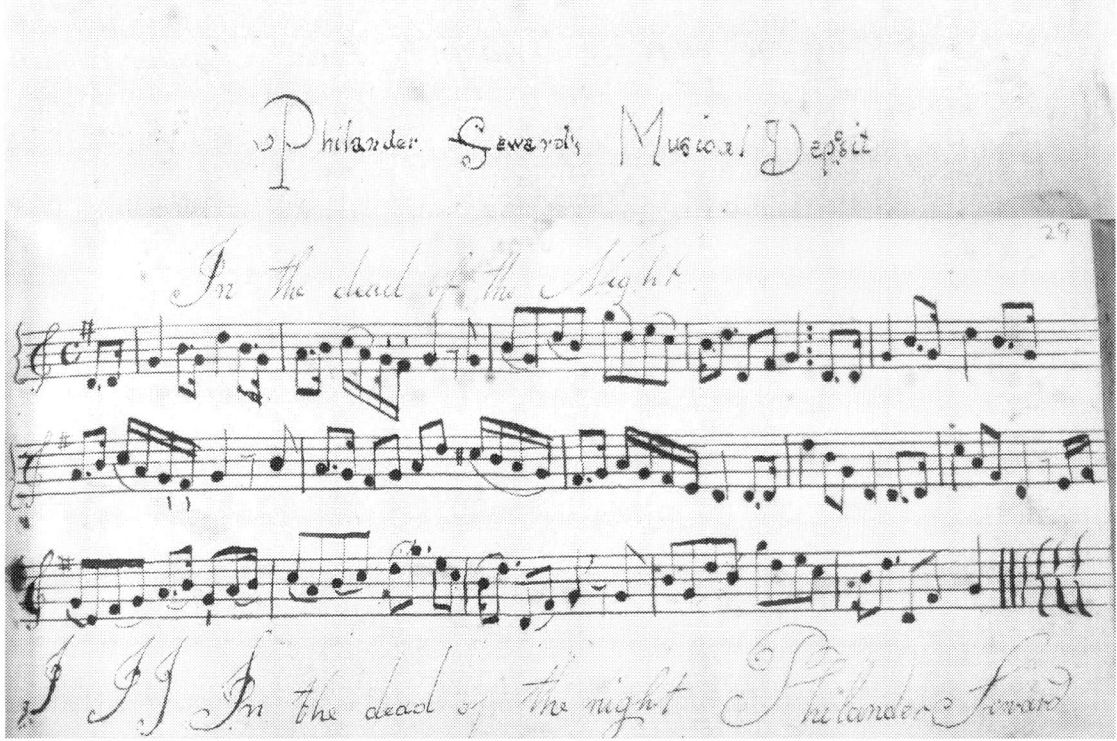

Figure 7. Philander Seward practiced his handwriting on facing pages in his music commonplace book, and thus identified himself for us. His writing out the grandiose title "Philander Seward's Musical Deposit" suggests that this teenager enjoyed imagining that his manuscript was like a published collection.

the manuscript before then; he and Arthur McArthur were learning music at the same time.

I list the contents of this typical music commonplace book in Figure 8. Reading left to right, following the names of the tunes (precisely as given by Philander Seward), I indicate the page number on which the piece can also be found in the music commonplace books of Seward (PS), Arthur McArthur (McA), Silas Dickinson (SD), and James Merrow (JM). "Riley" stands for a published collection, *Riley's Flute Melodies* (widely distributed in the early 1820s and reprinted in 1973). On the right side of that inventory, I summarize much of what I have learned about the individual pieces in Seward's manuscript: whether concordances with them match or not, whether variation between versions is of one or another type, and what specific uses given tunes had in Seward's day (with keys to that information placed at the bottom of the figure).

Tune ranges and a few marked fingerings suggest that Seward, like McArthur, played the violin. We don't know if he also played the flute or other wind instrument. Also, Seward, like McArthur and many other instrumentalists, yearned to play with other musicians. He didn't write out trios or larger ensemble pieces, but did notate the aforementioned handful of treble duets. He also ended the music portion of his commonplace book with bass lines for some tunes; perhaps he owned or had access to an additional manuscript or to a publication containing

FIGURE 8. THE CONTENTS OF THE SEWARD MANUSCRIPT

# of Item / Name of Tune	Page # in PS	McA	SD	JM	Riley	Treble or Bass	Surviving? Varied?	Uses*
1. Duke of York's March [C]	1r	13			I, 45	T		M
2. French Dance	1r					T		D?
3. Belisle's March	1v		35	28	I, 89	T	S?	M
4. Lesson by Morelli	1v	81	125	15		T	S	MDR
5. President's March	2r		7	27	I, 12	T	S	CM
6. Valencienn's March	2v					T		M
7. Through the Green Fields	2v					T	S	DR
8. Roslin Castle	3r		29		I, 8	T	S	CM
9. The Indian Philosopher	3r	101	147	12		T		?
10. The Haymakers	3v-4r		67	43	I, 36	T	S V	D
11. Flowers of Edinburgh	3v-4r		35	78	I, 5	T	S V	D
12. Fisher's Hornpipe	3v-4r	99	63	39	I, 52	T	S V	D
13. Primrose Hill	3v-4r		157			T	V	D?
14. Port Gordon	4v			2		T	S V	?
15. Tid Re I	5r			65		T		C
16. Boyn[e] Waters	5r	96			I, 80	T	S V	M…
17. Philadelphia March	6r					T		M?
18. Life Let Us Cherish	7r			6	I, 12	T	S	CD
19. The Garland of Love	8r				I, 42	T	S	CD
20. Valencienn's March 2nd	9r					T		M
21. Rickett's Hornpipe	11r				III, 81	T	S V	D
22. Lord Nelson's Hornpipe	12r					T	S	D
23. The Soldier's Return	13r				I, 9	T	S	C?
24. Caledonian March	14r					TT	S	M?
25. Gen'l Green's March	15r					T		M
26. Jefferson and Liberty	16r		129	37		T	S	M
27. Money Musk	17r	99	67		II, 72	T	S V	D
28. The Devil's Dream	18r		71	56		T	S V	D
29. Black Sloven	19r		17	57		T	S V	CM
30. New Jersey	19r		123			T	S	M?
31. Duke of Holstein's March	20r		73	25, 62		T		M
32. How Imperfect	21r			8	I, 31	T	S	D
33. Drink to Me Only with ..	21r				I, 9	T	S	CD
34. Go to the D__ and Shake .	22r			77	I, 48	T	S V	D
35. Away with Melancholy	23v				II, 56	TT	S	CD
36. Duke of York's Cottillion	25r			47		T	S	D
37. Duke of York's March [D]	26v		13		I, 45	T		M
38. Duett in Rosina	28r					TT		O

# of Item / Name of Tune	Page # in PS	McA	SD	JM	Riley	Treble or Bass	Surviving? Varied?	Uses*
39. In the Dead of the Night	29r				I, 53	T		C
40. March . . . Battle of Prague	30r			77	I, 48	T		CM
41. New Haven Green	31r					T	S V	D?
42. The Rose	31r				I, 19	T		C?
43. Bonaparte's March	32r				II, 55	T		M
44. First Monday in May	33r					T		C?
45. Irish Wedding	33r					T	S	D?
46. Washington's Ode	34r					T	S V	D?
47. Meig's March	34r					T		M
48. The Irish Washerwoman	35r	101		41	I, 52	T	S V	DC
49. The Honey Moon	36r				II, 56	T	S V	DO
50. Prelude in G Major	36r				II, 57	T		E
51. Highland Reel	37r		69			T	S V	D
52. Nelson's Victory	38r		39			T	S	?
53. One, Two, and Begin	39r	59				TTB		?
54. Farmer's Joy	40r					TT		?
55. Midnight Hour	41r					TT		C?
56. Shoe Strings	42r					TT	S	?
57. Oh Dear, What Can the . .	43r		5	44	I, 95	TT	S	C?
58. Ladies Excuse	44r					TT		?
59. Presidents March, bass	52r			??p		B	S	M
60. March in Blue Beard	53r	68		28	I, 94	B		MO
61. Greens March	54r		75	35		B		M
62. Humours of Glynn	55r	45	51	46		B	S V	D
63. Katies Rambles	56r					B	S V	D
64. Roslin Castle	56v	42	29		I, 8	B	S	MC
65. Major Minor	58r	65				B		E?
66. Rondo	59r					B		C?
67. The Blue Bird	60r		127	38		B		C?
68. Basses Comic Tune, 2nd	61r					B		O?
69. Caledonia: "Their Groves	70r					text		C?
70. To an Early Bee	71r					text		C?
71. Oh Say, Simple Maid . . .	74r					text		C?
*Key for Uses: March, Dance, Concert, Opera or Theater, Educational, Religious								

Figure 8. The contents of the Seward manuscript, plus where in that manuscript each tune is found, where in three other manuscripts (and in Riley's Flute Melodies) other versions are located, whether the versions of a tune vary in small ways, and uses of each tune.

the melodies of those tunes, or perhaps he knew them by ear and wanted to furnish a bass line from which a friend or family member could accompany him. He didn't include any hymns or other tunes whose normal usage was exclusively sacred. After all, he likely owned a hymnal, or, if not, could have walked to the church on his land to consult one. (In an inventory of McArthur's library that is among the family papers, a hymnal is listed—I suspect he acquired it *after* he had entered some hymns in his commonplace book.)

Seward recorded plenty of songs, though untexted (he did record some lyrics at the end of his book, but they do not match any of his melodies), and he wrote out many other single-line tunes, including dances and marches. We do see a small gesture toward the didactic (Seward anthologized just one short "Prelude in G") and *perhaps* one religious tune. This "Lesson by Morelli" has a later life in the shape-note repertory as "Lesson by Murillo," but also was used often as a march; in this commonplace book, as in McArthur's, it sits among marches, so that function probably is the reason it is in both books ("Through the Green Fields" also lived on as a religious tune, "Green Fields"). Overall, "Philander Seward's Musical Deposit" is typical in contents and also in its size, which is manageable enough that I didn't just sample it, instead I transcribed the whole manuscript. This batch of tunes, the first of four anthologies in the current book, is given as Figure 12 at the end of this chapter. Each tune is numbered (by me) so that, for instance, the third piece in *Philander Seward's Musical Deposit*, "Belisle's March," is Figure 12, #3.

The melodies as Seward wrote them down lack idiomatic earmarks for the most part, and appeared commonly in collections for various instruments; it is only the pitch range of each tune that suggests the best instrument(s) on which to perform it. As mentioned previously, a handful of treble tunes do dip below the d marking the bottom of the range of the flute and fife, so Seward most likely played those tunes on the violin, and he could have played all the other treble tunes on the violin, too. The one entry that is explicitly an exercise provides strong support for the hypothesis that he played the violin. The "Prelude in G" marches up and down the G Major scale, starting on the open *g* string (below the range of the flute and fife), then offers a rising and a falling easy arpeggio, then ends with the simplest quadruple stop on the violin—the g chord including the open g and d strings, then the b on the a string and the g on the e string.

The proportions of airs, marches, and dances are roughly the same as in published collections of the day; Seward was a teenager making his own version of one of those, though minimizing the pedagogical materials (since he included just the one prelude, and one exercise aptly named "Major Minor"). How should I go about discovering what was most interesting about his collection of melodies? As I would do later when studying the McArthur manuscript, I employed a technique common to historical musicology and folklore, and searched out and compared multiple concordances of the collection's individual items.

In intensive work in the early 1980s—supplemented regularly in the decades since then—I compared the tunes as written out in the *Musical Deposit* with matching or similar melodies, titles, or both found in about fifty music commonplace books (penned from the 1780s to the 1820s in the cases in which I could establish dates), roughly two hundred printed collections (published from the 1780s through the 1950s; many of these collections housed in the Library of Congress or the New York Public Library, then Bayard 1982), and lists of tune titles and/or melodic incipits found in various bibliographies (in particular Sonneck and Upton 1945 and Wolfe 1964) and Internet lists (especially Kuntz n.d.). My initial conclusions hold: Seward compiled a wide range of tunes in terms of how common they were—neither just hits nor just rarities—and did not grant particular genres of pieces any more preference than had publishers whose collections he might have drawn on (Blake, Riley, and so on); the manuscript contains an average sampling of the published secular music of his day. Second, when a piece appeared in many of these collections, the fact that it was then common didn't necessarily mean that it would last longer: many pieces, even if widely heard then, vanished quickly. This was *popular* music, entering and leaving the scene like clockwork, though at a markedly slower pace than today.

Most interesting to me as a student of fiddling is that, although most concordances matched the versions found in the *Musical Deposit* or differed from them only in their keys, a few parted company from Seward's versions and from one another repeatedly and pervasively in matters of detail. These include tunes that had been common fiddle tunes before Seward's time, and which remain ubiquitous in the American folk fiddle repertory today: "Money Musk," "Rickett's Hornpipe," "Devil's Dream," "Fisher's Hornpipe," "Flowers of Edinburgh," and "The Irish Washerwoman." In Seward's time, printed (and manuscript) versions of these tunes varied in certain ways. General contours, diagnostic tones (notes that are metrically and harmonically prominent), and a few catchy melodic motives endured, but exact rhythms, passing tones, and other metrically weak notes were apt to vary.

Differences among these versions, like the differences between McArthur's tunes and other young instrumentalists' versions of them illustrated in Figure 6, correspond in a general way to differences in how performances of these tunes contrast in modern playing in New England, the part of the United States where Seward's six most "varied" and enduring hit tunes are most at home today (see Wells 1978). This affirms that these tunes were already in oral tradition early in the nineteenth century—that is, in the remembered repertoires of the English immigrants who were the main performers/teachers/publishers of the instrument compilations on which the American compilers of music commonplace books drew. See Figure 9 for a direct comparison of Seward's anthologized version of "The Flowers of Edinburgh" with three other contemporaneous versions, two from music commonplace books and one from the widely distributed *Riley's Flute Melodies* (1824–1826).

Playing through these four versions (plus the pairs of versions of tunes from McArthur) should give a modern fiddler a good sense of what details of musical language and what densities of effect would match the collective taste and

Figure 9. Four versions of the popular tune "The Flowers of Edinburgh."

Figure 10. In Seward's music commonplace book, the common tune "Garry Owen" received a title I haven't seen linked with it elsewhere, "Washington's Ode." Since the entry is written without hesitation, Seward must have copied this from a manuscript penned by someone else. That individual (or their source) seems to have written down the tune by ear, someone whose command of rhythm and meter was not strong: this melody is a jig, and should have been notated in 6/8.

collective creative proclivities of music literate fiddlers of young McArthur and young Seward's day. The variation between the versions isn't anything fancy: no one is making a point, showing off, adjusting key to fit a singer or other instrumentalist's needs, or anything like that. It's simply that "The Flowers of Edinburgh" and many other tunes had been around for a long time flourishing primarily in oral tradition. They were also printed now and again and thus figured into the pop music scene of the day, too. This melody's players did the forgetting and filling in and the slight adjusting to personal preferences that we would expect, so that various versions were equally available and equally plausible when publishers printed their personal takes on the tune and players adopted those versions in Seward's day. And the differences are pervasive: only one measure of "The Flowers of Edinburgh" has exactly the same pitches in all four versions in Figure 9. Tunes like this one have core identities, but flexible surfaces. The haze of detail created by regular variation in oral (and written) tradition has already worked like a lubricant easing their voyages through time. That is, these melodies are mature fiddle tunes. Their flourishing in this way symptomized a high level of interest and also offered alternative simultaneous shadings, nuances that could appeal to the next batches of fiddlers' regional and generational and individual tastes over and over.

Seward notated two fiddle tunes with rare Americanized titles in his *Musical Deposit*: his versions of the common British tunes "Garry Owen" and "Whistle O'er the Lave O't," tunes he titled instead "Washington's Ode" and "New Haven Green." That second transformation of title was both local and personal: Seward's father had attended Yale University. But "Washington's Ode" is striking for another reason. Figure 10 shows the page on which it appears.

Notice the treatment of time in this version of this tune! I urge the reader to carefully count this out, and compare it to any version of the tune of which it seems to be a relative, "Garry Owen." It's hard to imagine that any published source would have included such errors in note lengths, that is, in simple addition. My best explanation for this oddness is inspired by experience with modern fiddlers. Just as in Seward's day—and, as best as I can tell, throughout history—some fiddlers don't read music at all, and some read very well, but the majority work from notation laboriously. Many of the fiddlers I know today are good at parsing pitches, but are weaker in the reading and writing of rhythms. I would wager that Philander Seward knew such a mostly oral-tradition fiddler, a musician who had written down tunes by ear with mixed success. Seward copied his acquaintance's versions uncritically, and, if he played from his own notations, did just as many fiddlers probably did then and certainly do now—used the pitches as a solid reference, but filled in the rhythms himself. What matters here? The clumsy treatment of time in Seward's version of "Garry Owen" demonstrates something unsurprising—that some fiddlers back then were trying to do their own transcribing, even though most copying of tunes was from professionally filtered sources.

Editors and publishers of the collections from which Seward and his peers copied tunes, although British in training and preferences, did cater to American preferences by seeking out American content in marches and patriotic songs, which they arranged from American sheet music. Teenager Philander Seward endorsed that national trend when he wrote down the tunes for "General Green's March," "Philadelphia March," and the very common "President's March," which later acquired the text and title "Hail Columbia." Were these marches also in oral tradition? Several factors militated against the oral-tradition variation typical of dances affecting performance of marches very much. Patriotism-fueled respect would have supported careful efforts to remember tunes meticulously, the use of ensembles would have encouraged standardization, and, in any case, the general stylistic profile of marches left little room to express personal readings. Several typical features discouraged variation, including dotted rhythms (so many notes were longer than the shortest), lots of repeated pitches, frequent reliance on arpeggios and on neighbor-tone ornaments, and so on. In short, marches varied little, whether or not they were remembered rather than read from notation.

Seward's two versions of "The Duke of York's March" offer a good reference point to continue thinking about the marches of his day. Transposition to other keys, while not common, was an option—as illustrated by Seward's two forms of this piece—and the melodies (and any accompaniment lines) were not modified, just moved intact up or down. Also, versions of a given march might contain some or all sections of a piece. In fact, it is a little unusual that Seward's second version of "The Duke of York's March" does include the trio section. Last, pickup notes might vary, as in the "Lesson by Morelli" (see below in Figure 11). A few characteristics of many marches' melodies—apart from titles, pace, and use of lots of dotted rhythms—marked them as typical of that genre. About four-fifths of them include a few triplets in the penultimate measure of one or both sections (see Seward's "Belisle's March," "President's March," and several others). Also, some of these tunes include a few notes sharped or flatted to fit a moment's dipping into a related key (see his "Duke of York's March," mm. 13–14).

Lesson by Morelli

(Mc 81, 1808)

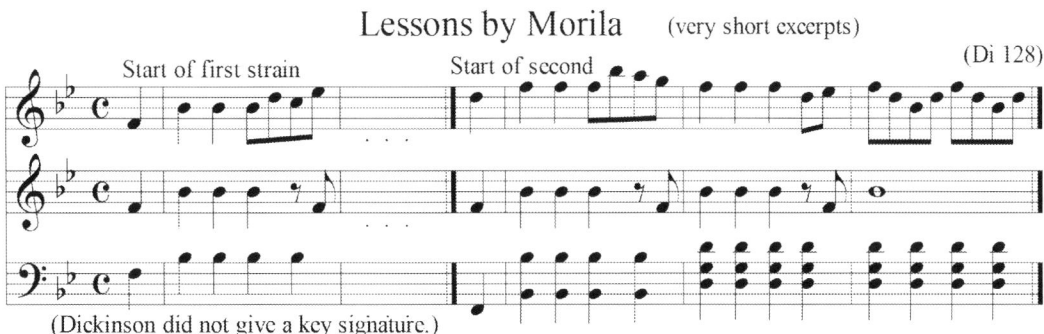

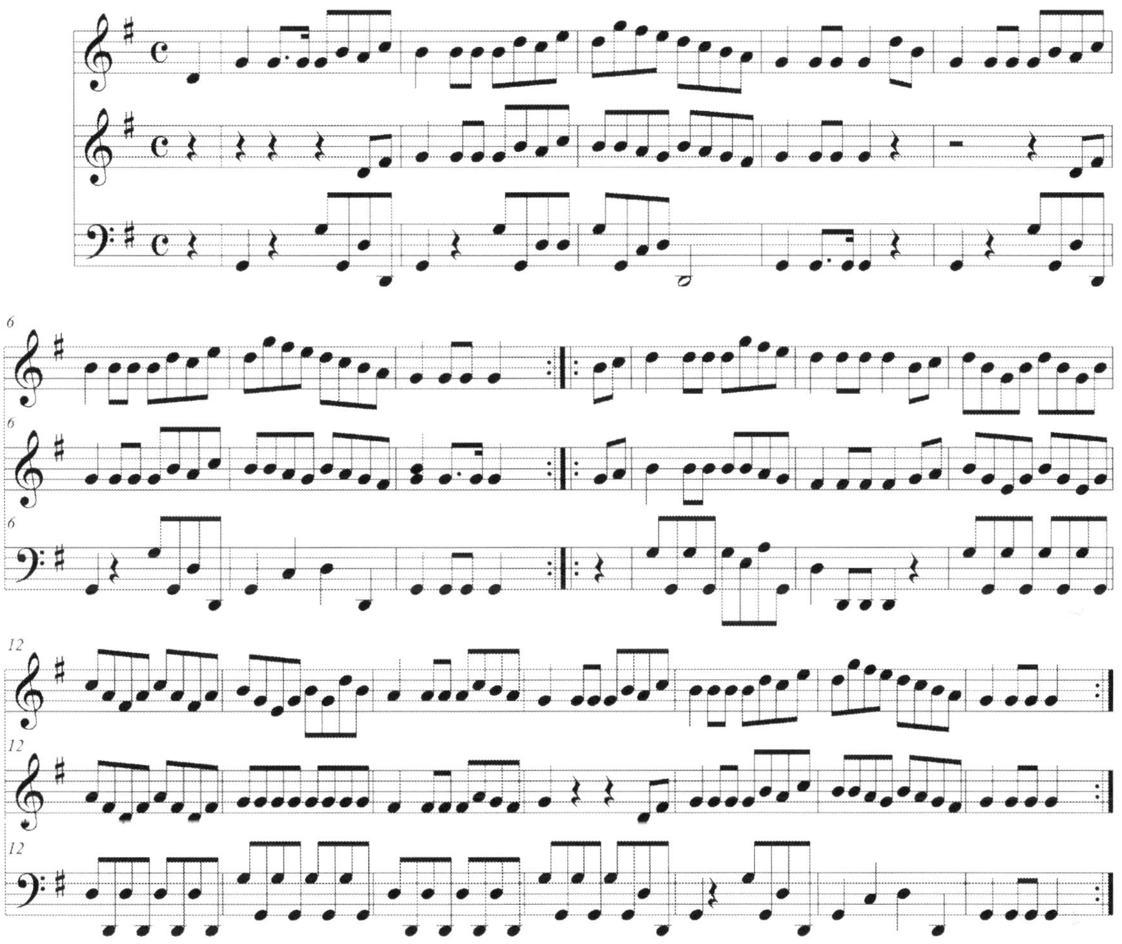

Lessons by Morila (very short excerpts)

(Di 128)

Figure 11. A versatile melody Seward recorded, "Lesson by Morelli," in the nice ensemble version given in the McArthur manuscript, plus bits of a less interesting ensemble version from the Dickinson manuscript (from about the same time).

Several of the tunes Seward played that were more often sung—then and through the decades since—have their own lengthy histories in oral tradition, notably "Boyne Water," which includes in its venerable resumé employment as the melody for many Child ballads, tunes including "Little Musgrave," "Fair Margaret," and the commonest one in the United States, "Barbara Allen." Bertrand Bronson found so many versions of those central old British (and American) traditional lyrics sung to this melody that he referred to "the always beckoning direction of 'Boyne Water'" (1959, IV, 424). Somewhat similarly, "The Soldier's Return" is a new texting of the oral-tradition tune "The Mill, the Mill, O," but this popular song didn't exhibit variation in Seward's day because of its recent attachment to its new lyrics (which offer an optimistic parallel to "Savourneen Delish"—the soldier, poor in booty but rich in honor, gets the girl). In general, Seward's many song tunes varied as little as did marches. When a fiddler or fifer played a song melody, even if the lyrics were not sung, they often would have echoed in the performer's memory, and helped minimize potential variation. Also, songs that Seward anthologized that were recent creations, such as "Jefferson and Liberty," "How Imperfect Is Expression," "Life Let Us Cherish," "The Garland of Love," and "In the Dead of the Night," hadn't had time to be partially forgotten and then interestingly recreated, but several would experience these processes eventually. The first three of those hits survive in a small way in oral tradition (see in Kuntz [n.d.]), and deserve a fresh hearing. This is part of the reason many more pieces are marked on the chart constituting Figure 7 as "surviving" than as "varied." These and many other melodies popular during this era weren't yet in oral tradition, but would ease into it.

Several tunes entered in *Philander Seward's Musical Deposit* started life as art music. "Away with Melancholy" is a much-anthologized retexting of "Das klinget so herrlich," from Mozart's *The Magic Flute* of 1791 (this excerpt remains a frequently arranged, separately performed tune). Jan Ladislav Dussek (1760–1812), a Czech piano virtuoso residing in London in 1789–1799, wrote "In the Dead of the Night" (ca. 1795). Swiss composer Hans Georg Nägeli composed "Life Let Us Cherish" in 1795; Seward's copy seems to have been from a piece of sheet music that included an instrumental section, and even specified that the solo instrument in that section was the oboe, doubtless echoing a sheet music arrangement. Last, two of Seward's pieces started life in ballad operas. His "Duett in Rosina" is the first sung piece in William Shield's *Rosina* (1783), and, late in the *Musical Deposit*, there is a bass line for a "Favorite March in Blue Beard," an indeed very popular excerpt from Michael Kelly's *Blue Beard* (1798). A similar source furnished McArthur's "Rose Tree," an old probably originally Scottish or Irish tune given new words and new life in Shield and O'Keefe's 1783 ballad opera *The Poor Soldier*, which drew heavily on Irish melodies. (I believe "Rose Tree" was later beefed up rhythmically to become the blackface minstrel hit "Old Zip Coon," which in turn furnished the melody for the ubiquitous fiddle tune "Turkey in the Straw.")

A few pieces show in their notation that they likely were taken not from collections, but rather from more visually elaborate settings in sheet music. These are the recent pop music hits, "Life Let Us Cherish," with its surprising (in a commonplace book) added "Moderato" section including the "Oboe Solo," the immediately following "Garland of Love," here "sung by Mrs. Bland," perhaps "Away with Melancholy" with its tempo marking, maybe "In the Dead of the Night" with its above-average specification of articulations, and perhaps a few others. In sum, the *Musical Deposit* contains melodies visiting the pop sphere from their established homes in oral tradition, pop tunes on the verge on entering oral tradition, hits from contemporary commercial popular music with their sheet-music-derived extra trimmings intact, and excerpts from fairly recent stage works ranging from opere buffe to ballad operas. There are marches, dances, and songs, a pair of tunes with futures in shape-note hymnody, a didactic tune or two, and several melodies that served multiple uses. The overall picture is one of multiple aesthetic and cultural functions captured in a compact musical language.

How representative of the fiddling of their day were McArthur's and Seward's manuscripts and the early American publications on which they drew? Young fiddlers in settled areas were likely to have parents who could afford to support their teenagers' desires to learn to play an instrument, and who respected and encouraged music literacy. Settlers in the ever-moving frontier had less time and opportunity to perform music, and certainly to learn to read and write music. At any rate, fewer music books—whether publications or manuscripts—would have been in evidence. However, we must remember that most of the economy, rich or poor, was still based on agriculture. There remained something of a rural feel to what are now big cities, and, at the same time, any settled clump of farms would probably witness its citizens trying to have a civilized good time. Survivals of music publications in sparsely settled areas would be good evidence for a vigorous outreach of city life, but such evidence is slim. Nevertheless, the occasional music commonplace book illustrating practice in surprising regions does turn up.

In closing this section, I would like to note that two large collections of music commonplace books are now available through a recent project: *American Vernacular Music Manuscripts ca. 1730–1910: Digital Collections from the American Antiquarian Society and the Center for Popular Music*: http://popmusic.mtsu.edu/manuscriptmusic/. Sometimes a given collection can be associated with its owner (most often if they signed it), but often not. Some of these collections came out of attics recently, and their provenance is easily established, but others made their ways to those libraries through antiquarian book dealers, and the chain of provenance has not been recorded. It is especially exciting and helpful when we do have a name associated with a collection, and when that name is distinctive enough that the individual can be located in time, place, and cultural context.

I urge the reader to leaf through (digitally) some of the manuscripts available through that website. Just like the McArthur music commonplace book and "Philander Seward's Musical Deposit," each of these music commonplace books provides an idiosyncratic mirror of musical life. Perhaps rather than "mirrors" we should think of these manuscripts as illustrative and representative mosaics each portraying the musical life of a given time and place in interesting and interacting ways. In my inventory of the contents of *Philander Seward's Musical Deposit* in Figure 7, I noted concordances of his tunes in—reading from left to right—McArthur's book, one kept by Silas Dickinson (on deposit at the New York Public Library, like McArthur's), one kept by J. M. Merrow (on deposit at the Center for Popular Music, and among those offered digitally through the project mentioned above), and in *Riley's Flute Melodies*, the published collection most readily available, since it has been reissued in a Da Capo reprint, and is in many university libraries.

We can broaden the lens further and consider the largest multifaceted index of secular music of this age. Originally called the *National Tune Index*, this has matured into *Early America Secular Music and Its European Sources, 1589–1839* (https://www.cdss.org/elibrary/Easmes/index.html), which indexes hundreds of sources by text (titles and, for sung items, by first lines), musical incipits (thrice: by scale degree, by stressed notes—that is, pitches at the beginnings of halves of measures—and interval sequence), and by source. It's amazing how many sources have been indexed for this project, and nearly as astonishing how many had to be left out. Of the music commonplace books I found most useful for this study, only the Dickinson manuscript attracted the attention of this team of researchers. This large database is especially good for discovering alternative titles of given tunes, and for ferreting out interesting printed and manuscript sources that a given person can find near them.

What fiddling from the late eighteenth and early nineteenth centuries is left out of the picture presented in this section of this book and neglected in the sources cited? Most of it, of course. We know little about the music making of the many antebellum fiddlers who were not musically literate or, if they did read music, left no evidence of this. Much of what we do know about such fiddlers comes out of research on individuals interesting for other reasons, or work by regional historians and folklorists documenting the total music scene of given locations. Restricting research to a state or other physically bounded area makes completing a project possible; poring over letters and other basic historical documents in county historical societies can be fascinating, but is rarely efficient. And most of the evidence such research yields consists of frustratingly brief anecdotes. As a sample of such evidence, I will quote from Louis Pichierri, from his admirable discussion of musical life in New Hampshire during this era: "Colonel Archelaus Moore of Canterbury was the master of a noted Negro fiddler who he ultimately set free for fighting in the Revolutionary War. Sampson, as he was known, 'was a famous fiddler and for many years afforded fine fun for frolicsome fellows in Concord with his fiddle on election days'" (1960, 55). That's it—a few facts and some alliteration. What music did this black fiddler play, using what techniques? From whom did he learn? How little this tantalizing anecdote yields can stand for the limitations on our knowledge of fiddling from this time. Nevertheless, looking closely at the music commonplace books of McArthur and Seward yields a sample of what two young fiddlers of that era were like, and what tunes they played.

Anthology I: "Philander Seward's Musical Deposit"

Duke of York's March
(Seward, f. 1r)

(rests at end of each section inserted by CG)

French Dance
(Seward, f. 1r)

(probably should have specified f#, except in m. 6)

Belisle's March
(Seward, f. 1v)

Figure 12. Tune Anthology 1, 1–3.

Lesson by Morelli

(Seward, f. 1v)

President's March

(Seward, f. 2r)

Valencienn's March

(Seward, f. 2v)

Figure 12. Tune Anthology 1, 4–6.

Through the Green Fields
(Seward, f. 2v)

Roslin Castle
(Seward, f. 3r)

The Indian Philosopher
(Seward, f. 3r)

The Hay Makers
(Seward,, f. 3v-4r)

Figure 12. Tune Anthology 1, 7–10.

Flowers of Edinburgh

(Seward, f. 3v-4r)

Fishers Hornpipe

(Seward, f. 3v-4r)

(Seward omitted third measure; his second measure copied here to create third measure)

Primrose Hill

(Seward, f. 3v-4r)

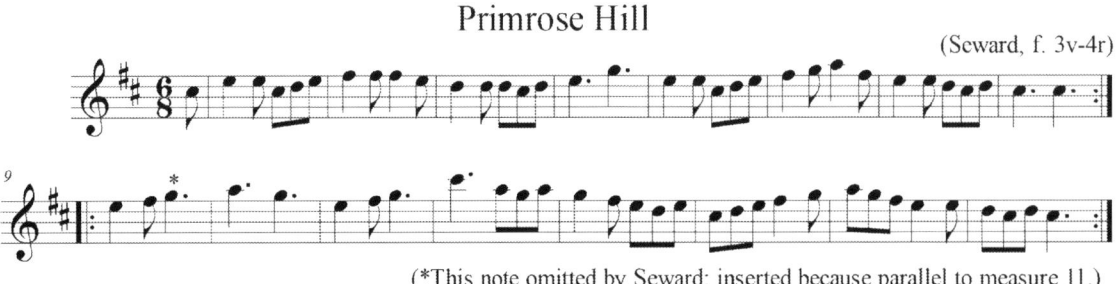

(*This note omitted by Seward; inserted because parallel to measure 11.)

Figure 12. Tune Anthology 1, 11–13.

Figure 12. Tune Anthology 1, 14–16.

Figure 12. Tune Anthology 1, 17–18.

The Garland of Love, Sung by Mrs. Bland
(Seward, f. 8r)

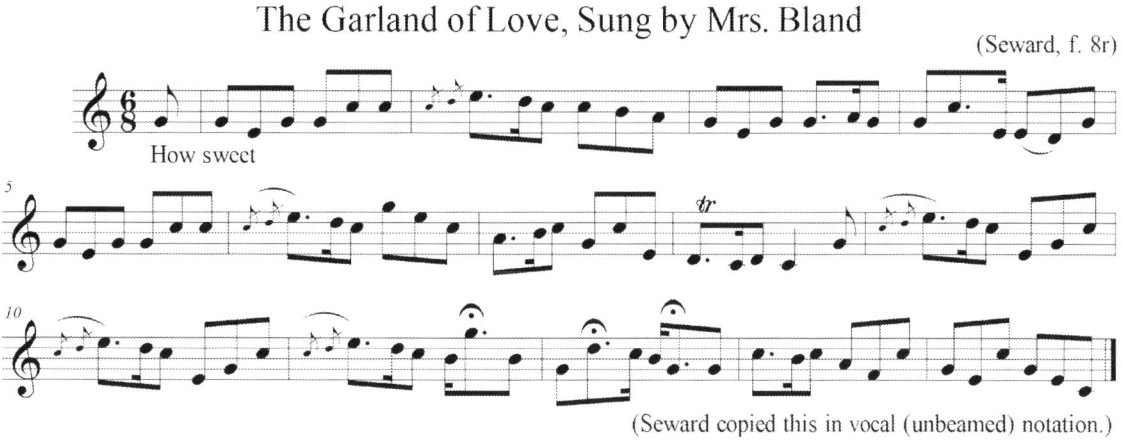

(Seward copied this in vocal (unbeamed) notation.)

Valencienn's March
(Seward, f. 9r)

Ricketts Hornpipe
(Seward, f. 11r)

Figure 12. Tune Anthology 1, 19–21.

Figure 12. Tune Anthology 1, 22–24.

Gen. Greens March
(Seward, f. 15r)

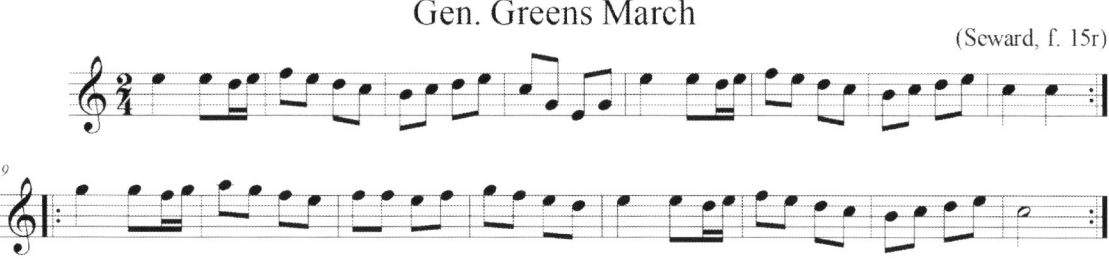

Jefferson & Liberty
(Seward, f. 16r)

Money Musk
(Seward, f. 17r)

(Seward left out the second measure, then wrote it at the end of the piece)

The Devil's Dream
(Seward, f. 18r)

Figure 12. Tune Anthology 1, 25–28.

FIDDLE TUNES IN MUSIC COMMONPLACE BOOKS

Black Sloven

(Seward, f. 19r)

(odd phrasing!)

New Jersey

(Seward, f. 19r)

(pickup notes not integrated; good luck!)

Duke of Holstein's March

(Seward, f. 20r)

How Imperfect

(Seward, f. 21r)

(Seward wrote the words "How Imperfect" a second time at the top of the page, practicing his penmanship.)

Figure 12. Tune Anthology 1, 29–32.

(Seward neglected to place a dot after the quarter note ending each section.)

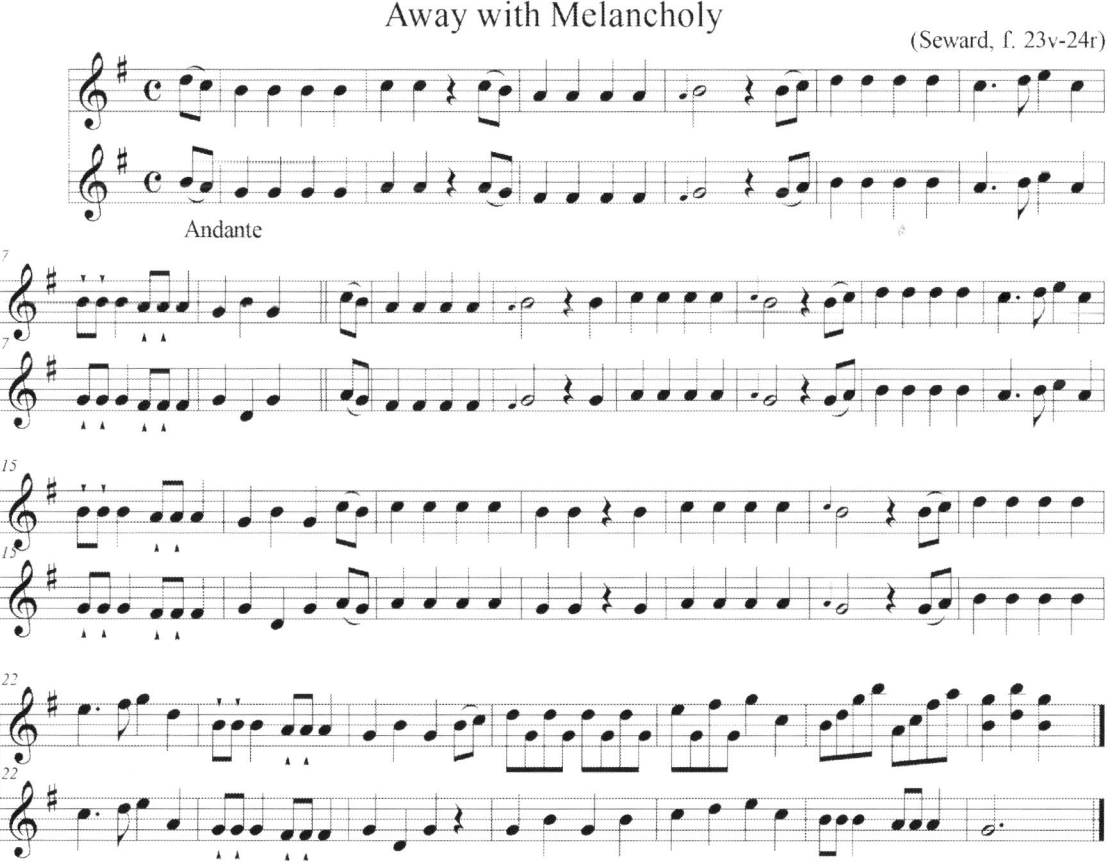

Figure 12. Tune Anthology 1, 33–35.

Duke of York's Cottillon

(Seward, f. 25r)

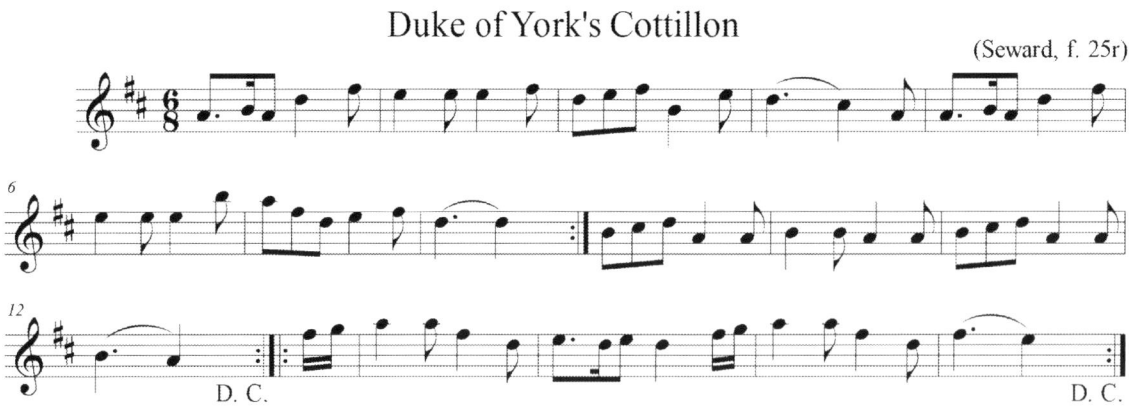

Duke of York's March

(Seward, f. 26v-27r)

(Seward omitted the last beat of the last measure of each half of the trio; I inserted rests)

Figure 12. Tune Anthology 1, 36–37.

F. 27v doesn't have any music on it. However, Seward wrote out these verses by Alexander Pope:

"Teach me to see another's woe to hide the faults I see,
That mercy I to others [show], that mercy show to me."

Duett in Rosina

(Seward, f. 28r)

[Seward's two sharps should be just one.]

Then, below the score, Seward quoted Shakespeare:

"Tis slander whose edge is sharper than a sword, whose tongue
Cut venoms all the worms of Nile who's breath rides
Posting, on the winds, & doth belie all corners of the world."
[above: reads "on the posting winds" in the original play]

PSMD p. 27v contains no music. However, Seward wrote down a name for his manuscript there:

"Philander Seward's Musical Deposit."

In the Dead of the Night

(Seward, f. 29r)

Seward continued practicing penmanship below this entry--especially his elegant cursive "I"--writing:

"I I I In the dead of the night. Philander Seward."

Figure 12. Tune Anthology 1, 38–39.

March in the Battle of Prague

(Seward, f. 30r)

New Haven Green

(Seward, f. 31r)

The Rose

(Seward, f. 31r)

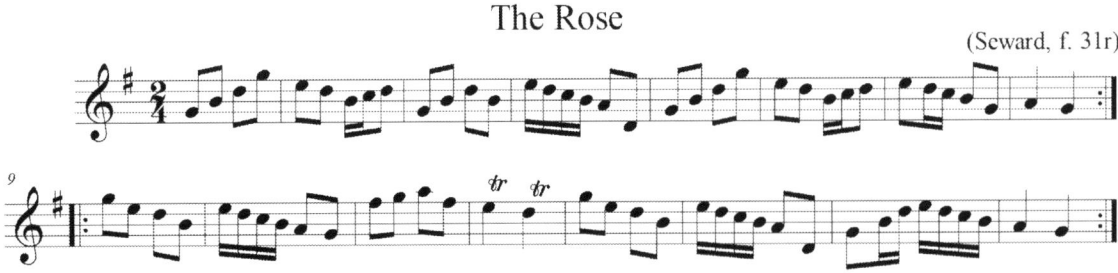

Figure 12. Tune Anthology 1, 40–42.

FIDDLE TUNES IN MUSIC COMMONPLACE BOOKS

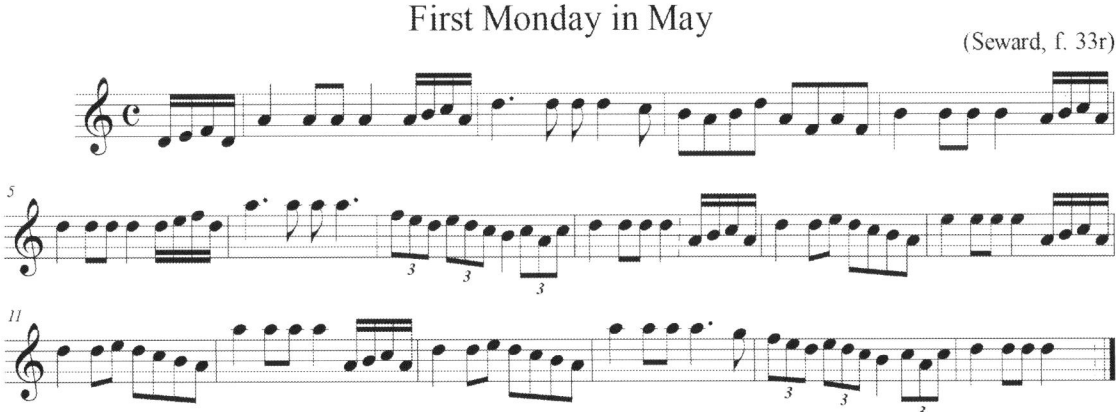

[The dotted line in measure 8 should probably be repeat signs pointing both ways, and the key signature should contain two sharps, for D Major]

Figure 12. Tune Anthology 1, 43–44.

Irish Wedding

(Seward, f. 33r)

This title was misspelled "Irish Weding" in PSMD. There is no key signature there, a common time meter, and implausible rhythms throughout. However, Seward's hand remained quite sure; I expect he copied this--and the previous piece, and the next two pieces--carefully from a remarkably bad source.

Washington's Ode

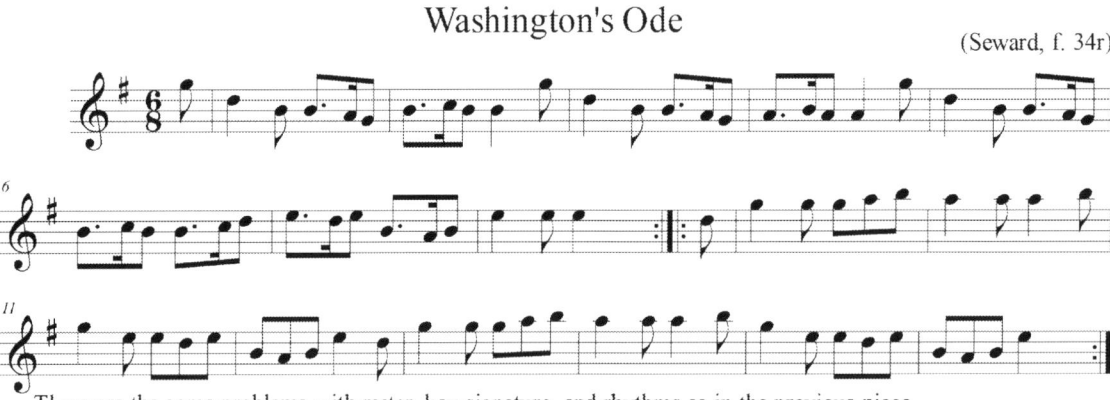

(Seward, f. 34r)

There are the same problems with meter, key signature, and rhythms as in the previous piece.

Meig's March

(Seward, f. 34r)

This is the third and last in this series having notation problems; I fixed the key signature and a few rhythms.

Figure 12. Tune Anthology 1, 45–47.

The Irish Washerwoman

(Seward, f. 35r)

The Honey Moon

(Seward f. 36r)

Prelude, Key of G Major

(Seward, f. 36r)

Highland Reel

(Seward, f. 37r)

Figure 12. Tune Anthology 1, 48–51.

FIDDLE TUNES IN MUSIC COMMONPLACE BOOKS

Nelson's Victory
(Seward, f. 38r)

One two and begin
(Seward f. 39)

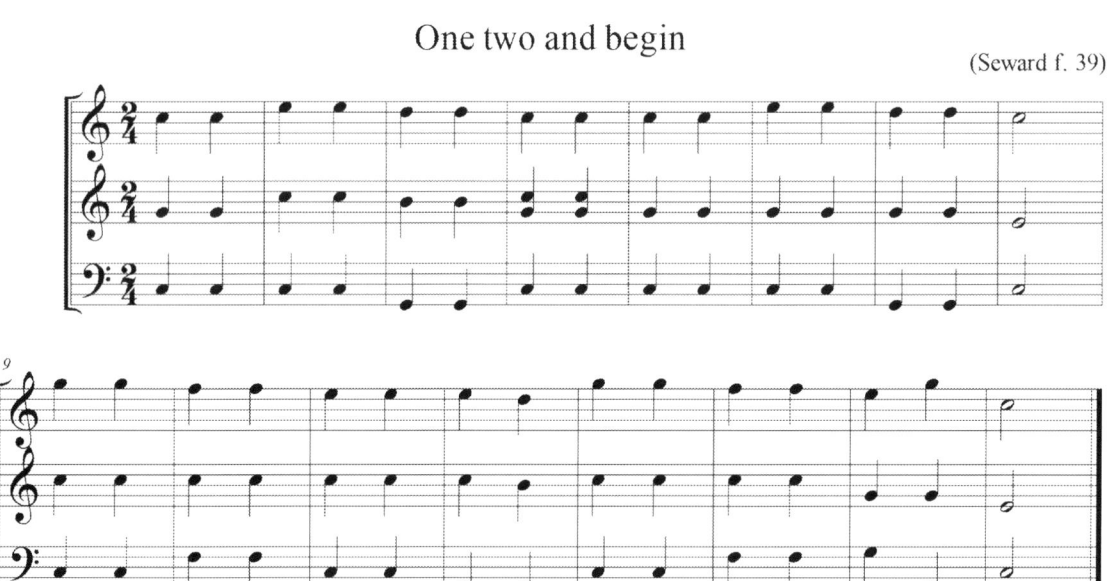

Farmers Joy
(Seward f. 40)

Seward mistakenly used two treble clefs; I found that the lower line needed a bass clef.

Figure 12. Tune Anthology 1, 52–54.

Figure 12. Tune Anthology 1, 55–56.

O Dear, what can the matter be?

(Seward f. 43r)

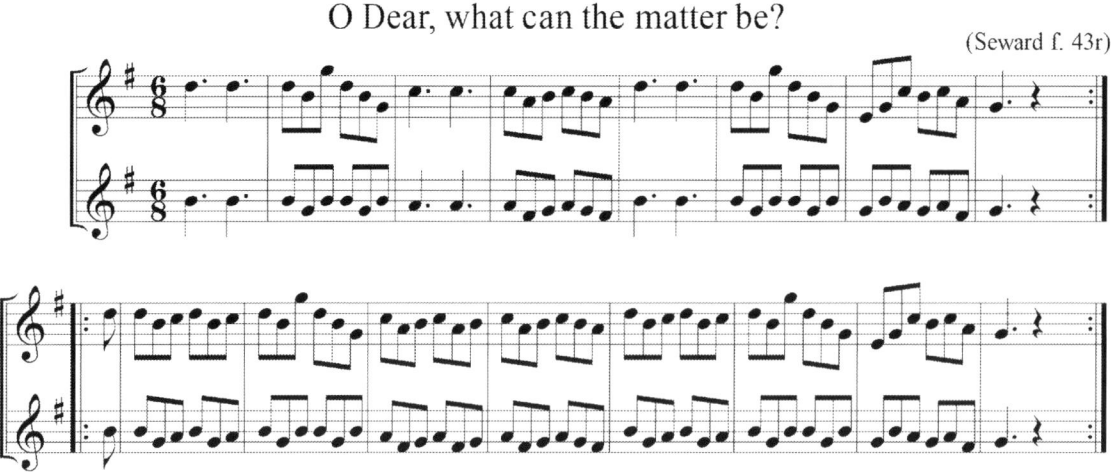

Ladies Excuse

(Seward f. 44r)

Figure 12. Tune Anthology 1, 57–58.

Here follow a few pages that either contain incomplete sketches or are empty. The sketches include:

Folio 44v: A partial (and unlabelled) "Duke of York's March," in D Major, the completed measures identical to those in Seward's version on f. 26v. Some attempt to begin to craft a bass part is evident. This sketch is in pencil.

Folio 46r: A few notes of an identified march in A Major (returning to pen).

Folio 47r: The beginning of "St. Patrick's Day in the Morning" (without a title here), in G Major, sounding very like Seward's "Washington's Ode" as I corrected it to fit into compound duple meter.

Figure 12. Tune Anthology 1, 59–60.

- 55 -

Green's March

(Seward, f. 54r)

Humours of Glynn

(Seward, f. 55r)

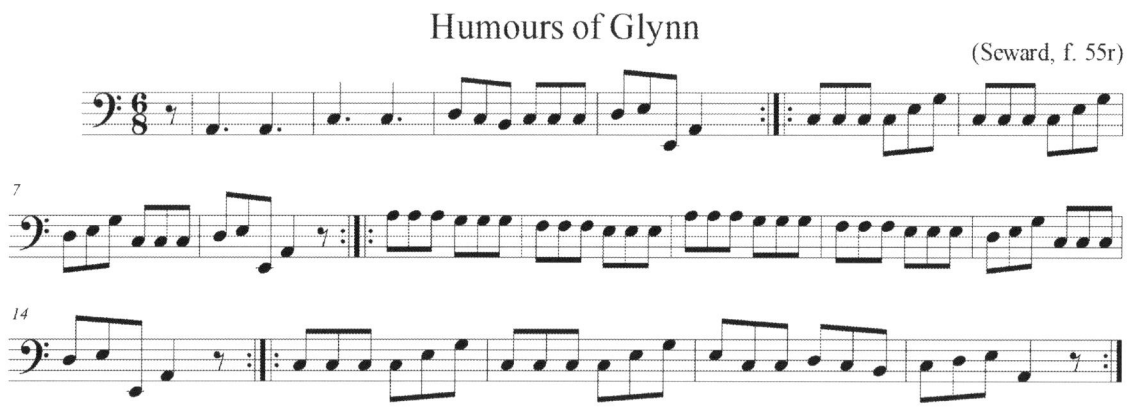

Katies Rambles

(Seward, f. 56r)

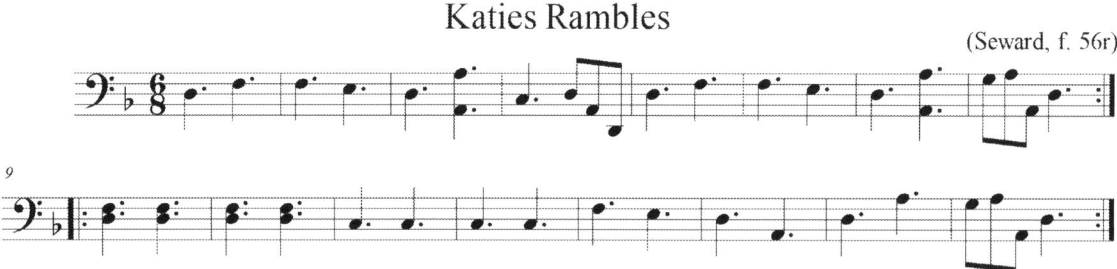

Figure 12. Tune Anthology 1, 61–63.

Figure 12. Tune Anthology 1, 64–66.

Figure 12. Tune Anthology 1, 67–68.

Last entries:

Duett

O say simple maid have you formed any notion
Of all the rude dangers in crossing the ocean,
When winds whistle shrilly ah won't they remind you
To sigh with regret for the grot left behind you.

    2
Oh no, I could follow, and sail the world over
Nor think of my grot when I look at my lover
The winds which blow round us, your arms for my pillow
Will lull us to sleep while we rock by each billow.

    3
Then say, lovely lass, what if happily spying
A rich gallant vessel with gay colors flying,
I'll journey with thee, love, to where the land narrows,
And fling all my waves at my back with my arrows.

    4
Oh say then my truelove we never will wonder,
Nor shrink from the tempest nor dread the big thunder.
While constant will laugh at all changes of weather
And journey all over the world both together

    5
How sweet are the flowers that grow by your fountain,
And sweet are the cowslips that spangle the grove.
And sweet is the breeze that blows over the mountain,
But sweeter by far is the lad that I love.
[next page, sideways]
Wanderer, your early search is vain.
Winter still shows his rugged form.
Still his cote arm lays waste the plain,
And hirls around the icy storm.
Epigram: On wining a ladies money at cards
How fairly fortune all her gifts imparts.
We win your money, Ann, and you our hearts.

To an Early Bee

Wanderer, your early search is vain.
Winter still shows his rugged form.
Still his cold arm lays waste the plain,
And hurls around the icy storm.
Return, oh wanderer, to thy cell
Still on thy treasured honey feast.
For yet no blossom hangs its bell,
Nor yet thy store can be increased.
Wait, wanderer, wait, and spring's bright hour
Shall soon assert its genial sway.
Shall spread the plain with every flower
Shall fill with music every spray.
Then, little Wanderer, thou mayest roam
And glean thy stores from every bloom.
With honey treasure seek thy home,
Nor dread the power of winter's gloom.
    J.M. Lacy

Caledonia [Robert Burns; these verses often sung with
"The Humours of Glynn"]

Their groves o' sweet myrtle let foreign lands reckon
Where bright-beaming summers exalt the perfume.
Far dearer to me yon lone glen o' green breckan
Wi' the burn stealing under the lang yellow broom.
Far dearer to me yon humble brown bowers
Where the blue-bell and gowan lurk, lowly, unseen
For there, lightly tripping among the wild flowers
A list'ing the linnet, aft wanders my Jean.

    2
Though rich is the breeze in their gay sunny valleys
And cauld Caledonia's blast on the wave
Their sweet-scented woodlands that skirt the proud palace,
What are they:—the haunt of the tyrant and slave!
The slave's spicy forests and gold bubbling fountain
The brave Caledonian views wi' disdain,
He wanders as free as the wind on his mountain,
Save love's willing fetters, the chains o' his Jean.

PART TWO

Charles Morris Cobb, William Sidney Mount, and Their Large Manuscript Music Collections from the 1840s to the 1850s

A generation after teenagers Philander Seward and Arthur McArthur were compiling their music commonplace books, the United States was very different. In the northeastern states, where most keepers of music commonplace books had lived, populations continued to mushroom. Despite considerable out-migration, cities burgeoned and rural areas became more densely settled, allowing increasing choices in both professional and leisure activities. Transportation became easier, so that if you couldn't find an object you wanted or information you sought near your home, going to get it or having it sent to you became more feasible. More specifically applicable to music in general and to fiddling in particular, printing music became cheaper, so that it was increasingly easy to buy scores for tunes—lots of them at once—in published collections that would likely contain plenty of melodies appealing to each individual. As a result, players of treble instruments had less need than in previous decades to arduously write down their own favorite melodies; the once-widespread practice of keeping music commonplace books waned.

Last, a general but important point: life got noisier. With more people crowded more closely, incidental, accidental, and deliberate sounds became more plentiful and probably louder, both on the average and in the aggregate. Pieces of music (and/or performance forces) had to be increasingly striking to achieve the same impact on the ear as simple melodies performed by a soloist had been previously. Also, ensembles—which became easier to assemble—became more important, indeed necessary in order for concerts or dance accompaniments to be heard by ever-larger crowds of listeners or dancers.

The most common type of personally organized music collection was no longer the music commonplace book, but instead the binder's volume. To create one of these, a musician would sort accumulated sheet music, often by genre. He or she (generally she) would then take the collection to a bookbinder to have the individual sheets sewn together and a cover added. Binder's volumes worked best for pianists and singers, that is, for musicians whose repertoires were in fact well represented in individual sheet music items. Just one antebellum binder's volume has been presented in a modern publication, one kept by Emily Esperanza McKissick (1836–1919) in Albany, New York, before her marriage in 1858 (Slobin 2011). It contains fifty-six pieces, nearly all conventional sentimental songs, with plantation songs mixed in unsystematically (these were leisurely paced very sentimental songs for the blackface minstrel stage that were popular at home). Only the first piece in "Emily's Book" lacks a text: It's a keyboard edition of the popular "Sontag Polka," which was also arranged in a medley for fiddle by William Sidney Mount, and is reproduced here (Figure 27, p. 16).

The situation was different for violinists, flutists, and other players of treble instruments. Publishers rather than customers themselves did most of the gathering of tunes for these musicians. Each individual tune took little space and cost very little to anthologize, so it made business sense to issue increasingly larger collections of instrumental tunes, collections that customers could then navigate selectively. Owning one or several of these big published collections would likely satisfy the needs of many a music literate violinist/fiddler or flutist. When a simple purchase of one or several of these large collections replaced the creating of a music commonplace book, less historical evidence of personal taste was left behind, even as the sheer number of tunes available to literate musicians increased exponentially. The process of looking through notated music to shape an intended repertoire had in a sense become more private: a performer could peruse the bounty of musical selections in one or a few big collections, and craft their personal gathering through informal and easily revised moments of leisurely selection, moments that would usually remain invisible to history. Bits of evidence of the process might be left behind through, for instance, the adding of fingerings, but such evidence was most common for the keyboard players who kept binders' volumes.

The fattest and most widely distributed published collections of tunes arranged for miscellaneous treble instruments in the antebellum United States were edited by Boston's Elias Howe Jr. There were two basic types of anthologies, one purportedly aimed at players of a given instrument and the other marketed as being shaped for all comers. Howe created both types. I will describe one of his instrument-specific compilations first. What for him was a relatively small collection came out in 1851: *Howe's School for the Violin: Containing New and Complete Instructions for the Violin, with a Large Collection of Favorite Marches, Quick-Steps, Waltzes, Hornpipes, Contra Dances, Songs, and Six Setts of Cotillions, Arranged with Figures. Containing Over 150 Pieces of Music.* This and parallel collections (that is, ones specifically for flute, or fife, or clarinet, etc.) followed a formula that departed little from that characteristic of instrument instruction books from Seward and McArthur's youth. These books were mainly anthologies. The initial didactic sections offered very little information about music and how to play it on the instrument in question. As was always the case, Howe's *Self Instructor for the Violin* leads off with the teaching portion, a brief section innocent of musical examples, just as the following anthology includes no instruction at all. In the instructional portion, two pages each describe note values and scales (major and melodic minor), and a page each treats meter, "Accidents" (accidentals), intervals, and chords. A total of three pages relate specifically to the violin, these treating tuning the instrument, bowing, fingering a G scale from the open g string to what can be reached on the e string without shifting—thus a total span of an octave plus a third—and shifting (to as high as third position, no further). Finally, there is a one-page dictionary of musical terms.

The bulk of Howe's book, the anthology of tunes, starts quite typically, with a parade of melodies of miscellaneous songs. Subsequent sections focus in turn on blackface minstrel songs, waltzes, hornpipes (and reels, that is, common-time contradance tunes), a handful of "Negro Jigs," and, surprisingly, just a pair of marches. In another and greater surprise, the minstrel songs and associated jigs fill a mere seven pages, less space than occupied by waltzes. Scholars of American music in general and of fiddling in particular are used to looking especially closely at the minstrel element in popular music of this time, since that was both fairly new and quite novel, and because it marked the beginning of reversing the flow of popular music from the long-lived Britain-to-colonies (and then US) pattern. But the statistics of the pop music scene as it relates to performing at home relegates minstrelsy to a less prominent position.

Howe published tutors for many individual instruments early in his career, and those books sold well enough for him to continue. However, if survival in modern library collections indicates success during the nineteenth century, Howe's larger *Instrumental Musician* (6 volumes, first of several editions 1843) and especially *The Musician's Companion* (4 volumes, first of several editions 1844) sold much better than did the tutors. The title page of the first volume of *The Musician's Companion* is given as Figure 13.

Even though there would seem to have been little reason to maintain a personal manuscript collection of melodies in the era of these massive collections, a few later fiddlers/violinists did maintain music commonplace books or other types of handwritten gatherings of melodies that they crafted to resemble commercial collections. The two largest surviving manuscript collections kept by fiddlers in the last two decades before the Civil War were made by men who were very different in background, in age, in livelihood, and in many other ways. But Charles M. Cobb (1835–1903) and William Sidney Mount (1807–1868) were active as fiddlers at about the same time (Cobb, although younger, was musically precocious). Mount and Cobb encountered the same published collections of pop music containing fiddle tunes. And these two very different men had quite a bit in common in the repertoire they played, in their ambitious violin/fiddle technique, and in various attitudes about fiddling. I will discuss Cobb's life first, then Mount's, then delve into factors that they shared. The anthology of tunes in this section of the book draws on both men's tune collections, and not just from their own conceptions of tunes, but also from the playing of other fiddlers whom either man knew well.

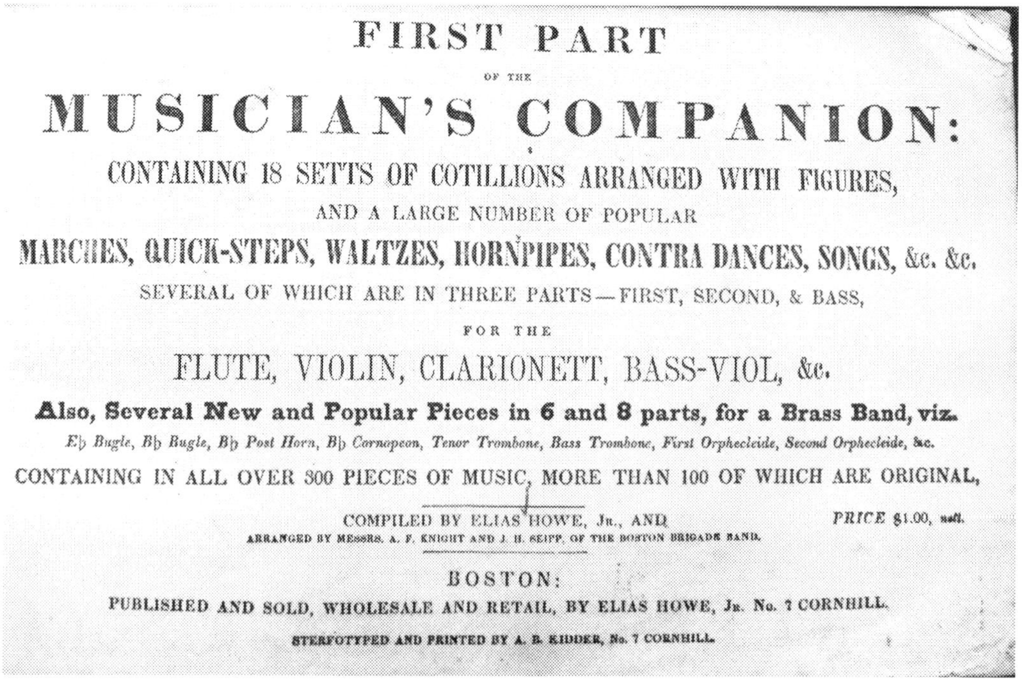

> FIRST PART
> OF THE
> MUSICIAN'S COMPANION:
> CONTAINING 18 SETTS OF COTILLIONS ARRANGED WITH FIGURES,
> AND A LARGE NUMBER OF POPULAR
> MARCHES, QUICK-STEPS, WALTZES, HORNPIPES, CONTRA DANCES, SONGS, &c. &c.
> SEVERAL OF WHICH ARE IN THREE PARTS—FIRST, SECOND, & BASS,
> FOR THE
> FLUTE, VIOLIN, CLARIONETT, BASS-VIOL, &c.
> Also, Several New and Popular Pieces in 6 and 8 parts, for a Brass Band, viz.
> E♭ Bugle, B♭ Bugle, B♭ Post Horn, B♭ Cornopeon, Tenor Trombone, Bass Trombone, First Orphecleide, Second Orphecleide, &c.
> CONTAINING IN ALL OVER 300 PIECES OF MUSIC, MORE THAN 100 OF WHICH ARE ORIGINAL,
> COMPILED BY ELIAS HOWE, Jr., AND
> ARRANGED BY MESSRS. A. F. KNIGHT AND J. H. SEIPP, OF THE BOSTON BRIGADE BAND.
> PRICE $1.00, nett.
> BOSTON:
> PUBLISHED AND SOLD, WHOLESALE AND RETAIL, BY ELIAS HOWE, Jr. No. 7 CORNHILL.
> STERFOTYPED AND PRINTED BY A. B. KIDDER, No. 7 CORNHILL.

Figure 13. The title page of Elias Howe's most popular publication, the first volume of his Musician's Companion (1844).

CHARLES M. COBB, JACK-OF-MANY-TRADES AND FIDDLER OF WOODSTOCK, VERMONT

With both Cobb and Mount, we are not dealing with lives pivoting on dramatic events, but rather with biographical textures full of music making. Charles Morris Cobb, of Woodstock, Vermont, lived most of his life in the house in which he had been born and would die. Woodstock was settled in the 1760s, had mills by the 1770s, and was incorporated in 1837. It grew swiftly, and had a population of some 3,000 by 1860 (its size today). While farming remained the main profession through the Civil War era, there were several factories in town by then. And the population base during Cobb's youth had grown enough that some local farmers gained significant income from more specialized work.[1]

Cobb's father, Gains P. Cobb, was a capricious, inattentive, and unsuccessful farmer. Charles Cobb said that his father lost money on the land and didn't collect efficiently for other work (*Journal* Feb. 21, 1852). Nevertheless, a modest stream of income from selling honey flowed reliably. Gains Cobb also made and repaired shoes and boots, and worked occasionally in A. W. Whitney Machine Shop in West Woodstock (Charles would do that also). Charles Cobb drew two maps in his journal, one to show where Vermont fit in New England, and one of his family's land. The latter drawing narrates his daily routine during the maple syrup boiling season, and also illustrates his mental processes—he drew the map in 1851, then added to it twice, with results passing from comprehensive to overcrowded (Figure 14).

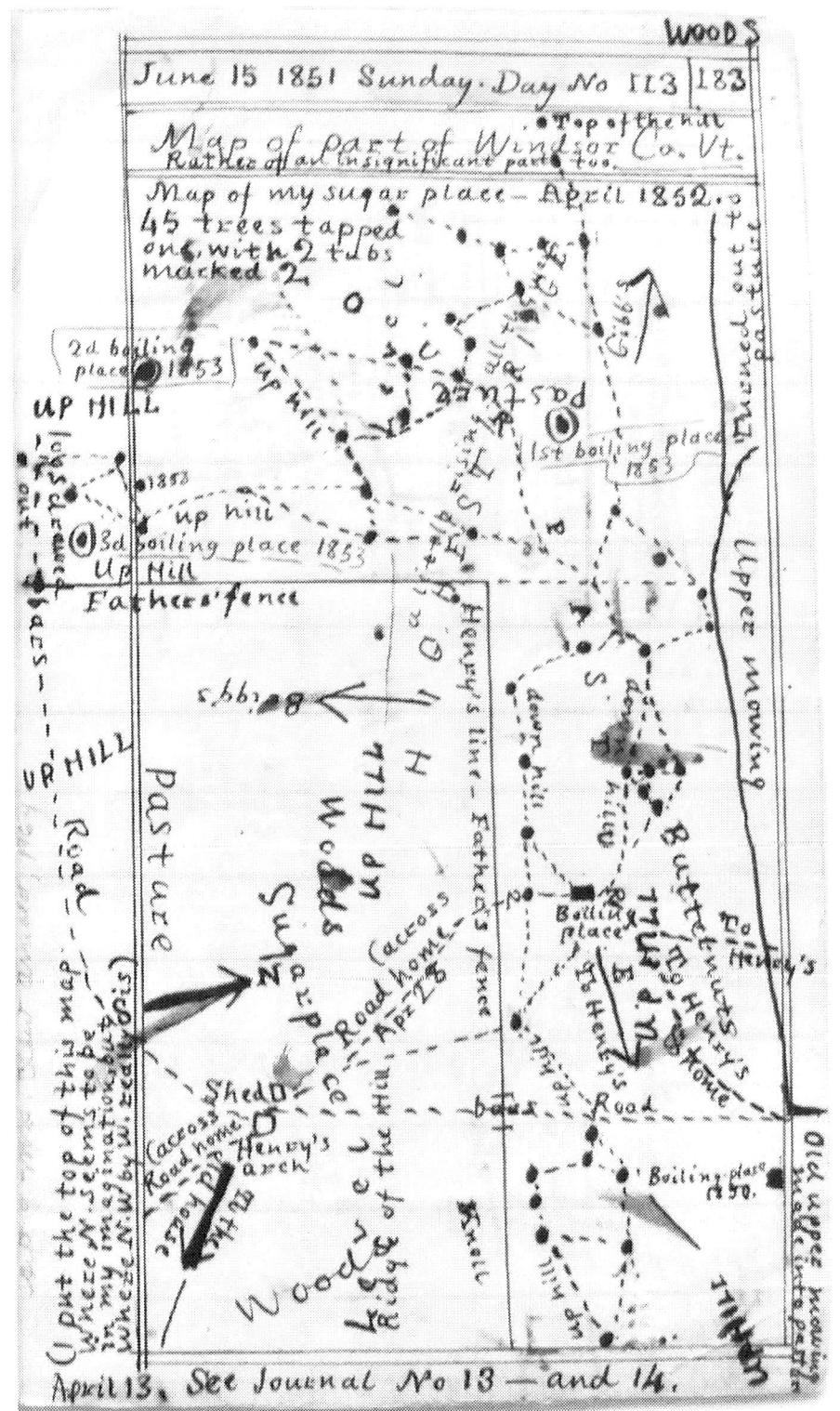

Figure 14. Map drawn by Charles M. Cobb of his neighborhood in Windsor County, Vermont. Courtesy of the Vermont Historical Society.

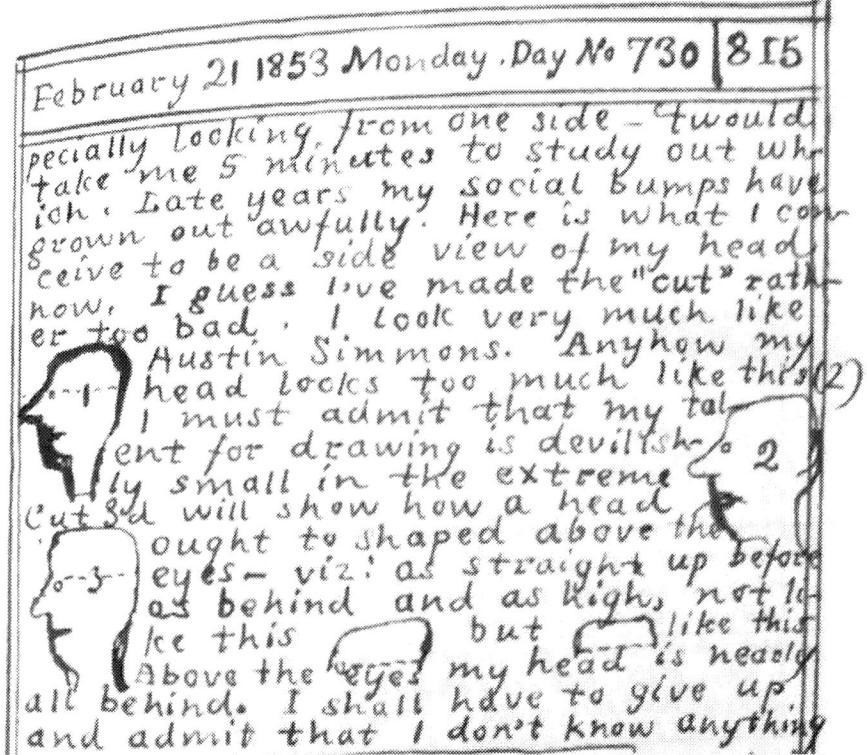

Figure 15. Our only likeness of Charles M. Cobb comes from his own pen. On the diary page previous to the one pictured here, he noted that he "used to have a square and erect forehead but now it is most devilish slanting and [his] nose sticks out awfully,—especially looking from one side." Austin Simmons, whom Cobb was afraid he resembled, was a local schoolteacher (and believer in the spiritual conversations conducted by "rapping"). Courtesy of Vermont Historical Society.

Cobb described his home as having "one inhabitable room, [that looked] from without like the abode of Satan's poverty stricken" (*Journal* Feb. 17, 1852). When they planned a move, he inventoried the family belongings. That list, transcribed as Figure 16, shows what a slim array of goods a family might own, and how surprisingly substantial a fraction of the Cobbs' belongings was music related (including copies of widely distributed tune collections). It also illustrates Charles Cobb's youthful but already wry sense of humor. Cobb drew the only representation we have of his appearance on another page in that journal (Figure 15).

Gains Cobb played the flute on occasion, but was more of a tinkerer than performer. He spent endless hours making fiddle cases and repairing fiddles and the common wind instruments of his day. Charles's mother, Lucia, was also musical—she played the melodeon and sang. She was sickly, and, according to her son, took plenty of verbal abuse from Gains Cobb. In a day of large families, Charles was an only child. Today he might be diagnosed as obsessive-compulsive with a luxuriant variety of collateral problems. But however unusual and socially awkward he swiftly manifested himself to be, his parents indulged his passion for music generously, surprisingly so given their always precarious finances.

FIGURE 16. INVENTORY OF THE COBB FAMILY BELONGINGS, MADE BY CHARLES M. COBB ON APRIL 8, 1852, JUST BEFORE THE FAMILY MOVED TO ANOTHER HOUSE IN WOODSTOCK, VERMONT.

Item	Value	Cost
First I will set down the OLD-HOUSE. $8 worth has been taken out & worked into the barn, say, well	[$]67	42
2. The wagon-house. It ought to be worth what it cost, but isn't	17	20
3. The new-waggon [It ought to be worth what it cost, but isn't]	60	80
4. The Melodeon. If it isn't worth what it cost us it's not because it has been injured, but because we were cheated in buying it	25	35
5. The Geo Scales fiddle-box. I will put it down for we never shall see Geo. Again. 'Tis now at Gibb's	1	6
6. My leather covered fiddle-box—made by Father of course	4	5
7. My fiddle. Gave H.B. Smith a violin that cost us $10 at first (fixed it $5 worth) gave a note for $10 to boot (the 1st fiddle cost 12.50 bow & all)	25	25
8. A fiddle-bow that we had with the Mile's fiddle	1.50	1.50
9. Another that we had of H.B. Smith (swapped) (cost 2.75)	.75	2.75
10. My watch. Prime cost $25—to us $15—has had it repaired, in all 3.87	18.00	18.87
11. Mother's watch. Cost us $9—Repaired 1.50. 1st cost $12.50, chain included, cost .75	12.00	10.50
12. Silk watch chain bought Dec. 1850 used up	[0]	.25
13. Silver Watch Key. Partly lost.	[0]	15.45
14. Our old clock Cost $18. Repairs $3 Mirror broken out Feb. 1850	3.00	21.00
15. Old clarionet. See Melodeon	2.50	2.50
16. Father's flute do	1.00	1.00
17. My accordian [sic]—lent to Ed Willis	1.00	.98
18. Thunderstruck fiddle. Not worth what it cost	.45	.63
19. Small flute. Swapped a flageolet that was given to me, for it—I might say that it cost nothing—or $5 because the flageolet cost that when new, but I'll keep clear of all extremes. If I'd bought the flag't it might have been for 25 cents	.34	.25
20. My large music book—containing 825 tunes—cost blank	7.00	5.00
21. Music B[ook].—Melodeon	.50	1.00
22. Music B[ook] American Violinist	.40	.80
23. Music B[ook] [Elias Howe's] Mus[ician]'s Companion	.30	.60
24. Music B[ook] Songs for the People	.62	1.25
25. Music B[ook] Modern Harp	.38	.75
26. Music B[ook] Carmina Sacra	.37	.75
27. Music B[ook] Modern Psalmist	.37	.75
28. Music B[ook] B[oston] Academy's Collect'n	.50	1.00
29. Amateur's Song B'k. Lent	[0]	.15
30. Blank music book that cost 50c out of the cover	.12	.50
31. My written Music Book. Paper 40c binding 50c	.12	.50

Item	Value	Cost
32. Leather cov'd Music Book	.10	.50
33. Shot-Gun	3.00	3.00
34. My 3 bladed knife	.50	.50
35. My Jack knife	.30	.37
36. The White Pen Knife	.12	.38
37. Father's Geo. Grow knife	.63	.63
38. Wormer belong to the Gun	.25	[o]
39. My Money Purse	.37	.37
40. Wallet, given to me by Orfa Marsh, cost 37 1/2	.12	.38
41. Lead pencils, & slate pencils 'round estimated	.05	.10
42. A small whetstone in my box	.12	.12
43. 12 cents in cash [in my box] Guess this is worth the cost	.12	.12
44. Another whetstone in my box	.05	.06
45. Our Light-stand	2.00	2.50
46. Hair-Brush given me by Aunt Laura	.20	.25
47. Pack of Cards lent [to?] Geo. Grow	.12	.25
48. A Burning Glass [lent to?] Geo. Grow	.08	.25
49. Jack-[k]nifes not reckoned—3 that I've lately lost	18.51	[?]
50. Father's old jackknife	.12	.25
51. His Pruning knife	.75	.75
52. My silk handkerchief	.46	.92
53. Father's "Fred" knife	.10	.25
54. My neck-handkerchief	.06	.12
55. Father's [neck-handkerchief]	.06	.12
56. My 2 pocket handkerchiefs	.12	.25
57. Some window curtains that "Granny" gave us—guess they won't be moved	___	.50
58. Our map of the U. States	2.50	5.00
59. [Our map] of Vermont	.75	1.50
60. My shoes or pumps, bo't Aug. 1850	.62	1.25
61. My old thin boots	.75	3.00
62. My new boots	2.00	2.50
63. Old thick pair	.12	2.50
64. Another!—won't be moved	___	2.50
65. Mother's shoes	.61	1.12
66. [Mother's] Old rubbers	.06	.92
67. [Mother's] Rubbers	.46	.92
68. [Mother's] Spectacles	2.50	2.50

Item	Value	Cost
69. [Mother's] Silver Thimble	.50	.50
70. Our tin tea-kettle	.63	1.25
71. Looking-glass	.50	.50
72. Oil Cloth for Table Cloth	.05	.75
73. Old Table	2.00	4.00
74.75.76 Our 3 bedsteads, cost $4, $4, and $6	9.00	14.00
77. New Table Cloth	.15	.30
78. My new Overcoat (unpaid)	8.00	8.00
79. My Big Cap	1.00	2.00
80. Summer [Cap] outgrown	.75	1.00
81. Father's fur cap	1.00	4.00
82. [Father's] new hat	2.00	4.00
83. Father's & my last summer palm-leafs	.25	.50
84. Small stove—had at 2d hand of Chas Raymond	3.50	3.50
85. Large Stove	5.00	15.00
86. Mother's small shawl	3.00	4.50
87. My gold-pen, case &c	1.25	2.50

Charles Cobb rarely went to school. He was sickly, but also not very interested. He summarized: "I don't go to school much" (*Journal* Feb. 17, 1852). Sometimes his parents needed him to help with the cycle of seasonal tasks—harvests on their small farm, tapping maple trees and working with the sap-to-syrup process, or the springtime repairing of fences, plus beekeeping year round. But he also disliked the regimented group learning experience, and seized on any reason to stay home. In any case, he learned more effectively outside of a structured plan, following his own interests and proceeding at his own pace (like many fiddlers today).

Cobb kept his journal assiduously as a teenager and young adult, from 1850 through 1862 (most enthusiastically in 1851–1854). He wrote about what he did during a given day (and recorded strong opinions on various topics) in a cramped hand in a series of tiny hand-sewn volumes, thirty-three of which have survived (now on deposit at the Vermont Historical Society). He also wrote out tunes in a large blank book given him as a Christmas present, often dozens of melodies on a page (he slackened the pace of entering tunes in this manuscript after the Civil War). Nearly everything we know about him comes directly from him, via these two sources. The journal/diary and tune collection overlapped: there are a handful of tunes in the journal, and both didactic prose and bits of trenchant commentary about tunes (and fellow fiddlers) here and there in his big book, which he named *The Universal Musician*. That title indicated his naïve but vigorously pursued intent: to assemble all of the melodies and all of the knowledge about music that mattered. That grand ambition eventually faded, and he crammed tunes into whatever space he found, and inserted multipart arrangements of tunes as he shifted his focus to playing horns in a band. The result is a delightful crowded mess. Figure 17 shows the title page, which was dramatically designed but accrued its own cramped population of melodies. Figure 18 shows another kind of crowding: Cobb tracked voting numerous times, and that crept into his book too.

Cobb's musical training flowed naturally from family and local fiddlers. His parents were musical, and the impoverished Cobbs had an upstairs boarder, a Mr. Hartwell, who gave singing schools, one of which he attended as early as 1845 (*Journal* May 20, 1850, and June 24, 1852). His interest in fiddling dates from late in 1846: "I got my first idea of fiddling from Fred's [?] having a 50c toy fiddle. Father bought me a fiddle at $2 of Wm King & fixed it up. Began to write music [meaning he copied tunes from publications]. . . . father bought the dun fiddle after having had others on trial all winter." (This was to be Cobb's favorite fiddle for years; Gains also purchased a melodeon that day.) For Christmas of 1849, Charles Cobb was given his "big book," which he would turn into his *Universal Musician* (*Journal* June 24, 1852). Cobb took about a dozen fiddle lessons from a local musician, Leverett Lull (*Journal* Feb. 28, 1851), and would eventually travel to Lebanon, New Hampshire, to study for a few weeks with the most prominent fiddler, dancing master, and band leader living nearby, Abram Pushee (1791–1868).

We know nothing about the musical community in young Philander Seward's Dutchess County, New York, and very little about music in Limington, Maine, when Arthur McArthur was a boy. Both young men doubtless collaborated musically with family members. But history left no traces of additional musicians in the Seward clan, and little about musicians among McArthur's siblings, though his daughter played the piano. A generation later, when these two men were grown and well ensconced in their professions, musical life in their towns had bloomed, and it is no surprise that we can learn plenty about musical life in Cobb's Woodstock, Vermont, and in Mount's Stony Brook, New York. In both places, fiddlers could count on regular musical interchange with other fiddlers and with other musicians.

Most of Cobb's fiddling acquaintances also lived in Woodstock. A young man might visit (or have Cobb visit him) and have the main activity of the evening be either playing checkers or fiddling, which Cobb would mention many times in his journal. Or family-to-family visits could include those activities. Most such occasions were shared with respectable people of similar socioeconomic status (though the Cobbs were on the poor side). However, one George Scales, an avid fiddler with whom Charles had traveled to Lebanon, New Hampshire, to study with Pushee, was an exception. Cobb looked down on Scales, partly due to their different approaches. Cobb valued the ability to read music, to transpose easily, and to maintain a large repertoire, while Scales read poorly and learned far fewer tunes (concentrating on what Cobb called "everlastings"). However, Scales did well enough that their mutual teacher Pushee arranged for him to lead dancing schools. This was while Cobb was a teenager, and Scales an adult, married and

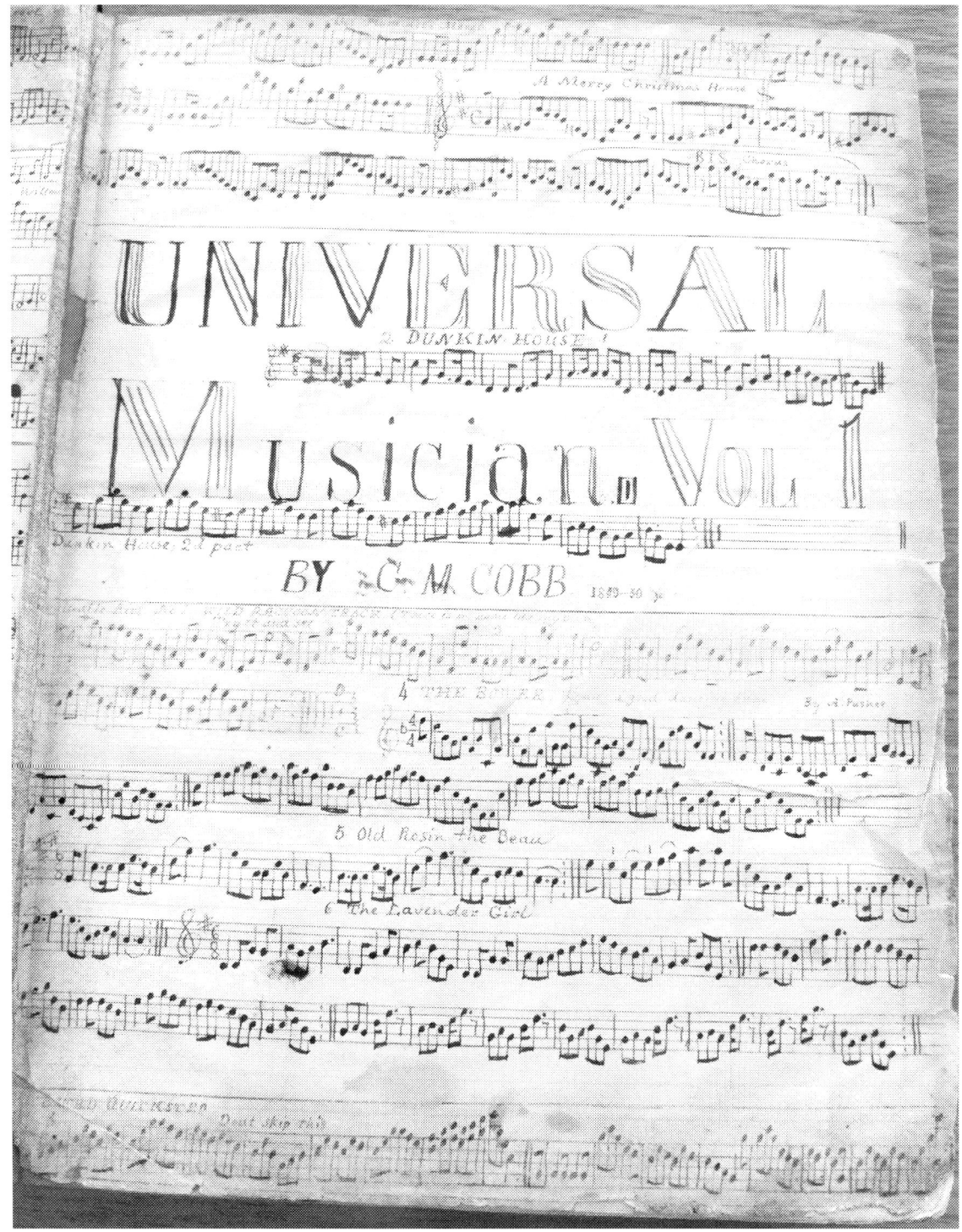

Figure 17. The title page of Charles Cobb's massive manuscript, his Universal Musician. Courtesy of Vermont Historical Society

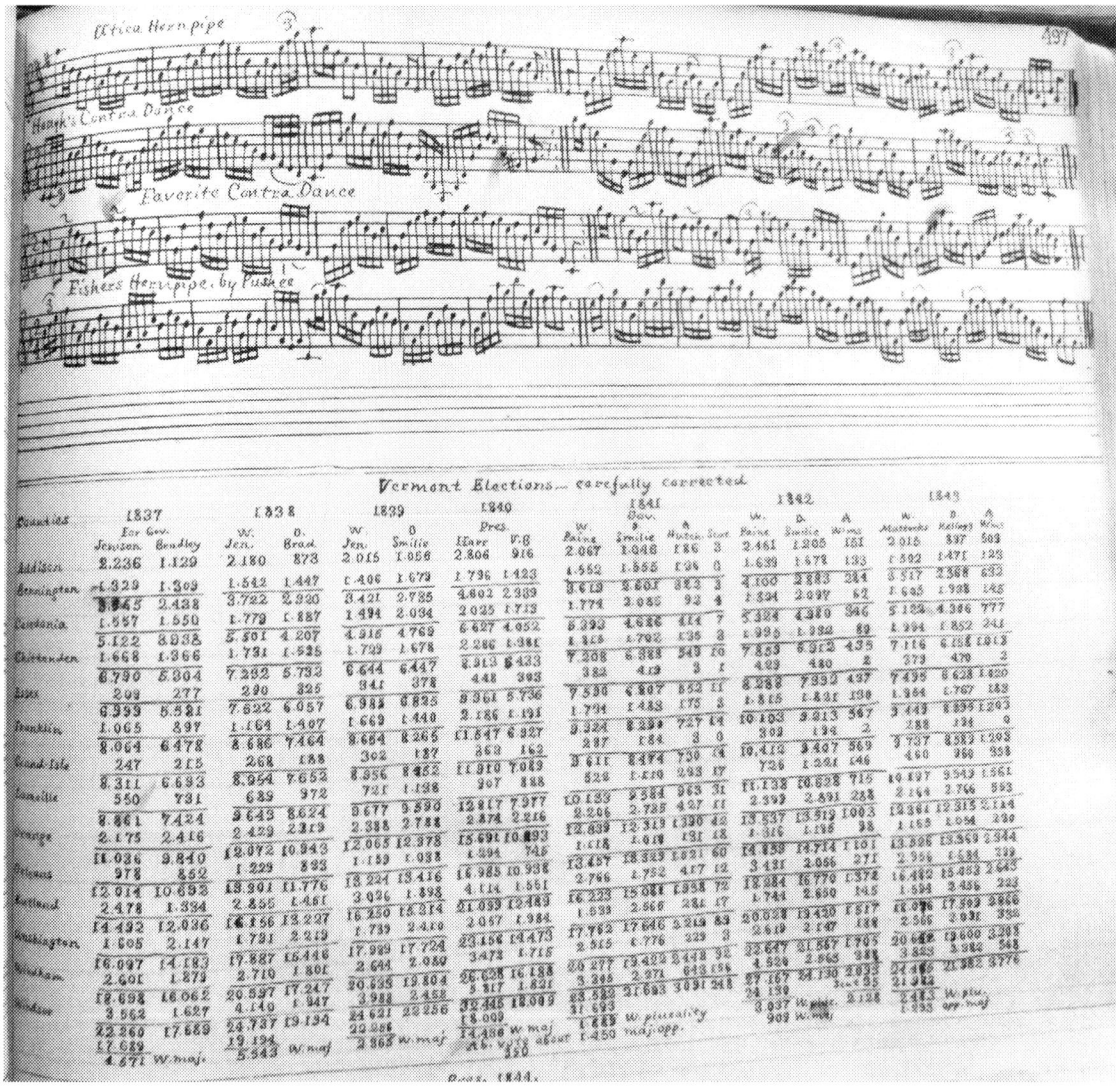

Figure 18. Page 497 of the Universal Musician, on which Cobb had copied a few tunes before dedicating most of the page to vote tallies for Vermont elections. Courtesy of Vermont Historical Society

with children, and with the expressed ambition to become a professional musician and dancing master—perhaps these factors swayed Pushee. Cobb was disappointed and skeptical . . . and gleeful when his negative assessment of Scales's character was confirmed. On June 21, 1852, Cobb wrote that he had learned that Scales had gone to Canada. "From there, he afterwards wrote to his wife that he had lost his best suit of clothes! Come to find out they tarred and feathered him & rode him on a rail! I asked Jerome [the bearer of this news] the reason & he said they 'found him where he SHOULDN'T HAVE BEEN.' This last about him was that he 'had gone to Illinois with two women one of whom was another man's wife!' Thus ends my acquaintance with and knowledge of George Scales. I ne'er shall see him no more nor will his wife."

There's almost nothing in the Cobb materials indicating contact with black fiddlers. His father purchased a broken fiddle from an individual Cobb called "Nigger Briggs," who turns up now and then in Cobb's journal as a local laborer. Cobb called the fiddle in question the "thunderstruck fiddle"; it needed a new top, which his father tried to craft. But we encounter indications that fiddling was then associated with African Americans: when Cobb's family learned of his intention to travel to New Hampshire to study fiddling with Abram Pushee, his uncle Eben Cobb mocked the plan, asking if young Charles thought he would "get to be a nigger in three weeks" (*Journal* May 23, 1851). Also, Cobb reported on a traveling show: "Last Saturday Barnum's Museum and Menagerie which was to be so very great came out small." Nevertheless, he saw a giant, and a mummy, and admired some songs and dances performed by "white niggers" (doubtless blackface minstrels; *Journal* Aug. 17, 1851). Given how thoroughly he narrated his life in his journal, he seems to have had little contact with African Americans or their imitators.

By the early 1860s, Cobb was thoroughly involved in the local wind band. His father had purchased a membership in the band for him in 1852; he would eventually play Eb alto sax horn (his first brass instrument), tenor and bass horns, string bass, clarinet, Bb and Eb cornet, and keyboards. The Woodstock Cornet Band became his focus as a young, poorly paid musician. The Cobbs accumulated more and better exemplars of wind instruments, and Gains Cobb tinkered with them, just as he had previously worked with fiddles and fiddle cases. Charles Cobb became competent and then skilled at performing and at arranging tunes for the band. His comments about fellow band members and their questionable abilities, about the band and its poorly paid performances, and so forth are amusing and a good source of information about this stage in the history of American band music. Cobb's work with bands became his musical focus, and the justification for his calling himself a professional musician in the census of 1900, although stints at local factories were likely more lucrative and so more important to him and his wife and children. His participation in the growing band movement was concomitant with the population becoming denser, and with dances and public celebrations getting bigger, requiring louder performances.

Nevertheless, Cobb's journal entries from shortly before the Civil War indicate that local fiddling continued during sociable evenings and neighborhood dances. We don't know how large, band-featuring events balanced with intimate fiddle-fueled affairs in Cobb's life or in general in his part of the country during and after the Civil War—he gradually stopped keeping his journal. But the growth of bands and their taking over the function of accompanying large dances did not overwhelm fiddling. In addition to a larger wind band, Cobb led Cobb's Quadrille Band, which consisted of him on first violin, a second violin/prompter (of dance instructions), clarinet, cornet, and bass (*Journal* Mar. 15, 1856). This served for occasions when the full band was not required—particularly dances—but for which a single fiddler would suffice. A helpful tally: He wrote that in 1856, he worked in a machine shop 207 days, was in band performances 5 days, and employed as a fiddler 33 nights.

Late in life, Cobb gathered up some poetry in a book he called *Song-Verses, Legends, Ballads and Other Sketches in Rhyme* (no publication information specified; the Library of Congress catalog guesses a date of appearance: 190?). These literary efforts evince his trenchant sense of humor. Most of the thirty-seven poems consist of several verses each including several rhymed couplets. He mocks dishonesty, greed, financial shortsightedness (and other fiscal foolishness), pretensions of all kinds, and patent medicines, with just two lyrics bearing a positive message. He ends with one of those: "Three Cheers for Old Vermont!" He rarely mentions music, and refers to fiddling just once, in this tongue-in-cheek series of admonitions:

Wise Counsel

Young men, don't go to see the girls, Don't get your coats against their curls,
Don't hang around with them to talk, Nor ever go with them to walk,
But stay at home to ply your trade And thus all wicked thoughts evade.
In doing this you'll wisdom heed, Oh, Yes! Oh yes indeed!
Young girls, don't let the boys come near, Don't let yourselves their discourse hear.
Don't let them make the least advance, Nor ever with them flirt or dance,
But stay at home and help your marm, And you'll be always safe from harm
And e'er your "title clear" can read Oh yes! Oh yes, indeed!
My friends, don't sugar candy eat Nor spoil your teeth with pound-cake sweet;
Don't e'er escalloped oysters try, Nor stuff yourselves with chicken pie,
But eat your beans and good corn-cake And graham bread in skimmed milk take,
On meal-and-water gruel feed, Oh yes! Oh yes indeed!
Young man, don't learn cigars to smoke Nor tonic beer drink till you choke;
Don't ever play at games of chance, Nor learn to fiddle, sing or dance,
But saw your wood and hoe your corn And milk the cows at early morn;
A life of honest labor lead, Oh yes! Oh yes indeed! (35–36).

WILLIAM SIDNEY MOUNT, PAINTER AND FIDDLER OF STONY BROOK, NEW YORK

William Sidney Mount, more of a public figure than Charles Cobb, made a lasting mark in the history of American painting. There is quite a bit written about him, including a fair amount on his musical activities, so I can treat his biography briefly. He was the fourth of eight children in a comfortably propertied family in Stony Brook. Both sides of his family went back many generations in the United

States, and both parents were musical. His father died when he was seven. He and his elder brother Robert Nelson Mount were sent to live with their uncle Micah Hawkins (1777–1825) in New York. Hawkins instructed both in music: Robert Nelson Mount—henceforth Nelson, as he was normally addressed—would become a professional fiddler and dancing master, and William Sidney would fiddle for dances and in concert, too, albeit less ambitiously than he pursued his main profession of painting.

Micah Hawkins, born in Stony Brook, apprenticed in coach making, but spent most of his adult life as a grocer and hotelier. He was also a bon vivant deeply involved in the arts. He played flute, violin, and piano, and built a piano into a counter at his store. His ballad opera, *Saw-Mill, or The Yankee Trick* (1824) was the first American effort in that genre; to be performed several times. The published libretto remains: Two young men outwit two of the high-and-mighty (particularly the odious Count Phlegm), and eventually are united with their sweethearts. While we don't know precisely what music was attached, the song lyrics would fit many tunes. A waltz is danced along the way, a Dutch-dialect parody of "Yankee Doodle" must have been sung to that tune, and "Possum Up a Gum Tree" is mentioned (Hawkins 1824, 48, 34–35, and 50; Ford 1940, 19).

Hawkins bought lots of sheet music, focusing on sentimental songs, often from ballad operas (this collection is now in the Library of Congress). A pair of flowery songs by London resident Frantisek Kotzwara remind us that the composer of "The Battle of Prague" was a multifaceted composer of pop music and low-rung art music, not just the creator of his most famous piece. These songs, like the majority of Hawkins's sheets, were marked "printed and sold by George Gilfert, 177 Broadway," although some of Hawkins's individual sheets came from London publishers, and a few from Dublin. These were piano or piano-vocal scores, but many saved room in the lower right-hand corner of the second page for a plain version of the melody, this compact melody marked as being for "German flute" or for "flute or guitar."

But long before accumulating his collection of sheet music and writing his ballad opera, Hawkins kept a music commonplace book. His manuscript, which he labeled with the year 1794—he was seventeen or eighteen years old—was not unlike the slightly later efforts of Arthur McArthur and Philander Seward. However, the tunes Hawkins assembled ranged from straightforward song tunes and instrumental melodies like those that these two musicians gathered to fancier fare. On the simple end, he notated the warhorse "Soldier's Joy" (see Figure 19). The minor variations between versions from the late eighteenth and early nineteenth centuries remind us that such tunes lived in the memories of most instrumentalists, even city boys like Hawkins . . . though the ubiquity of Elias Howe's publications later tended to squelch variation among music readers. The version of "Soldier's Joy" printed in 1864 in Howe's massive *Musician's Omnibus* is in a section devoted to contradances, and has the dance figures specified. The pitches replicate those in Howe's 1851 *School for the Violin* and in the 1844 *Musician's Companion*; in none of these books was there any consideration of violin idiom.

Soldier's Joy

Figure 19. The extremely common fiddle tune "Soldier's Joy" as recorded by Micah Hawkins, uncle of William Sidney Mount, in his commonplace book (1794), in Silas Dickinson's music commonplace book ([180-?]), and in the mid-nineteenth-century publications of Elias Howe.

Hawkins left out the first half-measure of the second strain (I reconstructed it by borrowing from later in the strain). It would be unthinkable for a skilled musician to skip a half measure in performance, particularly at the beginning of a strain. This omission must reflect hasty copying by this youngster. He probably played this common tune from memory, and likely varied it in performance, with the incidental changes coming at the same places in the tune where the artificially concrete versions I juxtaposed in this figure differ.

At the other end of a spectrum of difficulty of pieces Hawkins copied was his entering of "Felton's Gavot[te]" with the original variations. This extravaganza came from England—from parson, keyboardist, and occasional composer William Felton (1713–1769), a fan of Handel of whom Handel was not fond. "Felton's Gavotte" was originally the "Andante with Variations" from Felton's third harpsichord concerto (of 1744). It was later texted ("Come Fill the Glass," 1748), and was said by Charles Burney to have been performed in Ciampi's opera *Bertold* (1762). But, Burney added, the tune was "too common and vulgar for an opera audience" (IV, 477, quoted and discussed in Sonneck 1911, 527; as of this writing, there are several performances of it available on YouTube).

Hawkins's music is important when studying the Mount brothers because his knowledge forms the backdrop for their musical training. While William Sidney Mount's background was, like Charles Cobb, grounded in straightforward popular tunes (many of them also or soon to be in oral tradition, and many not), his upbringing in the hands of a sophisticated musician automatically inclined him to value not just homespun melodies and brash theater pieces, but also more cultivated music. Cobbs would reach in that direction, too, but because of personal curiosity and ambition. The center of the lesson is that the categories of art music and non-art music overlapped considerably at this time, and the mix was especially vigorous outside of the biggest cities of Europe. New York was not London in size or in terms of culture; it was not even Edinburgh. There was no substantial population in the mold of Charles Burney, whose education led to snobbery—no group to echo him in damning "Felton's Gavotte" as unworthy of a gentleman's attention.

Another oft-cited early influence on Mount's playing was that of Anthony Hannibal Clapp ("Black Tony," 1749–1816), an African American described as a Hawkins family slave or retainer, and a fiddler (Kaplan 1999, 14). However, Mount identified just one tune in his manuscripts as having come from Clapp. Perhaps the influence was less in repertoire than in performance techniques. Or, if I am correct in holding that the patterns of tune attributions in the Mount manuscripts indicated a plan to assemble a saleable book, invoking Clapp's name might not have supported that goal.

Mount studied art formally, and visited New York regularly, even after settling in the family hearth in Stony Brook on Long Island. Like many people with several homes, he remained restless. He complained of New York's crowding and dirt, then groused in turn about the intellectual isolation of Stony Brook (Frankenstein 1975, 8).

Mount's interactions with other fiddlers come to light through his tune annotations, plus testimony in his letters. These musicians include his brother, professional dancing master Robert Nelson Mount; his friend, second cousin Shepard Smith Jones; members of the German immigrant Pfeiffer family; and Mount's most problematic fiddler associate, fiddler and dancing master Nelson Matthewson.

Figure 20. The most elaborate melody entered in "Micah Hawkins' Book," "Felton's Gavot[te]" with fancy variations.

Of course, the fiddler to whom Mount felt the closest kinship was his brother Nelson, whose wife and children stayed home in Stony Brook while he traveled, leading dancing schools and fiddling for the dances that resulted. The letters between the brothers yield much of what we know about William Sidney Mount's attitudes toward fiddling. The brothers also exchanged tunes, though that traffic was heavily weighted on the side of William Sidney sending to Nelson.

Much of the music Mount mailed was gathered from another Nelson, Nelson Mathewson, who seems to have been originally from the South. Just as Charles Cobb knew many respectable fiddlers and one disreputable one, Mount had this single unprincipled fiddling friend. In the end, Mount described him in summary fashion as "drunk and improvident" (letter, July 7, 1839, to his brother Nelson), but that was after lengthy musical contact, and after obtaining quite a few compositions from him to send to Nelson Mount. Mathewson worked on Long Island in the 1840s and 1850s, though he intended to join Nelson Mount in the South (Hessler n.d. #2, 15). William Sidney wrote that "Mr. Mathewson has set up for himself a promising [dancing] school—fifty to sixty scholars at 10 dollars a head"

Figure 20b. The most elaborate melody entered in "Micah Hawkins' Book," "Felton's Gavot[te]" with fancy variations continued.

(Jan. 30, 1839). Mathewson had some trouble dealing with groups of students. He created a list of "Rules and Regulations" that forbade "pushing, pulling, loud talking, spitting, and fantastical dress" (Hessler n.d. #2, 16).

In another letter to his brother, Mount bragged in a way suggesting that he deeply respected Mathewson's musical judgment: "Mathewson was so well pleased with the style in which I played the above Waltz, that he wrote it, from hearing me play it. I had seen Fanny Essler dance 'The Cachuca' several times, and I believed caught the spirit of it. I am pleased that Mathewson always plays it as written above" (Aug. 29, 1841).

However, Mount's relationship with Mathewson tracked a swift trajectory from reportage and respect to dismay and disgust. In a later letter, he noted that "Mathewson spent two weeks with me in July. I had to dress him up (so reduced was he in appearance) from his head to his feet, with what clothes I could spare. He wrote me some music, which I paid him for. He appeared to be quite disappointed because you did not come home, as he had hopes of going with you to the South. He told me he thought he should go out to Georgia this fall with some friend. He said he was sorry he left the South . . . Success attend him, but he must reform for his own happiness and comfort" (date unknown).

And finally: "Mathewson is on Long Island, I believe. I suppose you are aware that I have not profited by his acquaintance much. I am sorry he makes such a beast . . . of himself. Rum is his idol. He has a violin with him that cost $100. It belongs to a young gentleman here by the name of Barry Dunbar who while Mathewson was here gave it to him to repair or glue up. He absconded with it. He promised me to send it back. He has not done it. Mr. Dunbar is about to authorize me to proceed and get it. That circumstance would prevent [Mathewson] from ever being able to obtain a school . . . Foolish man. I believe he was well liked on account of his being a good violinist. That was all that recommended him. He can't play so well now. Rum is the cause, poor fellow" (Aug. 29, [1841?]).

Mount also interacted with a musical family named Pfeiffer (that is the usual spelling, although Mount also used the homophonic alternatives Pfieffer and Fifer; I copy each of Mount's various spellings when quoting him). From Mount's tune attributions, we learn that the Pfeiffers were from Thuringia in Germany, where one A. Pfeiffer was born. One son was S. L. Pfeiffer of Mobile, Alabama, whose visit(s) to Stony Brook lasted long enough for Mount to copy many of his tunes. The local anchor for the family, Fred Pfeiffer, repaired and tuned pianos (and built them, in a basement shop that once suffered a "steam boiler explosion"; Hessler 1980). A portrait of Pfeiffer's young daughter Ida still hangs in the Long Island Museum of American Art, History and Carriages, one Mount made in exchange for Pfeiffer having fixed his piano (while Mount mainly played violin, he owned a keyboard, and also played fife with the Stony Brook and Smithtown Fusiliers; Hessler [1984]b, 5).

This museum's large collection of music associated with Mount includes sheet music (songs in piano-vocal score), published anthologies of tunes, and lots of loose pieces of paper of various sizes with tunes written on them in Mount's hand; this bounty of music constitutes the equivalent of a very large music commonplace book. One publication in the collection belonged to his brother: [Septimus] *Winner's Collection of Music for the Violin, Consisting of Marches, Waltzes, Polkas, Cotillions, Hornpipes, Reels, Jigs, Fancy Dances, Mazourkas, Schottisches, Polka Quadrilles, and all other Fashionable Airs, Arranged in an Easy Manner, in the First Position* (1853). R. N. (Robert Nelson) Mount wrote his name and the date 1854 on the cover. Nelson's owning this book suggests that his skills were less than William Sidney's, although one tune, "College or Sailor's Hornpipe," has a handwritten insertion that takes the fiddler to high g on the e string (probably fingered in fifth position with extended fourth finger). Also written in is a comment advising that one section might be played up an octave. Perhaps this was William Sidney writing, offering Nelson suggestions for a more artistic (but challenging) performance. One of the brothers also owned a copy of Howe's most widely distributed violin method (1851); a few individual pages from that method are in the collection.

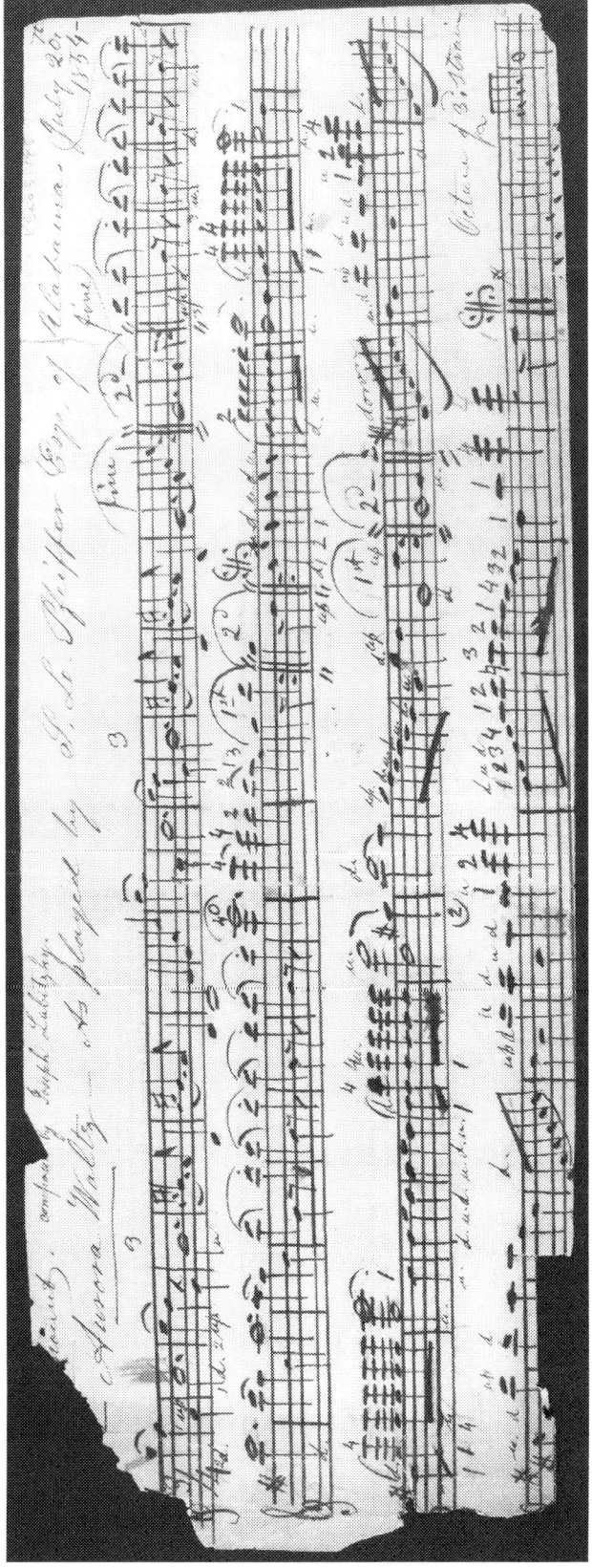

Figure 21. William Sidney Mount transcribed many performances of tunes by other fiddlers, and generally specified his sources. This very difficult version of Josef Labitsky's "Aurora Waltz" is from the playing of a brother of local piano builder and repairman Fred Pfeiffer. The brother, S. L. Pfeiffer, who lived in Mobile, Alabama, was a virtuoso both as performer and transcriber. Courtesy of The Long Island Museum of American Art, History & Carriages Collection.

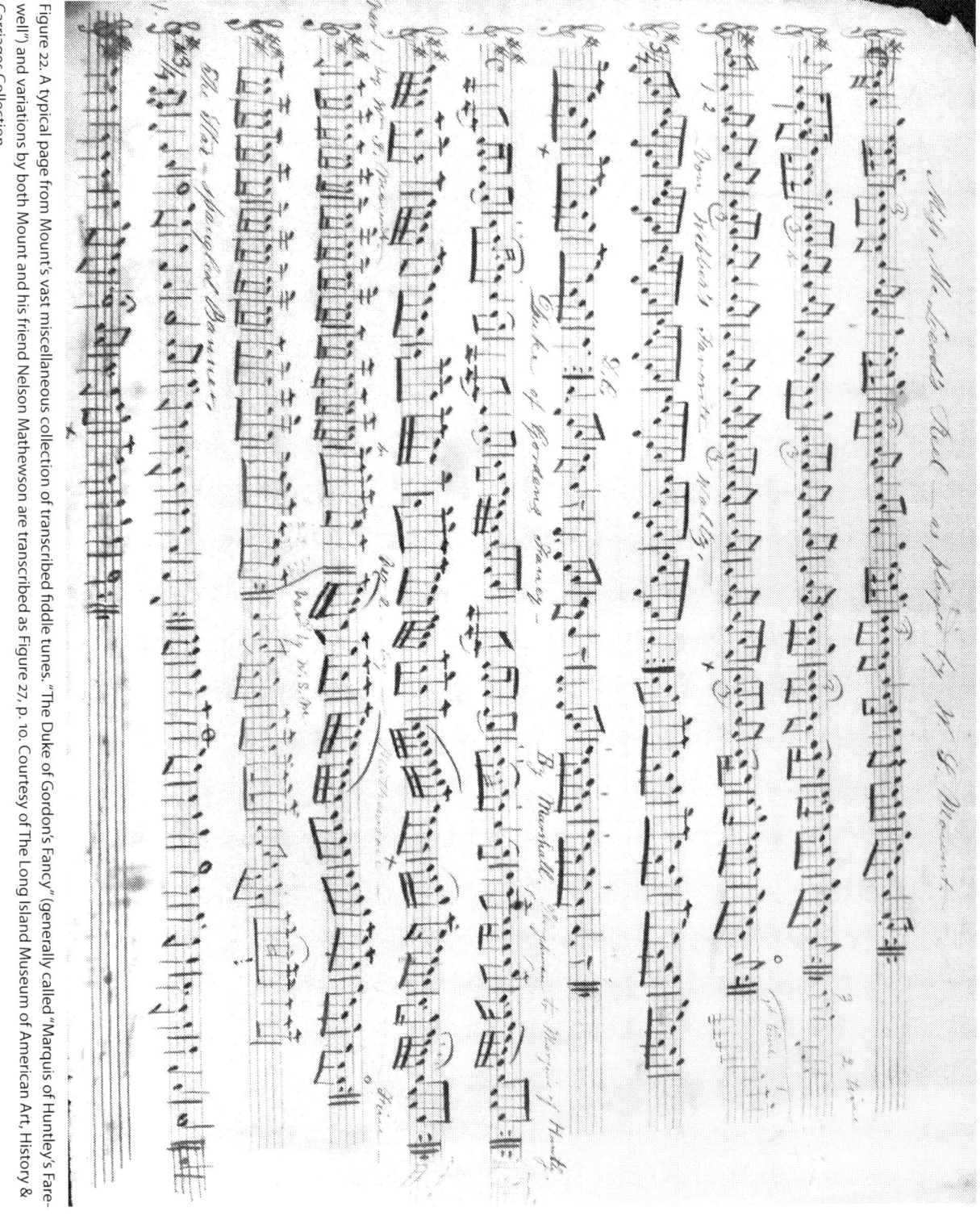

Figure 22. A typical page from Mount's vast miscellaneous collection of transcribed fiddle tunes. "The Duke of Gordon's Fancy" (generally called "Marquis of Huntley's Farewell") and variations by both Mount and his friend Nelson Mathewson are transcribed as Figure 27, p. 10. Courtesy of The Long Island Museum of American Art, History & Carriages Collection.

Mount's attributions of versions of tunes return us to the story of his contacts with other fiddlers. In this large assembly of manuscript pages, he notes over two dozen times that transcriptions of melodies or variations on melodies were from his own playing, and he links other tunes (or variations) with some twenty other musicians, ranging from his uncle Micah Hawkins to fiddlers living on Long Island and to many visiting musicians. Many fiddlers are represented with just one or two references, including Hawkins and also Mount's friend Shepard Jones. But some names appear numerous times, notably Nelson Mathewson and one or the other Pfeiffer brother, referenced in Figures 21 and 22. For the "Aurora Waltz," a new tune in Mount's day and the most technically difficult piece Mount transcribed, Mount notes both the composer (Labitsky) and his source for this ornate version, Alabama's S. L. Pfeiffer. Then for "Duke of Gordon's Fancy" (customary title: "Marquis of Huntley's Farewell"), a Scottish piece published several times late in the eighteenth century, Mount marks two variations as being by him, and one by his troubled but talented friend Nelson Mathewson (see also Figure 27, #4).

THE PHYSICAL FIDDLE, THE SOUND OF FIDDLING, AND PERFORMANCE TECHNIQUES

Most violinists/fiddlers are able to keep their instruments in playing trim, and some even start to learn on homemade approximations of fiddles. This offers a handyman-linked advantage to the instrument: wind and keyboard instruments certainly have to be purchased for substantial sums, and even routine repairs are relatively challenging. But it is not just that the violinist/fiddler *can* perform regular maintenance and even somewhat specialized tasks in instrument upkeep, they *must* do so. Periodically, their instruments need their varnish freshened, tuning pegs "soaped," strings and bridges replaced, sound posts set up, and bows rehaired. A few players carry this further, modifying or even building their own instruments, and perhaps challenging the basic inherited shape and specifications.

What we witness repeatedly in the antebellum era are attempts to make the violin louder. The most ambitious example that I have encountered is William Sidney Mount's invention (and patenting) of an unusual violin that he named "The Cradle of Harmony," one of several inventions reflecting his hobby of crafting interesting things with wood (he also made a few small boats, and a horse-drawn art studio; Frankenstein 1976). Mount's new violin was in an almond shape, with no inward curve; the neck end a bit narrower than the endpin end. Even more innovative was that the back was concave, thus parallel to the soundboard. The instrument was just 1 ¼ inches deep. Mount supplemented these major changes with adjustments to the sound post and the bass bar, and some thinning of the body wood. He believed that these revisions resulted in more volume, which is possible, and in better tone, which is doubtful. A devotee of the details of how paints were made up—he filled many pages of his diary with opinions about painting materials and techniques (Frankenstein 1975, 8)—he also experimented with violin varnishes.

Just a few of these oval violins were made (by other craftsmen, to his specifications), and a handful survive. Gilbert Ross played a number of Mount's tunes on one of these unusual violins for an LP entitled *The Cradle of Harmony*, issued in 1976 (subsequently available on CD). Of course, we can't tell if the violin is especially loud from a recording, but the tone, even in the hands of this fine musician, is thin and nasal, though not unattractive. The probable enhanced volume and certainly more cutting timbre in the upper register would have made it easier to hear over the rattles of dancers' shoes and the murmur of their swishing clothing, panting, and chatter. Ross praised Mount's innovative fiddle: "The viola-like darkness of the lower strings contrasts beautifully with the brightness of the instrument's upper register" (Frankenstein 1976). This puts a positive spin on Mount's violating a traditional desideratum for violins: having a smooth and slight graduation of timbre throughout the instrument's range. Mount went on to apply lessons learned from shaping the new violin to minor modifications of the sound post and the bass bar on conventional violins ("grooving both sides of the bass bar and thinning the bass side [and rubbing with sandpaper shavings])"; Frankenstein 1975, 343). In sum, timbre and especially volume were enduring concerns for Mount.

Cobb wrote about fiddle volume when reporting on playing at a dance with his friend George Scales: "George displayed his fiddle with a new addition, a stick running through the inside lengthwise (it was like a small ruler, up and down, and fastened to the end of the neck, and the block at the back end)... It had [written within it] 'Wm. B. Tilton and Co., patent, 1851' and he [Scales] said it cost him $10 to have it put in... It made the fiddle better in some respects and worse in others" (*Journal* Dec. 4, 1851; Cobb further noted that Pushee had a franchise from Tilton).[2] I believe that the "better" factor was a penetrating sound coupled with a modest increase in volume. Thus, when Mount transformed—indeed, re-invented—the fiddle, and when fiddlers whom Cobb knew inserted a reinforcing stick through their instruments lengthwise, they were pursuing that common goal, increased volume to suit bigger dances.

Cobb played many fiddles while he was learning, and settled on one he named by the tint of its varnish, his "dun fiddle." He once compared it to a quieter fiddle: the contrast was between "a fart and thunder" (Feb. 23, 1851). He wrote about it again on December 11, 1851: "The old dun fiddle. There are but few in these diggings so tremendous loud and yet so soft and mellow. Anything can be played on it with as much expression as could be wished. It will sound just as the person feels who plays on it." Nevertheless, he then reported that his father traded it (and an IOU for $10) for another fiddle, which was considerably louder (apparently written on Dec. 12, 1851; the ordering of entries in the journal are unclear at this point).

When Robert Nelson Mount became a professional fiddler and dancing master, William Sidney often located new music to send him, and also gave advice on fiddle technique. Nelson often traveled in the South, where dancing schools were popular; in the winter of 1841, he was in Monticello, Jasper County, Georgia. In a letter dated February 1841, William Sidney enclosed a cotillion, and suggested that "Some parts of the strains you must play softer than others, particularly the [strains in minor]; they are heartfelt. Play some of the strains in octaves above or below at pleasure. In shifting, slide your fingers up and down [employ portamento]. You know what I mean. Let your first two fingers work[?] it up in playing the whole sett." Nelson also sent his brother advice on technique, on employing scordatura: "If you wish to give it the Negro touch, you must raise the bass string one note" (letter to William Sidney, Jan. 17, 1841). Cobb noted that George Scales clamped the violin's neck with his wrist, making it impossible to shift smoothly (*Journal* Dec. 11, 1851). Thus, both Cobb and Mount valued shifting; their notated music indicates that they expected to go regularly to and from third position at a minimum.

Kaplan gathered Mount's testimony appreciating the value of music: "I am confident that music adds to my health and happiness." "Music is a softner [*sic*], people cannot fight very well when lively music is about. . . . On one occasion, I stopped a fight at an Election, by playing a lively hornpipe on my violin—from shoulder hitting they went to dancing" (1999, 14). "There is time for all things and music fills up a rich space" (1999, 13). "Allow me to say that no class of men should be more honored by the rising generation or better paid than the musician and dancing master" (Kaplan 1999, 13). Cobb didn't express a general opinion of the value of music in any surviving document, but his devotion to playing and to writing down tunes speaks for itself. Many journal entries read "We had some music," meaning that music was performed in his home by several people, including him. Many other entries read "I wrote some music," meaning that he entered tunes in his large book. He remarked that "I'd rather arrange music than visit or be visited strange to say, and consequently all the visiting I get or do is mighty small and I appear in public and private as tho' I never saw anybody before, nor wanted to again" (*Journal* Aug. 27, 1853).

Cobb generally used the word "music" to refer to human performances or musical notation, but he did write two journal entries describing outdoor sounds as music. From Monday, April 7, 1851: "The frogs in Hartwell swamp began to sing (cuss 'em) 2 or 3 days ago. I think it would be a good plan to go down there to night, and by dint of war, endeavor to stop the music. I would certainly stone a frog if I saw him sing out." Then just a few weeks later, on Monday, May 6, his opinion had mellowed (or a more acceptable animal chorus was heard, perhaps of birds): "We have a great deal of music, evenings now, gratis;—there appears to be a good many tiny warblers in the ponds and about."

ANNOTATIONS TO MUSIC ANTHOLOGY #2

For this music anthology, I conjoined pieces from Cobb's *Universal Musician* with music from Mount's manuscripts. Both fiddlers echo Seward's and others' shaping of their commonplace books on the general model of published collections. That is clear for Cobb, whose lengthy compilation went through a stage in which it resembled one of Elias Howe's gigantic collections of instrumental music—that is, the early stage, before Cobb filled in most blank space with tunes, copied lectures on music, and so on. But Mount seems to have had more concrete plans to publish much of what he wrote down. I can't think of a better reason for his meticulous attributions of tunes, especially his repeated writing of "as played by W.S. M." We know that he wanted to profit from his invention of a louder violin; here it appears that he contemplated publishing his versions of tunes plus versions by other fiddlers he knew. While Cobb would have competed with Howe on Howe's own terms through the sheer size of his collection, Mount would have sought a unique market niche by presenting personal takes on melodies, with specific directions for performance. We can be grateful for this plan, even though it remained unrealized, just as he never got his patented "Cradle of Harmony" fiddle into production. He pursued his intentions to publish far enough to yield a generous collection of carefully notated performances.

In this anthology, I join common and uncommon tunes, and chose melodies that were attractive in various ways; many of which illustrate points about tune transmission or details of performance practice. In ordering these tunes within the anthology, I gather many by genre, but others by topic. All of the tunes from Cobb are from his giant music commonplace book, "The Universal Musician," on deposit with the Vermont Historical Society; the page numbers are Cobb's. All of the tunes from Mount are from the collections of The Long Island Museum of American Art, History and Carriages; the numbers attached to each are the accession numbers assigned at that museum. All photographs in this book are my own, as are all transcriptions.

The basic order within Figure 12 is as follows:

p. 1.	Marches
p. 2.	Songs
pp. 3–6.	Hornpipes
pp. 8–11.	Reels and Strathspeys
p. 12.	Jigs
pp. 13–15.	Waltzes
pp. 16–17.	Other fashionable dances
p. 18.	Tunes in modes other than major
p. 19.	Tunes employing scordatura
p. 20.	Pastoral topics
pp. 21–23.	Blackface minstrel tunes
pp. 24–25.	Virtuoso display tunes, one of them composed by Mount
pp. 26–31.	Cotillions, plus tunes composed by Cobb as potential members of cotillions
pp. 32–33.	A concert selection made by Mount

This anthology leads off with two marches. Why not more? Over half of the marches from the Seward manuscript were still being played while Cobb and

Mount were fiddling, and appear without significant change in the Howe publications and in Cobb's *Universal Musician*. I also illustrate other common ones in the section below on the playing of Gideon Lincecum (Figure 31). Interest in this genre's literal wartime function ebbed in the late 1840s and 1850s. New marches in published anthologies were as likely to have been plucked from operas as to be named for actual military figures or battles. These were theater pieces rather than functional marches (though repertoire lists from Civil War bands may include marches originally from operas). In addition, marches were more frequently printed in collections intended for all treble instruments than in violin methods.

Here are some statistics: In Philander Seward's early nineteenth-century music commonplace book, sixteen of sixty-eight notated pieces have the word "march" in the title; somewhere between a sixth and a fourth of the tunes in most young men's music commonplace books of the time were marches (I am not including multifunction pieces sometimes used as marches such as "Lesson by Morelli" and "Soldier's Return"). Howe's *First Part of the Musician's Companion*, from about forty years later, includes twenty-eight pieces with "march" in their titles among some two hundred tunes. That's about 14 percent of the contents, compared with 24 percent for Seward. Howe's shorter *School for the Violin* (1843, but most surviving copies from 1851) also has 14 percent of its anthology devoted to marches, mostly the same ones found in the *First Part of the Musician's Companion*. That is because this *School for the Violin* is one of the many methods that, even though including brief instructions specific to the named instrument, then continue with the same repertoire of tunes as methods for other instruments; such collections were not shaped to suit any instrument specifically. In contrast, there are just two marches in Howe's very different, more specifically string-oriented *Self Instructor for the Violin* of 1851 (less than 2 percent of the contents). These two marches' titles aren't patriotic; the tunes started life as piano sheet music: "Fest [Festival] March" and "Suwarrow's Grand March" (both on p. 52, the latter title not referring to an American figure, but rather almost certainly Alexander Vasilyevich Suvorov (1730–1800), a Russian general important in the Russo-Turkish War and later in the Napoleanic Wars).[3] The *Musician's Companion* volumes had included players of wind instruments in the collective target customer base; now that one had a choice of listening to a trumpet (or band) versus a violin play a march, solo fiddlers/violinists played them infrequently.

The two marches I reproduce from Cobb and from Mount illustrate what was genuinely new in the genre. "Mackintosh's March" is simpler than earlier marches, and "March in Bellini's Grand Opera of *La Norma*" marks the opposite, elaborate extreme. "Mackintosh's March" has only its dotted rhythms and otherwise thin rhythmic texture to identify itself musically as a march. Apart from that, it's a simple bipartite dance, just like a fiddle tune. The first strain presents an antecedent and consequent form of one idea. Then the second strain starts with material similar in rhythmic feel, then returns with the consequent form of the first idea. The entire form, with repeats, is: a a' a a' b a' b a', the same as many fiddle tunes.

Mount's long title of the march from *Norma* relates the arrangement's history: "March in Bellini's Grand Opera of *La Norma* Arranged and Transposed by J.C. Smith for the Violin from a Piano Copy." A shorter arrangement appears in Howe's *Musician's Omnibus* (1864, 24). Both arrangements are in D Major, but Howe's version omits the trio (m. 25 and following in Mount's version; a truncated version in C Major had appeared in 1844 in *The Musician's Companion*, I, 138). *Norma* was a very popular opera to mine for popular music "singles" (Hamm 1983, 78–82), and this and another march from it appear in many collections. I chose to put it in my own anthology because Mount said it came from a fiddler making a personal version based on a commercial piano arrangement of a piece of art music; this sort of layered reworking to create a fiddle version happened often. The result remains a fully developed march featuring a ration of accidentals and retaining the trio section. It might not seem like a candidate for oral tradition, but Samuel Bayard collected a "Grand March o' Normal" that might be descended from the Bellini march (1982, 216–17). Bayard doubted that the tunes were related, but I hear the "Grand March o' Normal" as starting like an accompanying part to the march from *Norma*—that is, the melody outlines an arpeggio using members of the same chords as in the original, but one chord member higher. Perhaps someone who had performed the march in an ensemble remembered the "seconding" part rather than the melody, and passed that part on.

The most important general fact concerning this genre is that most of the marches that were popular early in the century were still played in mid-century. In fact, this was just as true of most of the genres gathered together in both publishers' and individuals' collections of music for treble instruments. We don't witness one body of tunes being abandoned to make room for another when new pieces and new genres of music entered the picture—the old need not go away; taste was broadening rather than shifting. Hornpipes and reels did not go out of use when polkas arrived. It made financial, social, and aesthetic sense that published and personal anthologies grew larger and larger.

The next short section in this anthology is of melodies from sentimental songs (very sentimental—nearly all song lyrics popular shortly before the Civil War seem histrionic today). The first, drawn from Charles M. Cobb's *Universal Musician*, actually takes us a few months into that conflict. It is Cobb's version of "The Vacant Chair," a song composed in 1861 yet still sung today (there are several performances on YouTube as of this writing). As in the case of nearly all of the tunes Cobb anthologized, he named neither composer (George F. Root) nor poet (H. S. Washburn). Nor did he relate the story inspiring the poem: eighteen-year-old John William Grout, of Worcester, Massachusetts, fell at the Battle of Ball's Bluff, on October 21, 1861. This early death at a particularly ineptly run battle (on Grout's side, the North) was a quick welcome to the arbitrary nature of war, a near-instant tragedy for the soldier and for his family. Here Cobb did something unusual for him. Rather than just printing the melody, or giving both tune and complete text, he chose an intermediate path, inserting just the first few words below the melody, those words constituting a reminder of what he felt were very well known lyrics. The poem is set at a family Thanksgiving after Grout's death. It begins:

> We shall meet, but we shall miss him, there will be one vacant chair,
> We shall linger to caress him, while we breathe our ev'ning prayer.
> When a year ago we gathered, joy was in his mild blue eye.
> Now the golden chord is severed, and our hopes in ruin lie.

It ends:

> Sleep today, O early fallen, in thy green and narrow bed,
> Dirges from the pine and cypress mingle with the tears we shed.

The second sentimental song is "Nelly Gray," written in 1856 by Benjamin Hanby, whose minister father was trying to right a moral wrong. A runaway slave learned that his sweetheart (Nelly Gray) had been sold south, which was considered to be much worse than remaining in Virginia. Could she be ransomed somehow? The end of the story as related in the song's lyrics is that the singer dies, and is reunited with his love after death. The story is as emotional as "The Vacant Chair," but less relatable to current US concerns save in the theme the songs share—love lost through physical separation and eventual death.

The final song, here in an instrumental version, comes from William Sidney Mount's own playing. "'Tis the Last Rose of Summer" remains one of the most popular of *Thomas Moore's Irish Melodies*, a collection widely distributed in the United States from the 1810s forward. The tune, an old one polished by oral tradition, received a new boost in popularity and thus distribution through Moore's adaptation. The new lyrics echo the general spirit of Moore's collection: Ireland as locus of nostalgia (that is, until Irish immigrants arrived in large numbers), nostalgia for a past home and, most importantly, for a past time when loved ones were together. The lyrics are thus compatible with those of the previous two songs. Charles Hamm's title of *Yesterdays* (1983) for his general history of American popular music pinpoints nostalgia as a central theme of American life; allied characterizations of the theme for our country of immigrants and of multiple moves could be "dislocation" or "personal loss." In his version of this well-known song, William Sidney Mount was transcribing—in considerable detail, and thus likely with considerable precision—just how he played it. He shaped a musical analog of the overwrought lyrics, melodic gymnastics just as over-the-top as this poem.

With the section of hornpipes we are arriving at the bread-and-butter core of fiddle tunes, melodies probably never texted, instead suitable for dancing and idiomatic for fiddle. The hornpipe is a fast enough dance that it's hard to imagine adding lots of ornaments—what we see on the page is probably fairly close to what we hear. A generous handful of the hornpipes anthologized by Cobb and/or Mount were ones common earlier in the century in the United States, and quite a few of those are still played today. One of Cobb's many notations of the venerable "Fisher's Hornpipe" is in the photograph given as Figure 18; it is a typical hornpipe in every way. In fact, the biggest surprise in the world of hornpipes is how they run in several streams: (1) old ones persisting, (2) new ones on the established model, and (3) new ones that take a certain hornpipe characteristic—difficulty, especially for the left hand—and carry it further.

"Fisher's Hornpipe," "Durang's Hornpipe," "Rickett's Hornpipe," and many other hornpipes already common in the early part of the century never flag in their popularity, and are still standard repertoire for fiddlers in parts of the United States. I reproduce one here, "Hulls' Victory," because it illustrates several factors. Cobb and his sometime teacher Abram Pushee didn't play it identically, and Cobb found those small differences interesting enough to put both versions in the *Universal Musician.* He also liked the tune enough to arrange it for two treble instruments and bass. Howe published it many times as a solo melody, but also with dance figures. In short, these old, sturdy, moderately difficult pieces retained a secure home in mid-century fiddling.

Many new hornpipes with similar melodic textures were written; some would fade away (for instance, "Jones' Favorite"—this referred to Mount's second cousin and friend Shepard Jones), and some would persist, including "Vinton's Hornpipe," which Cobb presented in several versions. The new, challenging hornpipes had poor prospects. For example, "X Hornpipe," which presents difficulties both for the left hand and for the right through an epidemic of string crossings, is no longer played, as far as I know. But the tessitura-sweeping arpeggios of "Pushee's Hornpipe" haven't kept it from maintaining a modest presence in modern New England playing. "Thunder Hornpipe," a pictorial novelty piece, is still with us, too.

Reels and strathspeys constitute a special corner of the antique fraction of the mid-century repertoire; they gave creative fiddlers room to imagine and to wander. On the average, melodies called reels move more conjunctly (stepwise) than hornpipes, and have been more apt to be ornamented in performance. But the two genres are close enough that they have melted into the general American category of "breakdown." "The Braes of Auchentyre," a distinctive Scottish tune from the 1780s, was adopted under that name in the United States; I reproduce a form that Cobb's teacher Pushee wrote into Cobb's collection. The tune also flourished with a new, local name, "Beaus of Albany." I give two versions bearing that title, one with dance figures. Cobb noticed that one of the most popular late eighteenth-century reels, "Lord McDonald's Reel," was identical to the lesser-known "McDaniel's Reel." The tune is now called "Leather Britches" in most of the United States, though the original title can still be encountered in contradance circles. I reproduce "The High Road to Linton" because it was one of the many tunes Mount acquired from the Pfeiffer clan.

I also include the venerable and very common "Money Musk" because Mount and friends had such fun writing Italianate variations for it. Such variations consist for the most part of virtuosic figuration unrelated to the "theme" (the two strains of the fiddle tune) except for their following the harmony of the original. These performances may startle the modern fiddler. But this link between tradition and the flashy emptiness of pop music variation sets actually illustrates an interaction that reaches back to late eighteenth-century Scottish fiddling, to Neil Gow and his contemporaries. The Scottish fiddlers/publishers included one to three such sets in many, many of their fiddle books.[4]

Mount enjoyed these Scottish tunes, and apparently acquired collections published by the Gows in Scotland early in the nineteenth century. He supplemented his "Duke of Gordon's Fancy" (usual name: "The Marquis of Huntley's Farewell") with two variations by himself and a bolder one by Nelson Mathewson; perhaps this difference in confidence and in musical imagination accounts for Mount putting up with so much bad behavior from his sometime friend. Strathspeys were slow pieces, rich in ornamentation, while jigs were quick and plain; I give four jigs with entertaining names taken from Cobb.

In the 1840s and 1850s, waltz melodies were transitioning from the rhythmically dense early waltz to the thinner, graceful, Strauss type. "Bailey's Waltz" and "Rifle Waltz" (Cobb recorded this tune as an exciting duet) represent the former type, as does the novelty piece "The Cachuca." Among examples of the new type, both Cobb and Mount selected pieces by a composer contemporary with them, Czech Joseph Labitsky (1802–1881). Cobb played and wrote out "Spring Waltz by J. Labitsky, from O.A. Whitmore" (a versatile musician from Boston), while Mount wrote out a version of Labitsky's widely distributed "Aurora Waltz" "As played by S. L. Pfeiffer Esq. of Alabama," who must have been a virtuoso. Both Mount and Cobb felt that these lengthy waltzes were at their best in elaborate, personalized performances; each individual's opinion about how to get the best out of such pieces mattered. This version of "The Aurora Waltz" is the hardest piece to play in this book, but, surprisingly, the tune made enough of an impression that it achieved a spot in oral tradition: Ira Ford printed a version in his *Traditional Music in America* (1940, 145). Interestingly, while single-line first-position skeletons of this waltz appear in the Howe collections (e.g., 1848, 44), the fiddler transcribed by Ford does essay a few ambitious double stops—he was clearly working from an ornate version of "The Aurora Waltz." The last waltz in this group, "New Orleans Waltz," is also of the younger Strauss type, but is notable for its pathos-infused melody; the bounty of falling half steps evokes the melodramatic melancholy suffusing so many songs of the time.

Howe grouped the remaining, younger dance genres under the rubric "fancy dances" in his publications. I give samples of the main types. Fiddlers still play some polkas, but few that date back this far. The "Sontag Polka Medley," recorded from his own playing by Mount, is notable for that personal touch. The polka as a genre also invaded the quadrille. A "polka quadrille," rather than evenly balancing 6/8 and 2/4 tunes, would generally have just a single melody in 6/8; all the others would be 2/4 polkas. Cobb's notating of the common "Rainbow Schottische" illustrates his scholarly bent. He labels it apparently as did his source fiddler, "Emerald Schottische," but writes in its usual title, too (Figure 27, p. 17).

Vivian Williams offers many fancy dances in her fascinating reproduction of music from a post–Civil War mining camp: *The Peter Beemer Manuscript: Dance Music Collected in the Gold Mining Camp of Warren's Diggins, Idaho in the 1860's* (2008). The over 120 tunes include ten polkas (including the "Sontag Polka"), seven mazurkas, fourteen schottisches (the last a potpourri of preexisting tunes recast in schottische rhythm), and four varsoviennes. In addition, this source includes sixteen waltzes, a dozen quicksteps or marches (including a version of "March in Norma"), a half-dozen miscellaneous tunes, and fourteen sets of quadrilles. It is in these quadrilles that the greatest overlap with the present book occurs; most of this batch of mining camp quadrilles draws on familiar tunes, including ones that I also anthologize: "Such a Getting Up Stairs," "Rickett's Hornpipe," "Boatman Dance," "Arkansas Traveller," "Mountain Hornpipe," "Life Let Us Cherish," and "Oh Susannah."

The next three pieces in Anthology #2 illustrate a variety of mode. They are neither in major nor in the also reasonably common pentatonic key that fits into major (that is, the anhemitonic pentatonic, the form that consists of the major scale minus its fourth and seventh degrees). I took these three pieces from Cobb, since he was interested enough in pieces exceptional in this way to mark them. Cobb didn't command a detailed vocabulary in music theory. He described "Tullochgorum" as having "flat sevenths"; we would think of it in Mixolydian mode. He called the mode for "Logan Water" "minor"; it's in dorian. The most interesting is the common tune he called "The Cuckoo," found elsewhere as "The Cuckoo Hornpipe" or "Cuckoo's Nest." Cobb said it was in minor, and his notation of it (a3, implicitly for at least two fiddles or other treble instruments and a bass instrument) is more or less in melodic minor. It is shoehorned into D Major in mainstream American publications of the time (e.g., Howe 1864, 44), but survives in a variety of modal approaches in modern fiddling. The general impression I have of tunes in these less common modes is that they're important opportunities for modal richness.

The next page of the anthology contains three pieces in scordaturae (cross-tunings). Nelson Mount opined that having the violin tuned ADAE gave it the "Negro touch," expressing that opinion in a letter in which he sent William Sidney his transcription of a tune called "Possum Hunt" (very similar to "Possum Up a Gum Tree"; see Ford 1940, 19). Oddly, this tune doesn't require the fiddler to play the retuned string! Perhaps Nelson chose not to transcribe open string double stops; perhaps the retuning just added resonance. "French Muse," as written out by Cobb, and "Black Walnut," as written out by Mount, employ the tuning now often used in old-time fiddling for tunes in the key of A, that is, AEAE. Resonance and parallel fingering are facilitated. What is most surprising about these examples is that there are not many more of them in both of these collections.

One more page precedes the section on blackface minstrel tunes, a few melodies from Cobb's *Universal Musician*, ones with rustic names. "Farmers Joy" isn't a new title—Seward wrote out a different tune called that—but it does provide as general a country reference as possible. "Cabbage Duett" gets more specific, though the music doesn't draw a picture of a cabbage—I'm not sure how it could. But "Hens March" has a second strain marked "Cackling Hen" that features repeated pitches meant to imitate that animal sound. It thus sets the scene for more animal imitations, for the place of such sounds in minstrel performances, and for tunes bearing related names that are still played today.

I included just a few pages of African American or blackface minstrel melodies in this second tune anthology. In a recent book, Christopher Smith argued thoroughly and convincingly that Mount's genre paintings, approached both as general cultural narrative and as portrayal of dancing, when combined with Mount's entering of certain minstrel tunes in his manuscripts, contribute greatly to our understanding of the coalescing of blackface minstrelsy and of the broader creole synthesis (2013). But the early history of minstrelsy, however fascinating it is to us today, remained a smallish source of repertoire for Mount. Of the some 350 tunes that survive written in Mount's hand, only about twenty have black or blackface connections. He wrote down more hornpipes, waltzes, reels, polkas, etc.; many more tunes from late eighteenth-century Scotland, and even many more technical studies than minstrel tunes. Also, one way he demonstrated interest in a tune was to append variations composed by him or by his fiddler friends. He did that no more for minstrel tunes than for fiddle tunes in other genres.

Mount must have seen minstrel performances when in New York, but he also had opportunities on Long Island. Helen Rogers of Cold Spring Harbor (just twenty-five miles from Stony Brook) wrote in her diary about a musical ensemble made up of lively young men living in her village. The Jawbone Band played the core blackface minstrel repertoire on "bass drum, wire triangle, violin, tambourine, jawbone, castinettes [sp], rattlers, gourd and shell, trumpets, fife, and flageolet" (Valentine 1981, 113; Stony Brook had been home to a similar-sized ensemble, the Huntington Brass Band since the 1840s; Hessler [1984]a, 21–22).

As a music-literate fiddler regularly visiting New York, Mount also had access to a growing body of publications that actually focused on blackface minstrel tunes. One group of books that he must have known about was purportedly authored by "Gumbo Chaff" (Elias Howe's blackface pseudonym). These widely distributed collections came out in 1848. In *The Ethiopian Violin Instructor, Containing Full and Complete Instruction with All the Popular Negro Melodies of the Day, Including Those of the Christy Minstrels. By Gumbo Chaff, A.M. A., Author of the Ethiopian Glee Book, Ethiopian Accordeon Instructor, Ethiopian Flute Instructor, &c, &c.*, seventy-five of the ninety-nine melodies are minstrel tunes. The flute version has exactly the same musical content, and the accordion version of most of those tunes (plus quite a few hymn tunes; imagine the accordion as a substitute for the reed organ). Mount has to have seen these and other minstrel-oriented collections, but he did not copy tunes from them, instead gathering his blackface tunes directly from other fiddlers.

As a youngster, Mount certainly witnessed and heard the fiddling of Hawkins family retainer African American Anthony Clapp. Smith asserts that Clapp was

Mount's initial violin teacher (2013, 88), since they lived in the same household for a time. Our best hints concerning the general nature of Clapp's playing come from consistent patterns in Mount's paintings featuring vernacular musicians (see any book on Mount, but especially Smith 2013). We can ignore that fact that both white and black fiddlers in those paintings play instruments that lack chin rests, which were not yet common (shoulder rests are a twentieth-century invention; Riggs 2016, 65). Each fiddler supports the body of his instrument against his chest (lower than the art violin position, which is just *above* the collarbone) and must firmly grip the violin neck with his left hand, palm against wood; this makes any left-hand shifts awkward at best. This seems to be more consistent in these rustic-themed paintings than it could have been in real life, since Mount himself, plus Nelson Mathewson and many other fiddlers whose playing Mount transcribed, men who played for dances but who performed tunes requiring position work, must have held their instruments more as in art violin performance, with the left hand cupped to facilitate vibrato and shifting rather than pressed again the instrument's neck.

Just one tune attributed to Clapp survives in the Mount manuscripts. "Black Toney's Juber, as Played by W.S. M." (Figure 27, p. 21) looks simple on the page, even with the brief dotted-note variation at the beginning of the second strain that Mount transcribed. Of course, the performance must on occasion have been filled out with the common practice of adding percussion called "patting juba," a method of enlivening melodies rhythmically by clapping hands together or on one's body, first documented in slave quarters and then transferred in some form(s) to blackface minstrelsy.

"Old Sussanna, don't you cry for me" departs in small but telling ways from Foster's "O! Susanna," which appears in Howe's anthologies in a simple, unornamented form much closer to Foster's original tune (e.g., 1848, 42). The small changes in contour of this Ethiopian walk-around hit our ears less vigorously than do the new dotted rhythms; Mount's source for the tune saw the essence of his interpretation as one of shifting bits of time. In contrast, in Mount's playing of "Camptown Races" (renamed "Bobtail Horse," as in, e.g., Ford 1940, 33), he pushed his melody forward with turns and swift arpeggios. This was an infusion of art ornamentation rather than of minstrel rhythm. The "Stop Jig" he wrote down (source not specified by him), with its short bits of melody and with gaps in time at the beginning of the main idea—gaps demanding to be filled with percussion—exemplifies the newer kind of "Negro Jig." In such tunes, percussive enlivenment is not just something about which to speculate, not a feature to imagine as an optional enhancement of performance, it is required.

Cobb wrote out the hit "Arkansas Traveller" once, and Mount recorded it in three contrasting versions. The original playlet (the "traveler" asks directions of a rural wit, who toys with him verbally until learning that the traveler knows the second half of the tune the wit has been trying to get through) was in circulation in oral tradition before the first publication of the story-plus-tune in 1847. The first published version, "arranged" by William Cumming, is full of dotted rhythms, which, in the notation of what is essentially a reel, probably were not indicating such rhythms literally, but rather eighth notes that "swing." And the alternation of fiddling with rustic witticism in the performance echoes on several levels in the music, with soft and loud sections being specified (low-pitched sections quiet, and high parts loud), and even on the micro level: In the first and second and all other parallel measures, crisp dotted rhythms fill the first half of the measure, then slurred plain eighths the other half. Another piano and spoken-voice version from about the same time, one offered as performed by blackface minstrel Mose Case, matches this one closely—dotted rhythms, specified dynamics, format alternating talking and fiddling. The only major difference is that the A strain is up an octave. Some version including that factor must have been the model for the version in Cobb's *Universal Musician.*

One of Mount's versions of this tune was simply a faithful copy of "Arkansas Traveller" as printed in the book of simple first-position violin tunes owned by his brother Nelson, the collection by Septimus Winner. It's in A Major, but has no other special characteristics. By being in that key, it avoids the use of the G string, and thus is available for performance by the flute also; it has been shoved into that pop mainstream, Howe's gigantic world of melodies playable on any instrument. But Mount's other two versions return this fiddle tune to the fiddle world and are worth reproducing here. The version "as played by T.J. Cook" anticipates modern performances, with smooth melodies and fluent bowings. The version "as played by S. L. Pfeiffer" is more distinctive. The section beginning in m.9 illustrates open-string double stops, and also the kind of rhythmic holes characteristic of the new jig (like the "Stop Jig"). Last, I reproduce a version published after the Civil War by George H. Coes (ca. 1828–97), a blackface minstrel banjoist and straight man. Coes worked in New York, moved to California in 1852, and worked subsequently there, in Boston, and back in New York. It's easy to imagine him crossing paths with Mount. Coes and his ensemble-mates must have been playing "Arkansas Traveller" before the Civil War. We have no way to know if his fancy 1876 version reflects how he played the tune back then, or if instead it represents him pushing the envelope of rhythmic complexity anew. But his variations—dense clusters of repeated notes rather than melodic turns—reinforce the most distinctive musical characteristic of the music of minstrelsy: it is about rhythm.

The only pieces in this middle anthology arguably harder to play than the trickier among the waltzes are novelty numbers from Mount's collection: "The Cuckoo" (Figure 27, p. 24) and his own composition "In the Cars on the Long Island Railroad" (Figure 27, p. 25). This particular "Cuckoo" joins a centuries-long tradition of musicians being interested in bird songs in general and that bird's calls in particular. It is a tightly structured showpiece. The opening phrases recur at the end, thus constituting a relatively calm frame for the ebullience making up most of the performance. After the pictorial but relatively placid first eight bars, technical demands build steadily in terms of articulations (e.g., accents and bouncing bow strokes), string crossings, and especially work in high positions.

Figure 23. Mount enjoyed imitating sounds from nature on his fiddle, as did many fiddlers. He also pursued other pictorial effects, here the "Motion of the Boat" in a strenuous hornpipe.

While "The Cuckoo" uses sounds from nature as points of reference and extravagant departure, "In the Cars on the Long Island Railroad" offers a mixture of imitation and parodic exaggeration, and thus darkly comic, perhaps even alienated symbolizing of new, human-made noises. According to Hessler, the Long Island Railroad reached Hicksville in 1836 (some thirty miles shy of Stony Brook) then made it to Greenport in 1844 (about fifty miles beyond Stony Brook; [1984] b, 22). This was early in the era of rapid expansion of railroads in America and of artistic engagement with this new mode of transportation; the first railroad song was written the year of the first commercial railroad trip, in 1828 (Cohen 1981, 39). While Mount already knew what railroads sounded like through his visits to New York City (and the Long Island Railroad was constructed west to east), the sounds of building and then running a railroad came home to him in the midst of his activity of writing down music at home. The new railroad changed the local sonic environment, and probably annoyed Mount, since it caused the big city part of his life to encroach on the peaceful, rural fraction. His rhythmically dense musical depiction of the railroad toys with acceleration and deceleration and features dissonances representing the new and shocking noises of trains—chugging, clanking, the Doppler effect, and sheer volume. The composition is not inspired as an architecture of pitches, but melodic appeal is not the point. Like the much more traditional "The Cuckoo," it represents an attempt to bring the sonic environment into music, and, while doing that, have an excuse to stretch the violin's technical possibilities.

These were not Mount's only occasions to imitate either the natural or the machine world in sound. Mount had already experimented with replicating percussive sounds from the environment. In "The Woodpecker Tapping the Hollow Beach [sic] Tree," one line includes repeated pitches, syncopated—the tapping. Just as this imitation pales in comparison to that featured in the ornate "Cuckoo," he anticipated his delineation of railroad sounds when he copied out

Figure 24. A catalog of how players of treble instruments—especially fiddlers—might imitate various extra-musical sounds taken from Howe's Musician's Omnibus (1864).

another explicit musical portrait of a human conveyance, "Motion of the Boat," written down in 1843 (Figure 23). But this avowedly pictorial tune could easily be mistaken for a hornpipe.

Interest in having the fiddle replicate both sounds from nature and from humans was growing in Mount's day. More and more nonmusical sounds were paralleled on the fiddle, with increasingly numerous and detailed duplication of these sounds. Previously, such imitations concentrated on bird songs and were meant to entertain and amaze through beauty, accuracy, and variety. Now, to serve the rustic edge of blackface minstrelsy, the factor of broad humor blossomed, and comic pictorial effects proliferated. Several instrumental anthologies included parades of short imitations ranging from the old-fashioned subject of the cuckoo—now in ever more versions—to lots of funny topics. In Figure 24, I give Elias Howe's one-page summary and celebration of these from the second volume of the *Musician's Omnibus* (1864).

Fiddlers and their publishers pressed ahead with new rationalizations for granting blanket permission for technical exploration, even when that resulted in empty virtuosity. But their central motivation was comedy, particularly that of the blackface minstrel stage. In 1855, James Buckley issued a collection with an informative long title: *Buckley's Violin Tunes; A Collection of Beautiful Marches, Waltzes, Quadrilles, Polkas, Schottisches, Operatic Melodies, Hornpipes, Reels, Jigs, etc. etc. and Many Other Melodies Never Before Published, Including Buckley's Celebrated Imitations of the Farm-Yard, and Briggs Power of Music. The Whole Selected, Arranged and Composed for the Violin by J. Buckley and & Sons of Buckley's Serenaders.* Populating the dozen pages of "celebrated imitations" ending this book were short bits of melody entitled "Duck," "Larch," "Sheep," "Counterfeit Shilling," "Crowing of the Cock" (in several versions), "The Village Bells," and "Imitation of the Old Woman of the Farm, Singing a Psalm, with a Pair of Spectacles on Her Nose."

In sum, Mount's "The Cuckoo" and "In the Cars on the Long Island Railroad" are neither mainstream fiddle tunes nor mainstream art music pieces, but rather descendants of long streams of bird song pieces and, for that matter, the mixtures of mood portrayals and imitations of guns and funerals in works like *The Battle of Prague*. And if performances fell short in terms of technical excellence, so what? Listeners could debate the realism of the sonic parallels, be amazed by the tricks, and enjoy these special flashy moments partly because they are fancy, and partly because they were temporary, yielding to more standard tunes right away during an evening of fiddling. The novelty pieces are fun, offer an excuse to show off, and they appeal to audience members who might not have the background or temperament to enjoy either a string of tunes like "Fisher's Hornpipe" or a violin concerto. That is, they serve a social and perhaps emotional need to link sounds from the environment to deliberate making of music, serving an entertainment need, and offering a change of pace. These pieces are in Mount's collection for essentially the same reasons that "Listen to the Mockingbird" and "Orange Blossom Special" are healthy (though often obnoxious) fraternal twins in the novelty end of modern fiddling.

While those pieces defined the outer edge of antebellum fiddling in terms of sheer difficulty, cotillions and quadrilles were the lengthiest "pieces" of that day. These two related terms describe series of phrases or complete tunes conjoined in prescribed ways to accompany sequences of dance figures. The term in greater use in Cobb's and Mount's worlds was "cotillion" (often spelled "cotillon," following the French), and I'll use it to stand for pieces going by either designation here. Some of these extended pieces were around early in the nineteenth century, but the genre became extremely popular only toward the end of the antebellum era.

Cotillions are not easy to understand; that is, it is hard to figure out why they were so appealing during their heyday, apart from their facilitating sustained, uninterrupted dancing. Elias Howe acknowledged the special and growing demand for them in the decades before the Civil War in a mechanical way in the contents of the three volumes of his *Musician's Companion*: part 1 included eighteen cotillions; part 2, thirty-six; and part 3, forty. Charles M. Cobb took the trouble to make a census of his sets of cotillions in the "Universal Musician" three times, and named dozens of cotillions and quadrilles in the longest of these lists (see Figure 26). William Sidney Mount stayed busy locating cotillions for the use of his brother Nelson, the dancing master; he even solicited these from his troublesome but talented friend Mathewson.

The word "cotillion" referred both to dances and the music that accompanied those dances. It could mean just one dance (or melody) but more often meant a "Sett" of dances and an array of melodies accompanying them (I will retain the spelling "Sett" to avoid confusion). In this second anthology, I copied one complete Sett from Cobb, then two from Mount (one of unknown source, but likely Mathewson, and one certainly from him), and finally some cotillion ingredient phrases from Cobb. I had never looked closely at cotillions before starting the work on this book, because the first member of each Sett I glanced at seemed boring—so why look further? But I realized that if Cobb and Mount spent considerable time with cotillions, I ought to figure out why they did so. To my surprise, close examination of even a handful of these long pieces was quite rewarding.

The general feel of a Sett of cotillions is somewhere between a medley and an integrated single piece. Some Setts are dull throughout, but others illustrate interesting compromises between art and popular music. The widely distributed cotillion I copied from Cobb, the "Beethoven Sett" (which has no connection with Beethoven, as far as I and several friends who specialize in Beethoven's music can tell). This "Sett" starts inoffensively—the first "number" seems like a moment of polite ritual introduction rather than of musical interest. A fiddle tune convention is observed: the three strains in this number each have their own pitch range, as do the two strains of a typical fiddle tune. The whole section is in a rondo form, once the two Da Capo signs are obeyed: after the first tune, we hear the second, then return to the first, then hear the third, and finally return to the first yet again, yielding an overall form for section #1 of ABACA. Each subsequent numbered section in the Sett is constructed similarly (if there are three strains, the performed form is ABACA, but if only two, ABA). This rondo idea is then paralleled at a larger level. The beginnings of numbers 2, 3, and 4 bear some similarity to the very start of the composite Sett, and number 5 also includes melodic gestures similar to ones encountered in numbers 2 and 3. Last, and intriguingly, there are two familiar melodies offered in the course of the Sett, the first half of the famous tune "Rose Tree" in the second half of #2 (compare with this tune in Figure 6), and both strains of "The Braes of Auchentyre" as tune #6 (compare with "The Braes of Ochintyre" in Figure 27, p. 7). These similarities, taken together, produce a subtle but real feel of a rondo on the larger level.

Many aspects of the "Beethoven Sett" mark nearly every other cotillion, but not that quotation of a pair of well-known preexistent tunes. But this exceptional feature is typical in a way: Many cotillions have some special conspicuous trait. The second cotillion I placed in the anthology features more variety in terms of key than do most. Of the three parts in section #1, the last is in minor (an intrusion on the prevailing major mode that is common, but often saved for a little later in a given Sett). The beginning of this Sett's section 2 reminds us of the very beginning, just as in the Beethoven Sett; this is a generic trait. But the second strain in this section has lots of leaps; such virtuosity typically comes later in a Sett. The next section, however, is the most virtuosic, so much so that further exploration in that direction would be odd. Instead, the next section, the penultimate one, is boldly in E Minor (the relative minor of G Major, so not so big of a surprise). The combination of key, gestures, and rhythms here yields a bit of a Janissary effect (the fashionable imitation of Turkish military wind bands indulged in by many composers in the late eighteenth and early nineteenth centuries). But that doesn't last long: we abruptly blossom into E Major. This is quite a splash of color, which is immediately tempered by the last section, an inoffensive 6/8 number back in G Major. In short, this untitled cotillion has as its distinguishing identity marker these striking key relationships.

The third cotillion given in this portion of the anthology is built similarly to the previous two Setts, but with interesting differences. The first number, like that number of the Beethoven Sett and the following untitled Sett, has three strains placed in three pitch ranges; it is distinctive that the third strain of this cotillion in C Major is in the subdominant (F Major). The second number, again like that of the Beethoven Sett, starts in a way reminiscent of the beginning of the first tune, but in a contrasting meter. By this point in this Sett, we notice that many of the melodies feature arpeggios reminding us of bugle calls; it is a military-honoring Sett. The third number explores three keys, the main one of C Major, the dominant (G Major) and vi (A Minor). The next number is also adventurous, with some accidentals, passages in upper positions, and reminders of the opening arpeggios. The Sett ends with a lessening of effects, reverting to unassuming good manners.

As apparent in Figure 25, all three of these cotillions have elements of rondos, all three have nondistinctive, polite beginnings and endings, all three have sections in 6/8 (like jigs) and also sections in 2/4 (like reels or polkas in flavor). Each contains one or several tunes in keys other than the tonic of the set or at least leaning away from that tonic through inclusion of some notes outside of the key. The three Setts are about the same length. While these Setts share those characteristics, each also has one aspect that stands out as special: in the "Beethoven Sett" the inclusion of a pair of preexistent hit melodies, in the untitled Sett a grand harmonic adventure, and in Mathewson's Sett in C Major lots of tunes with military-sounding arpeggios.

These "Setts" are indeed somewhere between a medley and a developed piece, one in which material is established, then there is a clear departure into a harmonic and/or thematic adventure, then finally a return with closure. Each total Sett is longer and more content-rich than are most dance tunes that antebellum fiddlers played, but also decidedly less sophisticated than most art music. Do they embody a viable intermediate stance in terms of demands put on the listener, or will fans of both traditional music and cultivated art music find these off-putting? They were clearly popular in their heyday, but have faded away since. Why was this so? Perhaps because a fiddler could simply play just one tune for a long time

FIGURE 25. MAPS OF THE THREE COTILLIONS TRANSCRIBED IN THE SECOND ANTHOLOGY

		Beethoven Sett (in C)		Untitled Sett (in G)		Sett in C, Mathewson
1	6/8	3 strains, each in own range; rhythmic feel of all 3 strains quite similar	2/4	1: in G, but some c# 2: busier, if less distinctive 3: in relative minor	6/8	3 strains, each in own range; third strain is marked Minore, but is really in IV (F Major)
2	2/4	First strain similar to that of #1, but in new meter, second is well-known tune "Rose Tree"	2/4	First strain starts similar to start of #1; 2 has lots of leaps, is more virtuosic	2/4	First strain starts similar to start of #1, has bland feel more normal for a #1
3	2/4	New feel due to lots of repeated pitches, pitch f sometimes sharped; third strain: ab, but f#	6/8	Mostly in third position; hardest	2/4	1: in tonic (C Major) 2: in V (G Major) 3: in vi (A Minor)
4	6/8	Very like #1; feel of a partial return	2/4	E Minor (Janissary?); magical surprising leap to parallel major, E Major	2/4	3 strains and ranges, some f#s, reminds of opening arpeggios
5	2/4	Like #2; but contains no familiar tune				
6	2/4	Well-known tune: "The Braes of Auch-tertyre"/"Beaus of Albany"	6/8	Polite tune; just a calm ending after previous storm	6/8	Inoffensive, simply ingratiating return

for later traditional dances, ones emphasizing exuberant fun more than a balance of good manners and pleasure.

Charles M. Cobb repeatedly made lists entitled "Cotillons." When he contemplated gathering up cotillions for dance evenings, he grouped members of this genre with arrays of other dances that would have been useful during the same social gatherings. In Figure 26, I give the longest list of the three lists Cobb inserted in *The Universal Musician*. He did not date this census, but its contents are nearly identical to those of a slightly shorter list that he dated March 6, 1856. I reproduce this one because it includes a few more composer attributions and words of commentary than his earlier lists. I retain Cobb's spelling, capitalizing, and punctuation as faithfully as I can.

This impressive roster of dances allows several observations. First, we can be grateful that the list exists, but curious about why. Cobb also made a single short list of quicksteps and attempted to index his entire manuscript. But only the cotillions/quadrilles received this level of attention—he felt a special need to keep track of them, doubtless because they were in high demand. They present quite a variety in several ways. First, this seems to be a genre with a strong gravitational force, bringing in participation beyond the core ingredients of pieces that remind us of jigs or reels. For instance, E. K. Eaton's "Minerva" is called a "Polka Quadrille," and there is a "Waltz Quadrille" from Alonzo Bond.

FIGURE 26. COBB'S LONGEST LIST OF COTILLONS &C

1. HORTENSIA QUADRILLE. Labitsky. Old and celebrated.
2. Clara Polka Sett. Arranged by C.M.C[obb]. With figure[s].
3. Sett of Contra Dances. No. I Old __ 2. Chorus Jigg. Fig. 3. Hull's Victory 4. Lara O'Gath. 5. College Hornpipe 6. Comin' Through the Rye and Highland Reel
4. People's Quadrille. By T.B. Paine
5. Grand Marches. 1. From Enchanted Beauty. Comer. 2. No. 2. By A[lonso] Bond 3. Bond's Grand March. Arr. By [?]
6. WALTZ QUADRILLE (No. 3). From A. Bond
7. BOB RIDLEY QUADRILLE
8. Set of Waltzes for Spanish Dance (6 & Allen's Dance). Arr. By C.M. C.
9. CALIFORNIA SETT. With changes. x-ln't
10. Old BEETHOVEN Sett (5 No.s) & Fig.
11. Contra Dances I. Gal I Left Behind Me — Patanelli. 2 Portland Fancy — fig. 3 Monny Musk — fig. 4 Speed the Plough 5. Pop Goes the Weasel — fig.
12. DEXTER'S SETT. By E.K. Eaton
13. LE SALON DES DELICES Quadrille by _____
14. Schottisches 1. DIAMOND Arr. By A. Bond 2. The Dream of Love by ——— 3. Bible Hill, Dinsmore 4.Coral, arr. by O.W.R. Flag 5 AMPHITRITE
15. POLKA SETT. Fig.
16. Fantasia Sett. Wake Dinah Wake. No. 6 off. 5 no.s fig. Arr. by C.M. C.
17. ERNANI QUADRILLE. Old & good.
18. BEN BOLT SETT & Fig.
19. FIREMEN'S SETT & Fest March. A. Bond
20. LE PRINTEMPS QUADRILLE. Pan Joaquin
21. Old Opera Sett 4 No.s & fig.
22. Polkas 1. Sontag 2 Jenny Lind 3 BUTTERFLY Th. Holtz 4 MARGARETTA. Wittman 5 POLKA REDOWA
23. MINERVA Polka Quadrille By E.K. Eaton
24. LE FILLES DE MARBRE. Quadrille by Schubert. Arr. by N. Bousquet
25. ANNIE LAURIE SETT. Arr. by C.M.C. fig. Good sett.
26. PENNSYLVANIA SETT. Arr. by C.M.C. fig. Better still
27. Jordan Medley Sett (No. 9 Bond) x-Int fig.
28. The BOSTONIAN (No. 1 Hall) By _____ Quadrille
29. Round Waltzes. 1 Last in Bond's Book 2 Next to do 3 Lucrezia Borgia next to last page 4 La Jola Arroyonese 5 4[?] in Hall's Music
30. THE WINTER BEAUTIES. Waltz Quadrille
31. AMERICAN QUADRILLE. Jullien.
32. Contra Dances 1 Old Zip Coon 2 _____ arr. by O.W.R. 3 Fisher's Hornpipe fig. Bond 4 Contra Dance in Bonds Book 5 Kendalls Hornpipe 6 Lady Walpole's Reel fig. 7 DEMOCRATIC RAGE arr. C.M. C.
33. MOUNTAIN ECHOS. Quadrille by _____.
34. Medley Sett (No. 5 Bond)
35. LE PATRICIEN. Quadrille by Basisio
36. BELLES OF AMERICA Bass in A
37. The VILLAGE FESTIVAL. Quadrille [sic] by Carbon
38. LA FETE DES LOUPS. Quadrille by Bousquet
39. LE CHASSE INFERNALE. In 4 sharps

Many of Cobb's cotillions/quadrilles are made up entirely of new music, but a fair number are named for a hit tune that they contain: "Ben Bolt Sett," "Annie Laurie Sett," and "Bob Ridley Quadrille." The first quadrille Cobb listed is by Labitsky, whom we met earlier as the composer of the fanciest waltz that Cobb played, and also of the most challenging waltz that Mount wrote down from the playing of his friend S. L. Pfeiffer. Indeed, the composers and arrangers of these Setts—apart from Cobb himself—range from the local and obscure, such as Cobb's Vermont acquaintance bandmaster Alonzo Bond, to international figures like Labitsky and Narcisse Bousquet (ca. 1800–1869), a French recorder player based in Paris but also active in England.

While Cobb revised some existing tunes, and arranged quite a few for ensemble performance, his only sizeable efforts in composition consisted of a group of 120 short tunes that he designed to appear in medleys with others: "New Music by C.M. Cobb, Arranged in Single Parts (For Cotillions) &c." He commented in his journal on August 7, 1851: "I have begun to write in my great music book, about page 650, to write some 'New Music' in numbers, of 8 or more measures each, and I name every number something—no matter what. This new music is I suppose—original—and every part has some AIR to it. But I wouldn't want to say that it is all original for some such parts that I have before fell to humming and wrote off supposing to be original, I have afterwards heard played note for note and no doubt I heard some time before I wrote it off."

Most of these efforts are just individual eight-measure strains; when he put two such strains under one title he numbered them separately (so that "Marengo," Number 1 in the series, is one eight-measure tune, while "Novi," with its two strains, is numbered 2–3). I fit the first sixteen named tunes into the anthology. The title "Marengo" must refer to Napoleon's important victory in northern Italy in 1800; there seems no end to America's fascination with Napoleon, and Cobb was a voracious reader with a teenager's imagination. Lots of Cotillions are named for places, but Cobb's choices of these are entertaining: "Symme's Hole," "Australia," etc. And titles like "Fire-fly" and "Circumcision" are certainly evocative. In order to capture the flavor of the whole collection, I'll list a handful of the titles of the remainder of the 120 sections: #25: "December," #29: "Bride's Bell's," #38: "Oppression," #53: "Santa Claus," #71: "Teneriffe," #87: "Pumpkin Vine," #96: "Satan," #98: "Indianapolis," #109: "Cuckoo" (yes, including a cuckoo call), #111: "Serious Family," and, last, #120: "Monterrey."

Most of Cobb's tunes are typical cotillion tunes—simple, unremarkable major-mode ideas presented in 6/8 or 2/4, thus much like jigs and reels. However, just as he included a few cotillions in *The Universal Musician* that included tunes fitting into other genres, there's a quickstep in Nos. 2–3, "Novi" (in 6/8, but with dotted rhythms), and #23 is "Kreith's Waltz." Also, several of the tunes are in minor—as are a fair share of cotillion tunes—and are quite compelling (see #5, "Lamp-Oil," with its syncopation, #11, "Stirling," and #15, "Symmes' Hole"). Others of his tunes lean in the direction of word-painting—the blinking rhythms of #6, "Fire-Fly," the high leaps of #12, "Man of the Moon," and the accent-punctuated nervousness of #7, "Circumcision." It is a surprise that Cobb didn't take the next step and put some of these together as full cotillions. Perhaps he couldn't bring himself to write unexciting parts that could offer a conventional environment framing his imaginative strains.

I close this second anthology with five tunes that Mount said he presented as a "medley at a concert given for the benefit of St. James Church in Stony Brook August 1855" (this phrase written immediately below his transcription of the pieces): "Rustic Reel," "Pop Goes the Weasel," "Gallopade," "Miss Johnson of Houston Hill," and "Lord McDonald's Reel." He didn't pursue his more exotic musical interests here—no chromatic waltzes, no fancy position work. Instead, he gathered up tunes for what he called a medley—thus presumably played without pause—that had quite a bit in common with a cotillion. There are several tunes each in 6/8 and 2/4, related keys for the tunes (here G Major and D Major), and just enough variety between melodies. Nevertheless, in just five tunes, he gathers up quite a bit of the cumulative history of American fiddling. He described "The Rustic Reel" in a letter to his brother Nelson as "new" and fashionable in New York (Jan. 30, 1839). The final tune, "Lord McDonald's Reel," was common in the Scottish collections of the late 1700s and early 1800s, common in English collections, ubiquitous in American music commonplace books, and still is well known today, under the title "Leather Britches." Just before that reel, Mount placed a much less well-distributed Scottish tune, "Miss Johnson of Houston Hill," which was usually called "Miss Johnston's." It bears that title in Niel Gow and Sons' *Fifth Collection of Strathspey Reels* ([1809], 30), where it includes more trills and fewer dotted notes than in Mount's version.

The first two tunes were common ones in 6/8, the "Rustic Reel" (really a jig) and the young but already ubiquitous "Pop Goes the Weasel" (Cobb listed it among his sets of contradances; see Figure 36). The extreme simplicity, small gimmick (at the fermata, the fiddler likely plucks the e string to mark the word "pop"), and especially the tune's familiarity gave Mount some license to then play the longer, more intricate polka-like "Gallopade." It is in that piece that Mount indulges in just a little bit of the Italianate variation that he enjoyed so much, in this case the common effect of making a strain a bit denser on repetition. Mount had judged that the five tunes fit together; the effect is aesthetically balanced and historically *cumulative*, a word I'm tempted to use over and over again to characterize the last antebellum years of American fiddling. But "Pop Goes the Weasel" and this "Gallopade" did represent opposing forces.

M. Hunt Hessler, a Stony Brook music professor recruited to write about Mount's music for the 1984 exhibition and celebration "Catching the Tune," characterized the sociocultural moment in a single sentence: "Musical culture was in a period of transition from a nebulous mixture of styles enjoyed by all classes to a more class-oriented and thus value-laden stratification of forms" ([1984]b, 7). The tensions were indeed becoming more visible, the rope joining art violin playing with folk fiddling still strong but more and more taut.

Figure 27. Tune Anthology II, p. 1. Marches.

Figure 27. Tune Anthology II, p. 2. Song melodies.

Figure 27. Tune Anthology II, p. 3. Challenging hornpipes.

Jones' Favorite

Noted down by S. L. Pfieffer, Esq.
(Mount, 00.515.6)

Hull's Victory

(Cobb, 414)

Hull's Victory, Arranged by A. Pushee, May 1851

(Cobb, 82)

Figure 27. Tune Anthology II, p. 4. "Hull's Victory," first versions.

Figure 27. Tune Anthology II, p. 5. "Hull's Victory," conclusion.

Figure 27. Tune Anthology II, p. 6. Last hornpipes.

Braes of Ochintyre, Written by A. Pushee May 28, 1851

(Cobb, 83)

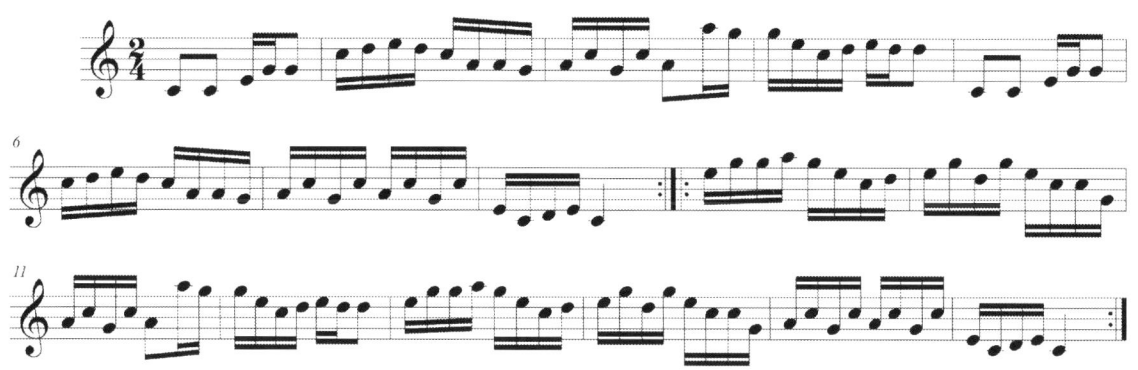

Beaus of Albany

(Howe 1864, 46, in section devoted to contradances)

1st and 2d couples balance, swing partners, both couples down the centre, back, 1st couple cast off, cross right hands and 2d couple, left hands back, right and left with 3d couple.

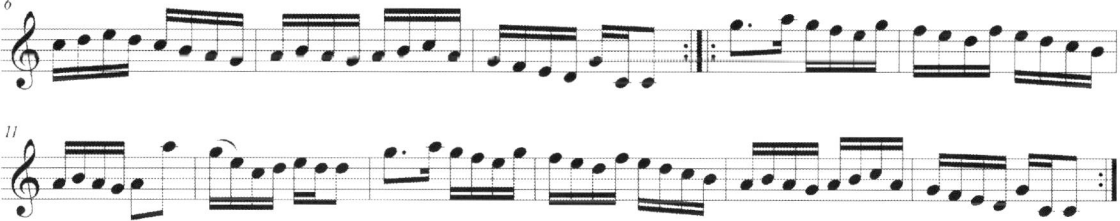

The High Road to Linton, Reel

From Mr. Fifer, March 15th, 1854

(Mount, 00.515.22)

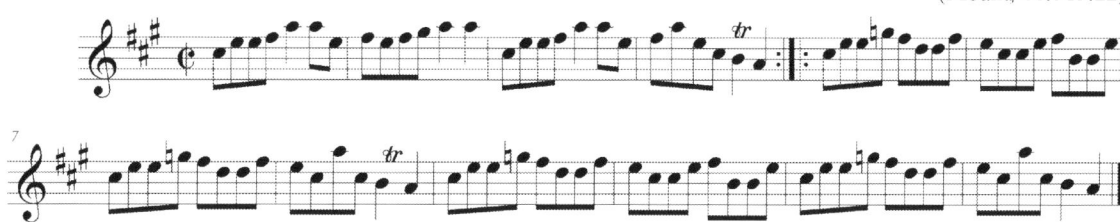

Figure 27. Tune Anthology II, p. 7. The Scottish reel "Braes of Ochintyre" and its frequently American descendant, "Beaus of Albany."

Figure 27. Tune Anthology II, p. 8. "Lord McDonald's Reel" and a rare retitling, "McDaniel's Reel."

Figure 27. Tune Anthology II, p. 9. The reel "Money Musk" and plenty of Italianate variations.

Figure 27. Tune Anthology II, p. 10. The strathspey "Duke of Gordon's Fancy" ("Marquis of Huntley's Farewell") with Italianate variations from Mount and from Nelson Mathewson.

Mrs. Wright of Salons [Laton]--a Strathspey
(Mount, 00.515.82)

The Braes of Tullymet. A Strathspey
(Mount, 00.515.1)

O'er the Hills and far awa'
(Mount, 00.515.2)

Figure 27. Tune Anthology II, p. 11. A few more Scottish dance tunes.

Kitty of Coleraine

(Cobb, 84)

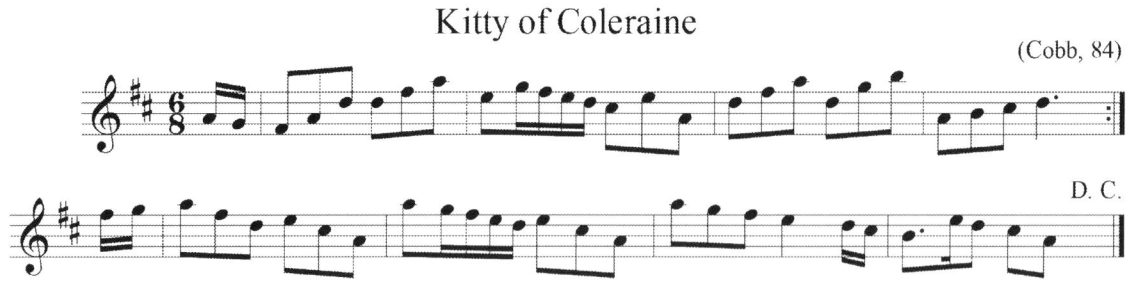

Flight of Fancy

(Cobb, 84)

Quarrel and Reconciliation

(Cobb, 84)

Dorothy Draggletail

(Cobb, 65)

Figure 27. Tune Anthology II, p. 12. Jigs.

Bailey's Waltz

(Cobb, 75)

Rifle Waltz

(Cobb, 85)

Waltz--The Cachuca

(Mount collection, from a letter sent to his brother Nelson on August 29, 1841)

Mount commented below his transcription: "Mathewson was so well pleased with the style in which I played the above waltz that he wrote it from hearing me play it. I had seen Fanny Essler Dance the Cachuca several times, and I believed caught the spirit of it. I am pleased to say that Mathewson always plays it as written above."

Figure 27. Tune Anthology II, p. 13. Waltzes, obscure to famous.

Spring Waltz, by J. Labitsky, From O. A. Whitmore
(Cobb, 226-27)

Figure 27. Tune Anthology II, p. 14. A modern waltz by Labitsky collected by Cobb.

Figure 27. Tune Anthology II, p. 15. A hard waltz by Labitsky and a chromatic waltz, by Mount.

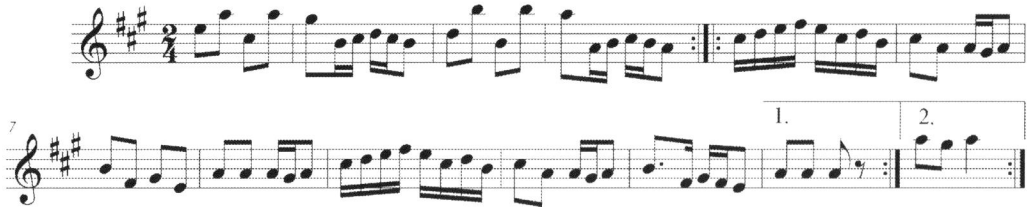

Figure 27. Tune Anthology II, p. 16. Polkas.

Figure 27. Tune Anthology II, p. 17. Fancy dances.

Figure 27. Tune Anthology II, p. 18. Modal melodies from Cobb.

French Muse

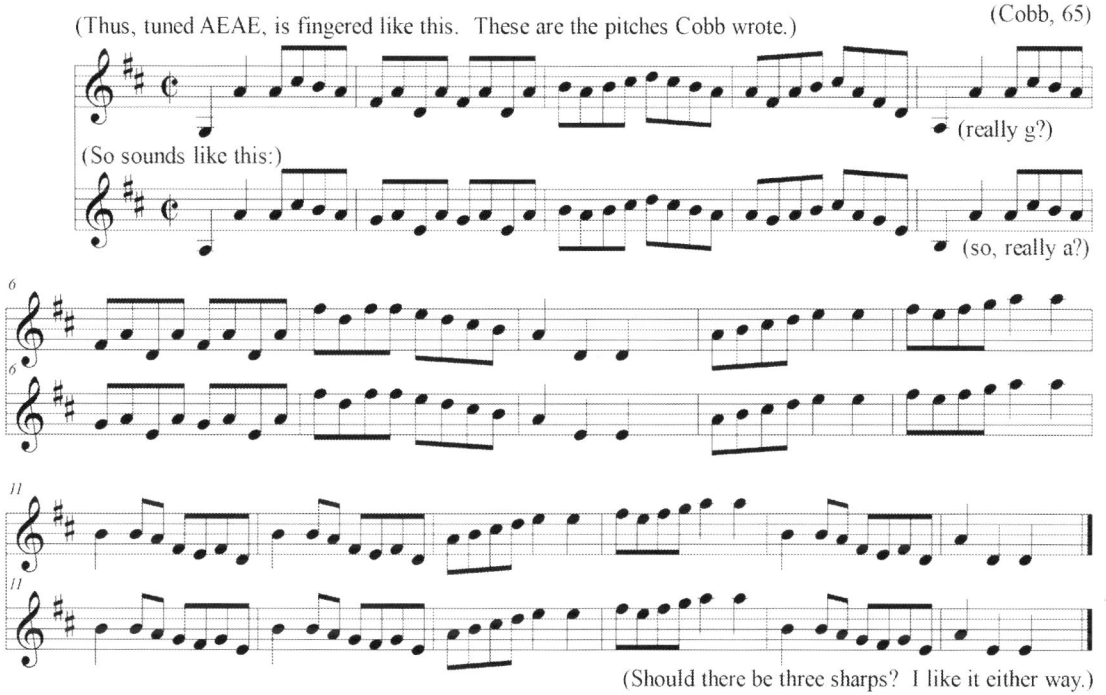

Figure 27. Tune Anthology II, p. 19. Melodies employing scordatura.

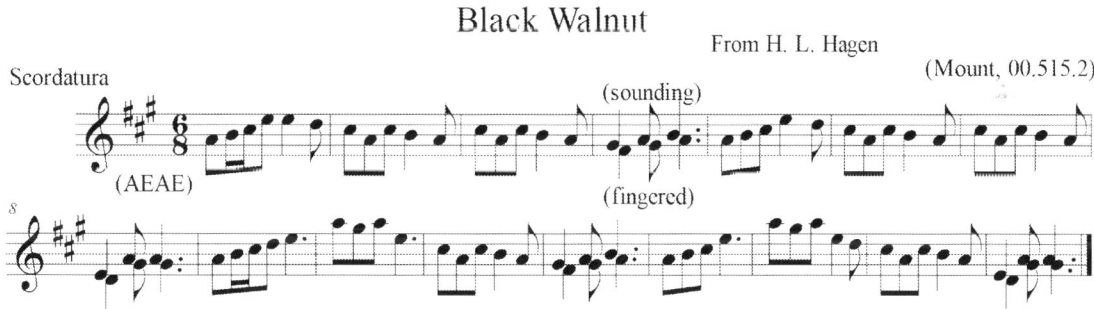

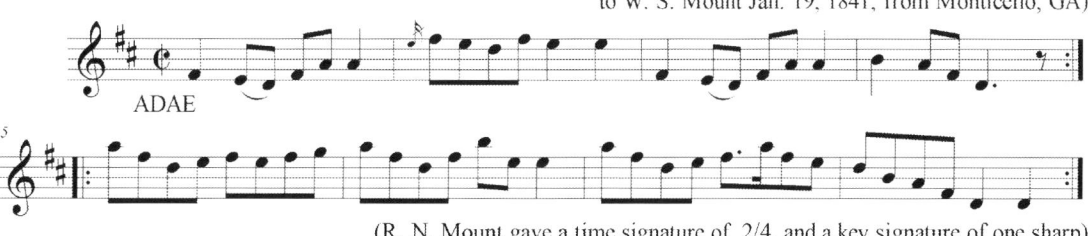

Figure 27. Tune Anthology II, p. 20. Tunes evoking the barnyard collected by Cobb.

Black Tony's Juber, as played by W. S. M.

(Mount, 00.515.1)

Old Sussanna, don't you cry for me

From Mr. Titus, in the spring of 1848

(Mount, 00.515.12)

(Yes, that's Mount's exact title. Oddly, he transcribed this piece in Ab immediately below this transcription in A.)

The Bobtail Horse, as Played by W. S. M.

written [down] by Thalo Pfieffer, Esq.

(Mount, 00.515.82)

Stop Jig

(Mount, 00.515.52)

Figure 27. Tune Anthology II, p. 21. Blackface minstrel tunes collected by Mount.

The Arkansas Traveller and Rackinsac Waltz
(Cumming 1847; treble line of first tune only)

Rackensack Jigg or the Arkansas Traveller
(Cobb, 227)

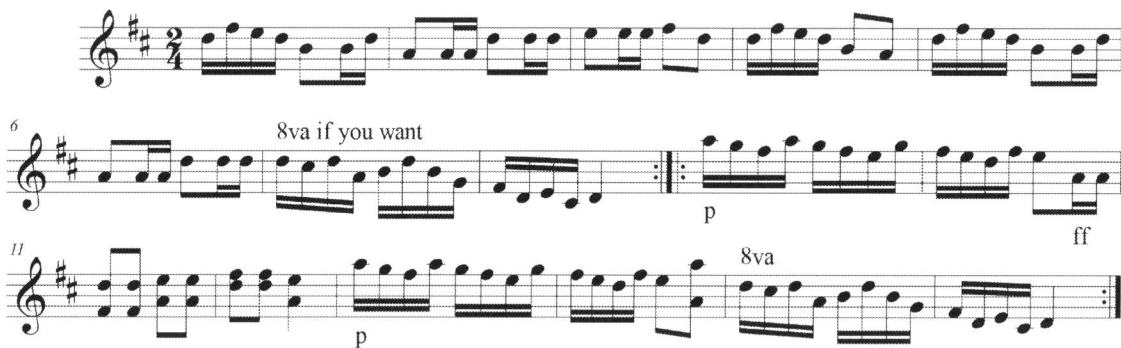

Arkansas Traveller, as Played by S. L. Pfeiffer of Alabama
(Mount, 00.515.6)

(I supplied measure 13, which I believe Mount omitted.)

Figure 27. Tune Anthology II, p. 22. "Arkansas Traveller," first versions.

Stony Brook, August 22, 1852

Arkansas Traveller, As Played by T. J. Cook

(Mount, 00.515.37)

(The last two measures Mount wrote in small notes in the upper right of the score. They offer an alternative ending.)

Arkansas Traveller

(Coes 1876, 57)

Figure 27. Tune Anthology II, p. 23. "Arkansas Traveller," concluded.

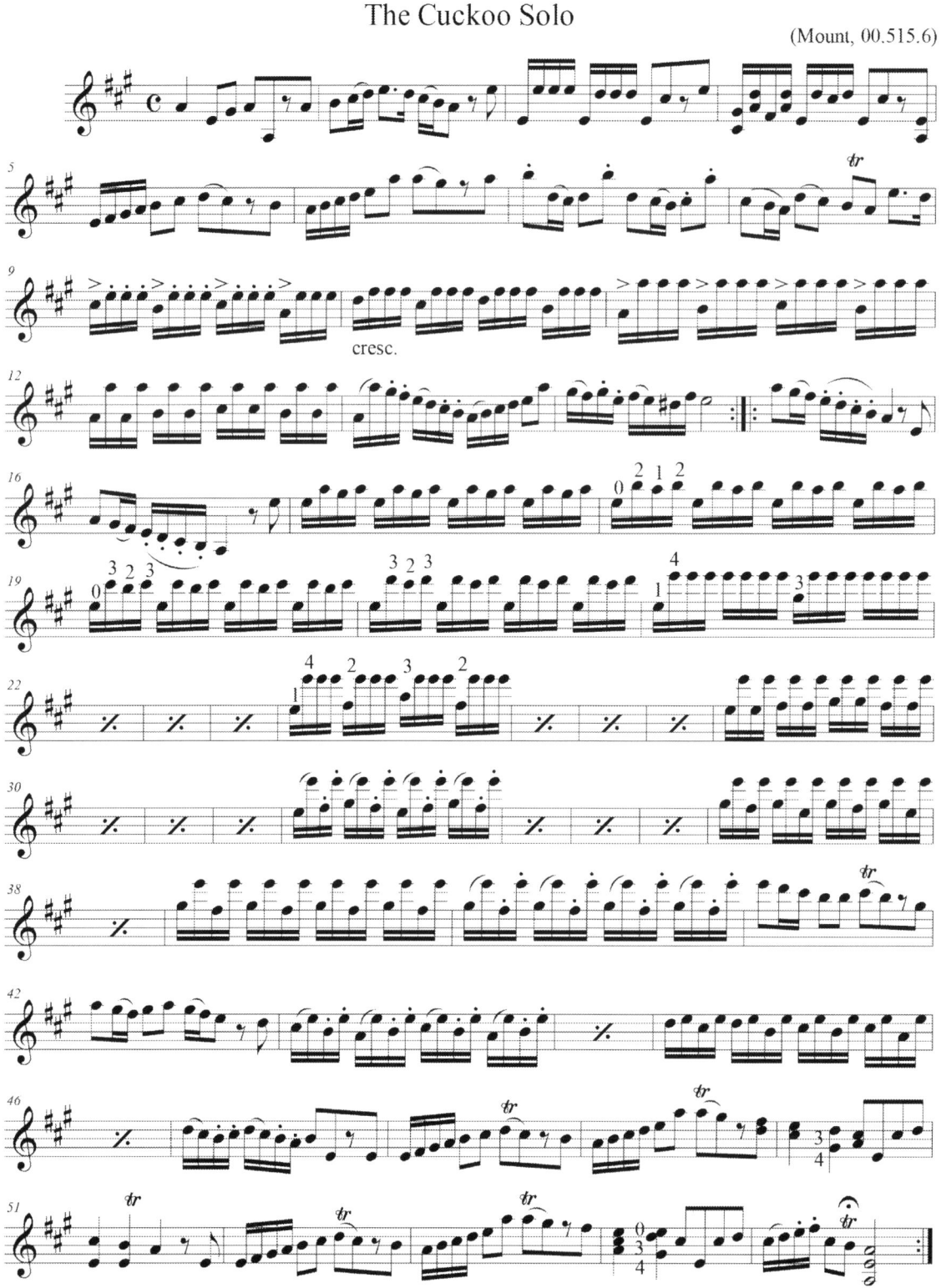

Figure 27. Tune Anthology II, p. 24. Mount's longest and most technically-challenging imitation of bird song.

In the Cars on the Long Island Railroad. By Wm. S. Mount

Stony Brook. Dec. 25[?], 1850.

(Mount, 00.515.39)

Figure 27. Tune Anthology II, p. 25. Mount's own composition, an imitation of train sounds.

Figure 27. Tune Anthology II, p. 26. A widely-distributed cotillion.

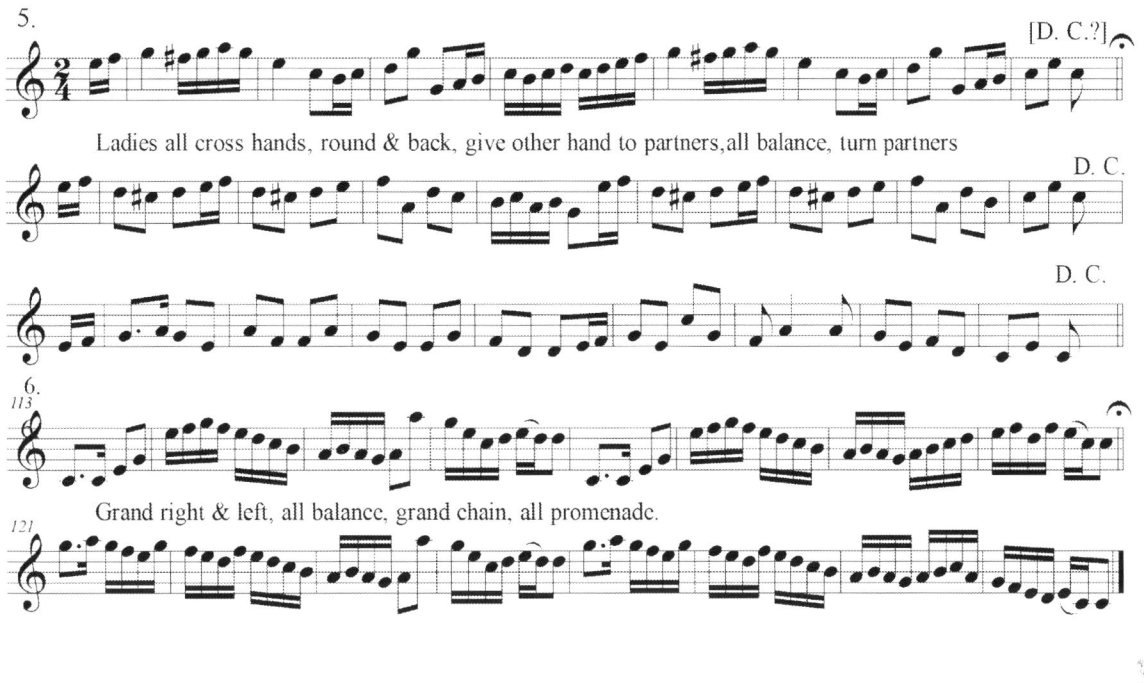

Figure 27. Tune Anthology II, p. 27. Previous cotillion concluded, and a rare one begun.

Figure 27. Tune Anthology II, p. 28. Rare cotillion concluded

A Sett of Cotillions in the Key of C. From Nelson Mathewson.

(Mount, sent in letter to brother Nelson, Feb. 4, 1841)

Figure 27. Tune Anthology II, p. 29. Cotillion from Mount by Mathewson, begun.

New Music by C. M. Cobb, Arranged in Single Parts (For Cotillions) &c.
(Cobb, 639)

Figure 27. Tune Anthology II, p. 30. Cotillion by Mount concluded; cotillion fragments by Cobb begun.

Figure 27. Tune Anthology II, p. 31. Cotillion ingredients by Cobb, continued.

Figure 27. Tune Anthology II, p. 32. First page of a concert medley played by Mount.

Figure 27. Tune Anthology II, p. 33. Concert medley played by Mount, concluded.

PART THREE

Fiddlers Moving South, and West, and away from Notation

Much of the history of nineteenth-century America centers on massive population shifts and associated cultural changes. Individuals, families, even major parts of communities moved south and west. Fiddlers were among the thousands packing up and leaving home for areas where populations were sparse and land cheap or even free. Most who headed west did so for reasons opposite to those that had inspired the Pilgrims and Puritans to cross the Atlantic. Those first settlers from Europe sacrificed material well-being for a critical change in culture—freedom of worship. While the nineteenth-century American movement west did include groups emigrating for religious reasons—for example, many Quakers' moves to Indiana, and the Mormons' treks to Utah—most migrants were sacrificing the valued social and cultural fabric of settled communities for the hope for elbow room coupled with economic betterment. They recreated aspects of expressive culture as best as they could in their new homes; fiddling was flexible and portable. Large parts of the McArthur and Seward families moved west. Mount had southern connections through his brother Nelson's professional travel and due to the Alabama wing of the extended Pfeiffer family visiting relatives in Stony Brook. Even Cobb had fiddler friends who headed west.

Little notated fiddle music has come down to us from the South or from the West before the Civil War, and speculation about what fiddling sounded like in less settled areas becomes ever more tenuous, verging on the fanciful. The beginning of this final section of the book summarizes what we can learn about southern antebellum fiddling from George P. Knauff's *Virginia Reels* of 1839 through 1851. This set of four publications came into being as an assemblage of thirty-five pieces that transcriber, editor, and profiteer Knauff arranged from fiddlers' oral traditions for young ladies who were his piano students. A second publisher soon got into the act, and another few pieces entered the collection. I have treated this rich source at length elsewhere (Goertzen 2017); I will summarize that work and add to it here. Second, I will look at an afternoon in the life of the garrulous farmer and botanic doctor Gideon Lincecum. While traveling in Texas in 1835, he fiddled at a picnic. Much later, he described the event and listed some of the tunes he played; this section explores what we can learn from such anecdotes. Third (and last), we will benefit from the energetic family folklore collecting of Armeanous Hamblen, who transcribed tunes from memory from the playing of his grandfather David Hamblen, tunes that he believed that the elder Hamblen had learned in western Virginia in the 1830s.

ORAL AND WRITTEN, BLACK AND WHITE, ENDURING AND EVOLVING: SOUTHERN FIDDLING AS REVEALED IN GEORGE P. KNAUFF'S *VIRGINIA REELS*

George Knauff was an industrious and inventive German immigrant. He married surprisingly well, and settled with his bride in Farmville, Virginia, in the 1830s. Their home and his music business (in the same building) were subsidized by his wife's prosperous planter father, and the young couple's social life must have joined in with that of the local upper crust, whose main evening entertainments were dances. Fiddlers—probably African Americans—enlivened those dances with performances that must have evinced interactions of white melodies with creolized performance style, of veteran and novel tunes, and of high-toned manners and down-home needs.

That we have inherited a published collection of distinctively southern antebellum American fiddle tunes is a pleasant surprise. George P. Knauff, the arranger, was a German immigrant trying to support his family following both conventional and unconventional strategies. But whose fiddling is represented in his publications? Knauff seized every chance to link his name with prominent local citizens on the title pages of his published sheet music through dedications or by acknowledging shared creative efforts, no doubt expecting this name-dropping to inspire purchases of the music. That the fiddler who played these tunes—a well-versed musician who expressed a demonstrably local take on American fiddling—remains anonymous suggests his name would not have helped Knauff sell the *Virginia Reels*. That fiddler must have lacked social standing, and so was probably a slave or free black.

A George Phillip Knauff and his brother John C. Knauff, originally of Marburg, Germany, arrived in the United States during the 1820s. The first massive wave of non-British European immigration would materialize during the two decades immediately preceding the Civil War; the arrival of the Knauffs just preceded that influx. Why does it matter to us that Knauff came from Germany, and did so as an adult? Knauff's formal training in music and also his initial acquaintance with tunes in oral tradition must have taken place while he grew up in Germany, he wouldn't have encountered the tunes that make up the *Virginia Reels* before coming to America. Also, he would not have been in as good a position to form concrete opinions concerning which types of music would be commercially viable in his new home as would American- or British-trained musicians.

George P. Knauff married Ann S. C. Bondurant of Farmville, Prince Edward County, Virginia, on November 21, 1832. She was a decade younger than he;

perhaps they met when he gave her piano lessons, likely in the context of a "female seminary" (finishing school) in Richmond. Farmville was still a small town when Knauff and his bride took up residence. It was laid out in 1798 and incorporated in 1832. The location was desirable, in slightly hilly land near the inward extent of the navigable portion of the Appomattox River. By Knauff's day, Farmville had already become the fourth-largest tobacco market in Virginia, although a town of only around eight hundred even by the mid-1830s (Ely 2004, 345). This crop could be shipped out by road to Richmond, but it was cheaper to send it by batteaux—flat-bottomed boats with a draft of no more than two feet when loaded (Ely 2004, 150), propelled by poling downriver to Petersburg.

In the Farmville Fancy Store, Knauff offered higher-end domestic goods and musical merchandise to his small town and rural clientele. He combined piano performance and teaching with his retail business, later built pianos (plus, in a sad coda, collected debts). Such a varied professional life was not unusual. Several planters in Prince Edward County doubled as physicians, lawyers, or land surveyors, while farmers were often qualified as blacksmiths or carpenters (Ely 2004, 107).

The Knauffs' daughter was born circa 1834, and a son followed in 1836. Sadly, Ann Knauff died a month later (Knauff-Waldrop n.d., 1–2). And between the two births, George Knauff suffered financial reverses. American businessmen faced a severe credit shortage in 1833, a massive crop failure in 1835, and a progressively less stable monetary situation culminating in the panic of 1837, which was followed by a depression lasting about six years. Late in 1835, Knauff attempted to auction off most or all of his inventory and much of his family's household goods (*Richmond Enquirer* May 6). A year later, fire consumed his house and store. The account of this in the *Richmond Enquirer* indicated that "two small families" in addition to the Knauffs lived in the building at the time, and that Knauff lost "every thing; his dwelling house, kitchen, smoke-house full of bacon, a number of very valuable Pianos and musical instruments, new furniture, music, and all his papers and books. Nothing was insured" (June 3, 1836).

In a remarkable show of resilience (and doubtless of steadfast support from the affluent Bondurants), Knauff reentered the business world as a piano builder less than a year later. But he faced sharp competition from the flamboyant and well-financed E. P. Nash of nearby Petersburg. Also, William Knabe—another recent German immigrant—would open a piano factory in Baltimore in 1838. Knauff's business failed, and he mortgaged most of his remaining belongings. These included a parcel of land in Farmville (likely the one on which the piano factory stood), "a negro woman named Susan, a negro child Maria, and a negro boy named George," two horses, a sulky (a lightweight two-wheeled cart), ten used pianos, two new pianos, an unspecified amount of music, a gold watch, and "all debts due unto me, the said George P. Knauff" (as listed in the *Prince Edward County Deed Book* 22, 264–65). The stage was set for another major change in his life.

The 1839 catalog of the Buckingham Female Collegiate Institute—just a few miles from Farmville—lists Knauff as "Professor of Instrumental" (West 1990, 18). This was the year he was most prolific as a composer and arranger of sheet music, indeed, probably the year of the first printing of the first three of the four pamphlets making up the *Virginia Reels.* The "female seminary"—the Buckingham Female Collegiate Institute was an ambitious entry in that crowded category—was the environment in which daughters of prosperous citizens received an advanced education. Both Prince Edward County and neighboring Buckingham County had long been dotted with "various small private schools of a temporary nature," often staffed by teachers from the North, since teaching was not considered "an especially 'high calling' in the South" (Shepard 1940, 168 and 365). But for impoverished Knauff, this job was a step up.

Music courses were the most popular of the pedagogical offerings classified as "extras" in these schools, even though fees for lessons and for instrument use added up. Farnham asserted that "the purpose of a musical education was home entertainment. Consequently, instruction was organized with a view towards developing a repertoire of pieces that might be enjoyed by family and friends," these focusing on sentimental numbers cast in easy keys (1994, 87). A typical young lady's binder's volume focused on current sentimental songs and, by the mid-1840s, included a few comic songs coming out of blackface minstrelsy. The last third or so of many collections included easy dances and marches, perhaps capped by a few variation sets or other relatively challenging selections. Playing such an assortment of pieces may have afforded young women chances for self-expression that were otherwise in short supply.

This institute's faculty consisted of five teachers in 1839; rosters rarely exceeded a half dozen, and always included a music teacher. But Knauff's tenure was brief. A student referred in several letters later that year to learning music, French, and Spanish from Mr. [Arnaud] Préot. A letter dated December 14, 1839, added that Mrs. Préot helped the writer "to make tapestry" (Shepard 1940, 184). Perhaps the keys to Knauff's being so swiftly supplanted lay in Mr. Préot's pedagogical versatility, and because he was married.

Knauff continued to sell pianos to the school, to repair those instruments, and, briefly, to create sheet music that the students could be persuaded to buy. His output was largely in 1839—perhaps while he worked at the institute—and in 1851–1853, when his daughter was enrolled at a similar school; the main batches of printings of the *Virginia Reels* are from those periods. The *Virginia Reels* were issued several times, and by two publishers. The broad outline is this: Knauff issued pamphlets 1 and 2 through George Willig Jr. of Baltimore, during or shortly before 1839, without plate numbers. Then, emboldened by interest evinced in the music, Willig reissued those two pamphlets and added a third (all now bearing consecutive plate numbers) in 1839. Willig's Baltimore competitor F. D. Benteen put out his own editions of pamphlets 1–3 in the early 1840s, omitting any reference to Knauff, and adding a few pieces to pamphlets 1 and 3.

Knauff's later flurry of publication—both of the *Virginia Reels* and of his other sheet music—started in 1851, and responded to the popularity of blackface minstrelsy, and thus to a part of fiddlers' repertoires not openly celebrated in pamphlets 1–3 of the *Virginia Reels.* Willig did publish pamphlet 4, which contains minstrel tunes. However, on the title page, he retained the elegant decoration common to the title pages of the first three pamphlets, apparently seeking sales of pamphlet 4 to the people who had bought numbers 1–3, and for the same reasons. That is, even the most lively, aurally crude minstrel melodies were now to be reinterpreted as decorous dances for girls being channeled toward elegant domesticity. Benteen eventually followed the opposite visual and thus sales strategy. Although he initially printed his pirate editions of the first three numbers of the *Virginia Reels* with tame decorations, he printed number 4—now with Knauff's name attached—featuring the bold black lines more characteristic of minstrel sheet music covers. Benteen also reissued his versions of numbers 1–3 with new covers to match that of number 4; his goal was to capitalize on the minstrel associations of tunes in pamphlet 4 to increase the sales of pamphlets 1–3 (see Figure 28). The main market would still be upper-class young women, but Benteen was more aggressively exploiting the bizarre but very real overlap between rough-edged minstrelsy and refined parlor music. I reprint all of the tunes from all editions. Benteen added a half-dozen tunes, and subtracted a few: all changes from the original Willig edition are noted in the course of Anthology III.

What was Knauff's understanding of the term "Virginia reel?" Reels were line dances, done throughout British culture and defined as much by the music to which they were done (duple time, rhythmic texture basically of eighth notes in cut time) as by the precise steps, which could vary. The lines of men and women couldn't be too close, because much of the dancing was done by the outer couples, and took place on diagonals within the lines. Elias Howe printed a "Virginia Reel" in his *Quadruple Musician's Omnibus* within a section devoted to line dances. The tune, named simply "Virginia Reel," was the common one entitled "Lord MacDonald's Reel," and still called that in the North, but now known as "Leather Britches" in the South. This page of the *Musician's Omnibus* is crammed full of dance tunes and their figures, the nine dances including this "Virginia Reel," and several of the tunes Knauff gathered into his *Virginia Reels*, "Money Musk" (which he called "Killie Krankie"), "Speed the Plough," "Miss Brown's Reel" (he called it "The Hero"), and some others (1864, 41). The lengthy but not really elaborate dance directions for Howe's "Virginia Reel" read:

> First lady down the centre half way (foot gentleman up at the same time to meet lady), balance there and return to places, 1st gent. and foot lady the same, 1st lady and foot gent meet and swing with left hand and back to places. 1st gent and foot lady the same, 1st lady and foot gent meet and swing with right hand and back to places, 1st gent and foot lady the same, 1st lady and foot gent meet and swing with both hands and back to places, 1st gent and foot lady the same, 1st couple give right hands and swing one and a half round, swing 2nd with right hand, partner with left, 3rd with right, partner with left, 4th with right, pt. with left, 5th with right, pt. with left, 6th with right, pt. left, centre with pt. and swing, all lead round (ladies to right, gents to left), all up centre, 1st couple down centre to stop.

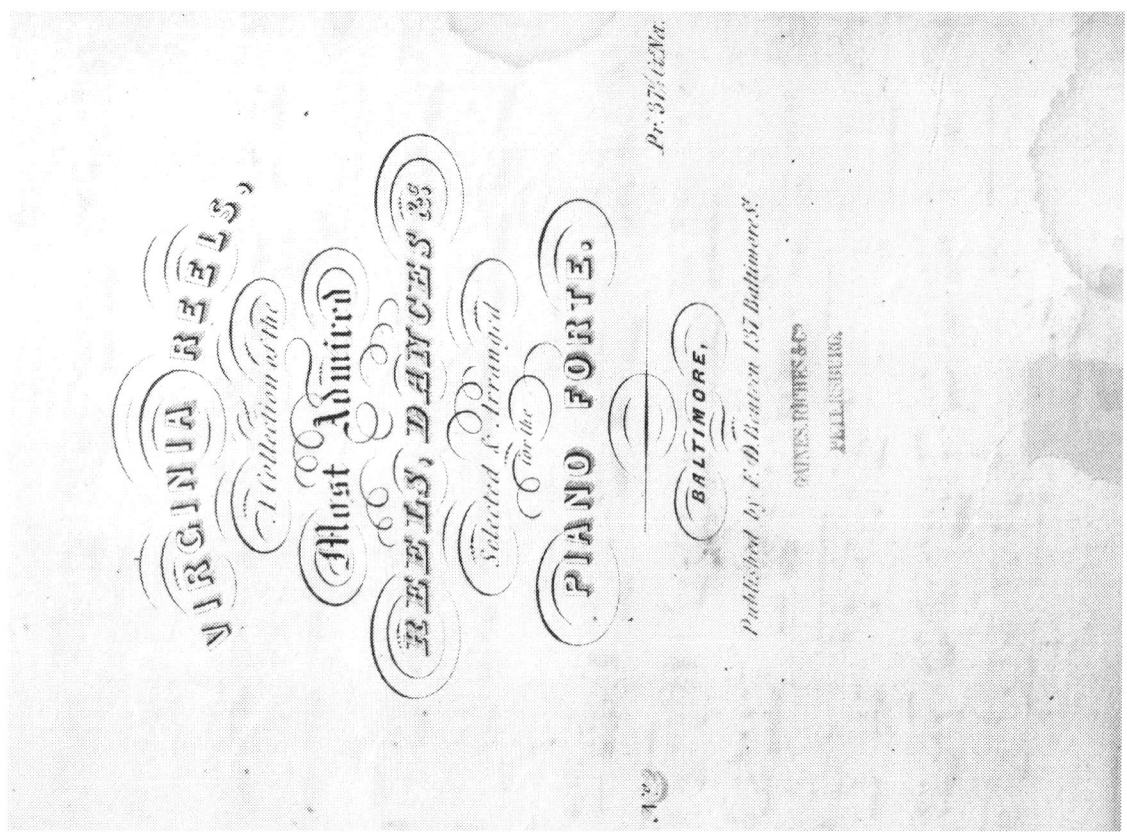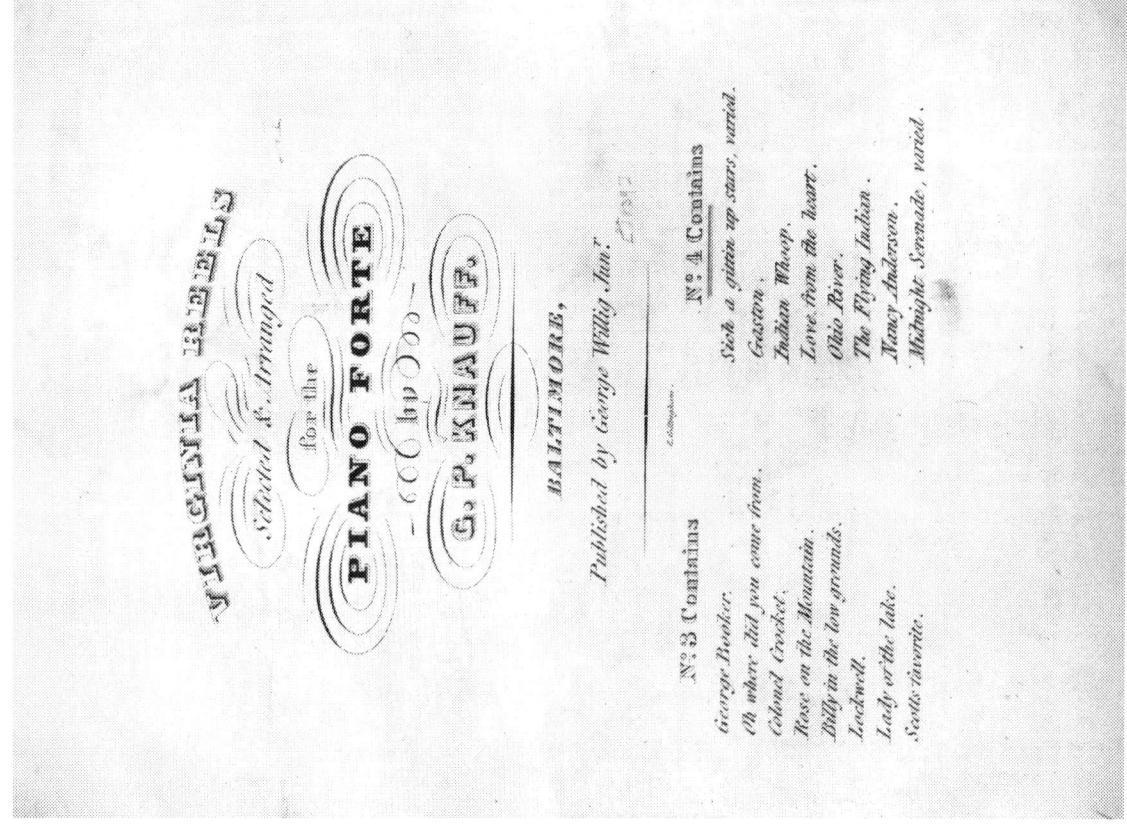

Figure 28. Sheet music covers advertise selling strategies. The original Willig covers for Knauff's Virginia Reels suit the decorous world of young female pianists—even the fourth volume, which is packed with blackface minstrel tunes (a). The first pirate edition from fellow Baltimore publisher Benteen follows that strategy too (b). Then Benteen opted for more minstrel-oriented heavy black lines in his 1850s reprint, in which Knauff now was credited (c), although still using refined decorations for Knauff works that were not in the minstrel vein (d).

Why did Knauff believe that he could make money by arranging and selling oral-tradition pieces? The opportunity may have dawned on him gradually, as he noticed that there was a body of music in regular use in his part of Virginia that included tunes few of which were published. As a musician trained in Germany, he may have reflected on the histories of the waltz and the Ländler—that is, that these were folk dances first, and then became fashionable, popular genres. When versatile musician and entrepreneur Knauff heard a fiddler playing the *Virginia Reels* melodies for dancing at social events held at the farm owned by his wife's educated and socially prominent parents, he sensed a similar chance to enhance his income.

Thus, Knauff wanted this music from oral tradition to become marketable, to be "popular" music, too, as a few items in Volume 1 already were. These established hits were "Speed the Plough" and "Killie Krankie" (under its usual name, "Money Musk"), plus the first tune in Volume 2, "Old Virginia" (arguably a version of the widely distributed "Flowers of Edinburgh"). The first pamphlet also includes fiddle tunes that were new—at least in print—but which would last: "Forked Deer," "Natchez on the Hill" (now "Natchez under the Hill"—I suspect that Knauff heard today's title but revised it, since he likely didn't know that the colorful entertainment district of Natchez was indeed "under the hill" next to the Mississippi River), and the title "Mississippi Sawyer" (though today's tune by that name isn't in this pamphlet, instead appearing in the fourth volume under the title "Love from the Heart"). Other tunes in this volume were and remain less common, and the last tune, "Love in the Village," looks to be a novelty piece drawn from some version of the ballad opera bearing that name. Volume 2 would emphasize local titles, pamphlet 3 miscellaneous tunes in oral tradition, and the possibly much later volume 4 melodies with blackface minstrel associations.

How do Knauff's arrangements reflect their intended use by young pianists? And how do we return his interpretations of these tunes to fiddle idiom? Knauff wrote harmonically elementary left-hand parts to accompany the melodies he transcribed by ear. If a modern fiddler opts for piano accompaniment, Knauff's parts can suggest chord choices and perhaps even textures. A reader of this book who wishes to see those accompaniments can consult volumes of the *Virginia Reels* available online or look at the photographed complete Willig edition that forms the appendix of my book on the *Virginia Reels* (2017). But in the current book, leaving out the accompaniments makes room for performer-friendly good-sized notation of the melodies. Similarly, Knauff's additions to the melody in the student pianist's right-hand part—such as parallel thirds and occasional harmonies in cadential chords—would not have been played by fiddlers back then, so I have omitted these pitches. I retain Knauff's slurs and other articulations; modern fiddlers must decide whether or not to heed those; that is, whether they feel that those performance indications are meant only for pianists or that they reflect something about how Knauff's source fiddler(s) played a given tune.

This is a good point to revisit the fact that the *Virginia Reels* were issued first by the Baltimore published George Willig Jr., then in pirated editions by F. D.

Benteen, also of Baltimore. The first three numbers of the Willig edition were most likely from 1839, and these three numbers came out in the early 1840s in the parallel but not identical Benteen versions. Willig's number 4 came out sometime between 1839 and 1851—likely nearer to but not within 1851, by which time Knauff was working mostly with Benteen; the Benteen version came out that year. Why did Knauff shift from Willig to the erstwhile publication poacher Benteen? I don't have a good answer for that, but can note that Willig's father, George Willig Sr., music publisher in Philadelphia, died in 1851. Perhaps Willig Jr. chose at that time to reconfigure his business in such a way that Knauff was a less suitable source of music for Willig to print.

The Benteen fourth number of the *Virginia Reels*, the only one in the original Benteen series to bear Knauff's name, is nearly identical to the Willig edition. The few tiny changes do not affect sound (a few pieces divide differently in terms of line shifts, and the vocal "whoop" in "Indian Whoop" acquires a clef). But the earlier first and third numbers printed by Benteen are different from the parallel numbers in the Willig edition, probably reflecting the repertoire and playing style of a different consulted fiddler than the one from whom Knauff borrowed. First, while a few of Knauff's tunes were removed by Benteen, most of the repertoire changes are additions, of two tunes to Pamphlet #1 and of more to Knauff's skimpy Pamphlet #3. In just one case, Benteen's fiddler played a different version of a tune, that being "Speed the Plough"; I give both versions in the anthology, aligned for easy comparison. The Benteen fiddler's version is closer to other published versions of the time and to today's versions.

The Benteen edition's new tunes and versions of the majority of tunes shared with the Willig edition are less adjusted for piano performance. The melodies are single line (that is, lacking most of the treble clef harmony notes found in the Willig forms as shaped by pianist Knauff), and articulations are simplified, consisting almost entirely of slurs indicating piano phrasing rather than anything a fiddler might do. I provide historical context for one of these in Figure 29. The newly added "Mrs. McLeod's Reel," like *Virginia Reels* tunes "Money Musk" (called "Killie Krankie" in the *Virginia Reels*, probably in error), "Flowers of Edinburgh" ("Old Virginia" in the *Virginia Reels*), and "Marquis of Huntley's Farewell" ("George Booker" in the *Virginia Reels*), had been a hit already in late eighteenth-century Scotland. I align the original printed Scottish version with an example from an early American music commonplace book, both in A Major, then add two American versions in G Major, which is the main key for the tune today. That the Benteen *Virginia Reels* version is in A and incorporates some rhythmic complexity makes it more like the Scottish model, that is, older in style.

Knauff's tune titles, like current American fiddle tune titles, illustrate multiple historical layers. Subjects among newer titles in the *Virginia Reels* include "Richmond Blues" (then a militia unit with newly adopted blue uniforms), "Peter Francisco" (the Revolutionary War enlisted-man hero, deceased in 1831), "Lady of the Lake" (a legendary figure, but here doubtless referring to Walter Scott's novel of 1810), and "22nd of February" (Washington's birthday, post–Revolutionary

Figure 29. Versions of "Mrs. McLeod's Reel," two in the original key of A (a Scottish print, and a less ornamented American manuscript version) and two in today's more common key of G (from later in the same American manuscript, then the ubiquitous printed version from Howe).

War as a national celebration). The *Reels* titles (and today's titles) also include ones that reach back into the late eighteenth century, such as "Speed the Plough." Perhaps the most striking characteristic of the titles assembled as the *Virginia Reels*—apart from their degree of departure from the usual titles of older tunes, helping demonstrate that Knauff was working from someone's oral tradition—is that they already evoked nostalgia. The word "old" in "Old Virginia" resonates on several levels. Fiddling had become less fashionable than flute playing decades earlier, and the genre of the reel, though far from ancient, paled in novelty when compared to younger dance types, notably the waltz and the polka. But continuity of both style and of local associations had their own powerful appeal. Most importantly, Virginia's past was already willfully remembered as idyllic. There was some justification for this: by the 1830s, much of the state's soil had been leached bare of nutrients, and out-migration to the west had become a serious economic problem. "Old" Virginia was celebrated in numerous poems, some of which would be set to music. This part of the South was already the "Old South."

With the appearance of the last pamphlet of the *Virginia Reels* in the early 1850s, the topic of blackface minstrelsy raises its complicated head. During the possible extended pause between Willig's publication of the first three pamphlets of the *Virginia Reels* and of the last pamphlet, minstrelsy transformed the American music environment, shifting from being primarily street fare—mostly performed by and for members of the working classes—to dominating popular entertainment. "Boatman Dance" ("Ohio River" in the *Virginia Reels*) may have been around for some time before Knauff printed it; minstrelsy's move into a broader range of acceptability must have changed how he viewed such tunes. Music that he might not have initially considered marketable to his affluent neighbors and to the parents of his female students had become fashionable.

When white "minstrels" in blackface copied and parodied African American practice, they drew on several streams of black performance. There were many slave fiddlers; hearing them play was the easiest route for these white entertainers to sample black music making, at the same time that it presented slaves' least specifically African American sounds. There were legions of slave fiddlers as early as the late seventeenth century (Wells 2003, 135). Also, free black fiddlers were common in the North (Wells 1978, 3); Anthony Clapp was among them. After painstaking research, Dena Epstein concluded that there were more black than white fiddlers in the antebellum United States (1983, 99). But distribution was uneven. There were few in Cobb's Vermont, probably more in Mount's Long Island, but certainly many in Knauff's Virginia. Social events centered on dancing in "Old Virginia," and none of the planters present at a dance wanted to be stuck in a corner fiddling: they had black servants to do that.

Dale Cockrell, while immersed in the holdings of the American Antiquarian Society, came upon a newspaper article from the early 1840s that illustrated informal, lower-class use of venerable fiddle tunes along with minstrel items in a mixed-race entertainment. This article, entitled "Grand Trial between Nance Holmes and Suse Bryant, on Long Wharf, Boston," narrated a dance competition between two prostitutes, accompanied by a "half-Negro fiddler" (1997, 8–10). The tune to accompany a hornpipe was "Fisher's Hornpipe," which goes back at least to the 1780s in England (see Kuntz 2012). Tunes played for a dance named a "Virginia Breakdown" included minstrel standards: "The Camptown Hornpipe" (from Foster's "Camptown Races"), "Grapevine," "Lucy Long," and "Jenny Get Your Hoecake Done" (Cockrell 1997, 10). Even earlier than this "contest"—well before the Virginia Minstrels became famous—John Hill Hewitt arranged eight minstrel tunes as *The Crow Quadrilles*, including "Sich a Gittin Up Stairs" and "Long Time Ago," "Sittin' on a Rail," "Clare de Kitchen," "Zip Coon," "Jim Brown," "Gumbo Chaff," and "My Long Tail Blue, Arranged with Figures for the Piano Forte" (1837). In short, even before the Virginia Minstrels asserted that their show would be newly refined and morally unassailable, the minstrel repertoire, while certainly having its palpably crude moments, also established a beachhead in polite society. This tug-of-war between piquant roughness and gentility would be central to shaping minstrelsy and especially how it was advertised: The genre was based on crude caricature and raunchiness in general, but needed to appeal to all classes in terms of both concert attendance and sheet music sales to be maximally profitable. How could performers—often composers and arrangers, too—consistently find that mercantile sweet spot?

Knauff cannot have helped but hear black fiddlers, black banjoists, *and* early minstrel music well before he began arranging and publishing sheet music, before 1839. Prince Edward County's black population certainly included musicians, although evidence remains spotty. I haven't found documentation of a black fiddler—or any fiddler—living there when Knauff did, but Melvin Ely, in his study of an antebellum community of freed blacks in that county, touched on this topic while discussing a Farmville court case from 1858. The disputants "share[d] a culture: much of the testimony resolved around black men playing the fiddle for gatherings of their peers" (2004, 348). Ely further noted that "as in earlier times, whites and free Afro-Virginians in the 1850s could readily find themselves rubbing shoulders at estate sales, public events, or places of business" (364).

Also, Knauff must have heard the banjo as transformed into a blackface minstrel instrument. Joel Sweeney (1810–1860), the first documented white banjo player, grew up on a farm about thirty miles from Knauff's home in Farmville and just as close to Knauff's later base, the Buckingham Female Collegiate Institute. Sweeney, who said he learned the banjo from local blacks, started performing publicly in the 1830s, just when Knauff was getting established in Farmville (Fischer and Kelly 2000, 66). He played at local court sessions (!) and toured Virginia and North Carolina with a circus. In any case, Knauff probably heard blackface tunes by 1839; gaining access to the music would not have been a barrier to publishing #4 of the *Virginia Reels* that early, even if that pamphlet came out physically later. In the most likely scenario, he would have been hesitant to publish the "minstrel" volume of the *Virginia Reels* before minstrelsy made a clear, decisive jump to being part of fashionable national entertainment. On the other hand, he might have hurried to get in on the profits earned by the early arrangers of blackface tunes. In any case, the publication of the Virginia Reels seem not to have inspired imitation. The foothold that blackface minstrelsy gained in popular music, that genre's complex and novel psychological appeal, was shared only by the tunes among the *Reels* that were indeed part of the minstrel repertoire. The remainder were oral-tradition tunes that might have shared in earlier overlaps of tradition with popular music, and might be among the old tunes that helped swell the size of giant anthologies such as those assembled by Elias Howe, but most liked any "new" cachet to keep them commercially viable as a separate group. Being among the *Virginia Reels* were their last strong gasp in the pop sphere.

How did Virginia's black fiddlers sound? They were taught by musical owners, or traveling violin tutors, or each other. Lower-class white Virginians may have been in the mix, too, among them Scots-Irish immigrants, many of whom filtered through Piedmont Virginia on their way to the mountains and better chances of landownership. I suspect that black fiddlers (enslaved or not) would have enjoyed the Scottish component of British fiddling, since Scottish tunes and Scottish ways of performing seem to have been more rhythmically dense and varied. Also, many Scottish fiddle tunes turn up in minstrelsy (see Goertzen 1995).

Published notation is not very helpful in reconstructing the sound of antebellum blackface minstrel fiddling. Perhaps some fiddlers "swung" the rhythms, as explored above in the discussion of "Arkansas Traveller." Additional excitement when such tunes were played by black fiddlers and by their imitators/exaggerators on the minstrel stage must have reposed in elements of fiddle performance that were not easy to transcribe (rubato, glissandos, accents), in the heterophony with the banjo, and through the contributions of the percussion.

Song lyrics and enduring cultural associations mattered, too. Let us return to Knauff's "Ohio River," best known as "Boatman Dance." Quite a few boatmen lived in Farmville and environs during Knauff's lifetime. The 1850 census of this county identified 529 men as farmers, in addition to 43 overseers, 44 carpenters, 24 blacksmiths, and 22 wheelwrights. In less primary occupations, there were 52 merchants, 25 shoemakers, 24 doctors, 20 tailors, 19 factory hands, and 16 each school teachers and clergymen listed. Finally, there were several millers, bricklayers, lawyers, cabinet makers, clerks, and "tobonists" (tobacconists), plus one or two representatives of each of various occupations marking Farmville as an established city. These included the professions of jeweler, confectioner, mattress maker, gunsmith, butcher, druggist, tavern keeper, and boot maker. Workers in transportation-related occupations included—in addition to the wheelwrights listed above—11 coach makers and 3 carriage makers. There were just 5 wagoners listed, compared to 54 boatmen. Prince Edward County boatmen might be slaves, free blacks, or whites (Ely 2004, 68 and 155). Knauff must have known some of these boatmen; their crowded quarters in Farmville were just a few blocks from his home. Why "Ohio River" rather than "Boatman Dance?" The Ohio is the river named in the lyrics of the song, and the word "Ohio" scans and rhymes, but we should also keep in mind that this major river was a boundary between slave and free states, and thus likely of special importance to Knauff's source fiddler(s), if they were black.

The lively interracial assemblage of boatmen bore reputations for being rowdy, not any more respectful of private property than they needed to be, and liable to dance! Christopher Smith, in his study of William Sidney Mount and early minstrelsy, credited waterways with great importance in spreading minstrelsy. He noted that "mobile boundaries and arteries—rivers and canals, harbors and bays, wharves, highways and early railroads—were both the earliest incubators and the ongoing conduits by which minstrelsy's urban synthesis could reach out again across the North American continent, more extensively, comprehensively, and far earlier than has been presumed" (2013, 33). It comes as no surprise that waterway-related titles abound within the *Virginia Reels*. And the importance of waterways for the spread of traditional music certainly did not start or end with minstrelsy; fiddling was at the center of this picture for centuries. Mark Twain felt that music was so essential to river life that he had Huckleberry Finn witness fiddling boatmen: "They stumped back and had a drink around and went to talking and singing again. Next they got out an old fiddle, and one played, and another patted juba, and the rest turned themselves loose on a regular old-fashioned keelboat breakdown" (1917, 23). And Twain peppered his description of *Life on the Mississippi* with evidence for vernacular music traveling there. One anecdote from his days as a steamboat pilot reads:

> Once at night, in one of those forest-bordered crevices (behind an island) which steamboatmen intensely describe with the phrase "as dark as the inside of a cow," we should have eaten up a Posey County family, fruit, furniture, and all, but that they happened to be fiddling down below and just caught the sound of the music in time to sheer off, doing no serious damage, unfortunately, but coming so near it that we had high hopes for a moment. These people brought up the lantern, then, of course; and as we backed and filled to get away, the precious family stood in the light of it—both sexes and various ages—and cursed us till everything turned blue. (1917, 88)

Many factors come together in "The Boatman's Dance." It came out under that title in 1843; Virginia minstrel Daniel Decatur Emmett claimed authorship. But he also said he wrote "Dixie," which Howard and Judith Rose Sacks have demonstrated probably came out of Emmett's visits with the Snowdens, a black family living in Emmett's hometown of Mount Vernon, Ohio (1993). The Snowden Papers contain no mention of "Boatman's Dance" (H. Sacks 2015). However, Robert Winans believes that "Boatman's Dance" is also among Emmett's compositions that "were at least partially 'borrowed' for the [Virginia Minstrels'] shows from preexisting oral tradition" (1984; 88), and I agree. Did Knauff's fiddler(s) get the tune from pop music, that is, from minstrelsy, or instead from some part of the oral tradition that may have separately supplied serial-adapter Emmett? Whatever the case, Knauff's employing the unusual title "Ohio River" suggests some oral/aural connection, as do so many of his titles.

Should we be surprised to see the titles "Indian Whoop" and "Flying Indian" in a volume of the *Virginia Reels* that focuses on blackface minstrel tunes? Indians were rare in Knauff's part of Virginia by this time, but retained at least a double presence in local consciousness. The well-established noble (and doomed) Indian of fiction and the visual arts was celebrated in many songs. That figure coexisted in American psychology with the threatening (and less spiritually elevated) living Indians with whom there was sporadic friction on the not-so-distant frontier. And a third thread emerged during Knauff's lifetime, one that reoriented the infinitely wise pagan of legend toward rollicking entertainment—the patent medicine and thus the medicine show connection with minstrelsy. In short, there was not just one informed and coherent image of the Indian in the air, but rather bizarrely coexisting and interlaced models: the eternal Indian, the inconvenient Indian (both frontier warlike savages and peaceful Indians who owned land whites wanted), and the jester embodied in the medicine show Indian, that is, the shaman demoted to clown.

The raucous side of minstrelsy exemplified by "Indian Whoop" also coexisted with attempts to tap the genteel market for minstrel airs in pamphlet #4 of the *Virginia Reels*—that is, having "Sich a Gittin Up Stairs" and "Midnight Serenade" ("Buffalo Gals") presented in "varied" versions. These do not exemplify how *fiddlers* typically ornamented tunes during repetitions, but rather were Knauff's attempts to plug into piano variation technique. The point of theme and variation sets in the pop sphere was not nuanced musical eloquence, but rather progressive difficulty, the conquering of which made the listener's amazement and thus pleasure grow. Typical examples might or might not start with a brief, flowery introduction akin to those often introducing songs. Then, the real beginning was a well-known tune played in a simple form. Progressively more difficult elaborations of that theme followed, generally contrasting in techniques and therefore effects. Such variation sets presented problems of technical facility rather than of interpretation to the performer and carried the listener on a straightforward journey from the familiar to a common result, astonishment at the performer's skill.

Knauff's essays in this form were easy in comparison with most of the independent theme and variation sets published at about this time, but nevertheless have a bit in common with those flashy monstrosities. "Sich a Gittin Up Stairs" is the closer of these two arrangements to the common practice. The sections are unsurprising: introduction, thinly textured theme, and just a few easily negotiated variations. What is most striking is that the last two variations have the pianist's right hand hitting chords off the beat. This type of variation was a common option in the big variation sets of the day. Those variations were harmonically based and distant enough from the main theme to require some temporal separation from the initial presentation of that theme. But they were not so hard that they needed to appear near the end of the form; they were most at home near the middle of the sequence of variations. Knauff used this option twice, both times *ending* with it. His concentrating on this figure is clever: this variation type belongs to conventional variation practice, but is also syncopated, suiting the fact that the "varied" tune belongs to minstrelsy.

Now, returning to "Indian Whoop," the most notable feature of which is the "whoop!" If we see minstrelsy as ranging from rough-hewn to refined approaches that wouldn't alienate crinoline-clad debutantes and other upper-crust customers, it is the whoop that places this tune near the rustic end of the continuum, despite Knauff's choosing to insert it in the female-student-oriented *Virginia Reels*. In addition, "Indian Whoop" belongs to a select group of tunes that have long served as bridges between fiddlers and a broad popular audience: tunes based on gimmicks, on featuring sounds plucked from the natural. This returns us to the world of novelty tunes named "The Cuckoo" and Mount's pictorial railroad fiddle tune. Knauff's "Indian Whoop" is the first use of that title that I've found. William Sidney Mount recorded exactly the same tune by the same title a few years later, entering it just below the minstrel tune "Old Molly Hare." He annotated his version of "Indian Whoop," noting that he had gotten it "from the brothers Pfeiffers." And he wrote sideways to the left of the tune: "As sung & played by some of the musical Southern Negroes." This reinforces my impression that Knauff either notated "Indian Whoop" firsthand from a local black fiddler or acquired the tune secondhand from Joel Sweeney or another local blackface minstrel.

Knauff's "Indian Whoop" is not intriguing as a melody. Its hook is its gimmick. In the end, that is the lesson of pamphlet #4 of Knauff's *Virginia Reels*. These tunes show fiddling reaching out into various musical and cultural spheres, and being rewarded by support from outside of the central constituency of fiddling. "Ohio River" ("Boatman") celebrates physical travel on real waterways, the spread of fiddling through minstrelsy, and the complex overlapping of working-class and upper-class sensibilities and those classes' entertainments. "Indian Whoop" travels in subject matter from labored ideology—the noble, doomed Indian—to slapstick, and thus to audiences of minstrelsy. "Sich a Getting Up Stairs," in Knauff's arrangement targeting the complementary, genteel fraction of the nineteenth-century popular music audience, helped define multiple simultaneous uses for pop music items in general, and for fiddling in particular.

Killie Krankie

VR I, #1

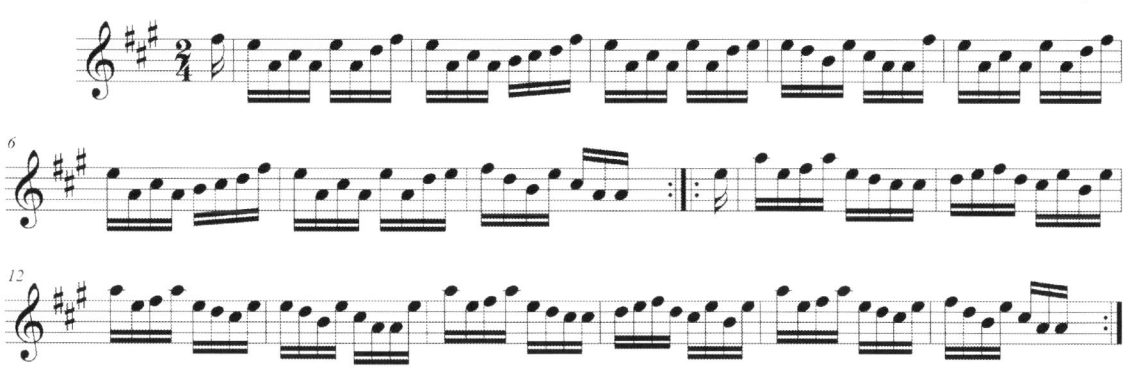

Republican Spirit

VR I, #2

Natchez on the Hill

VR I, 3

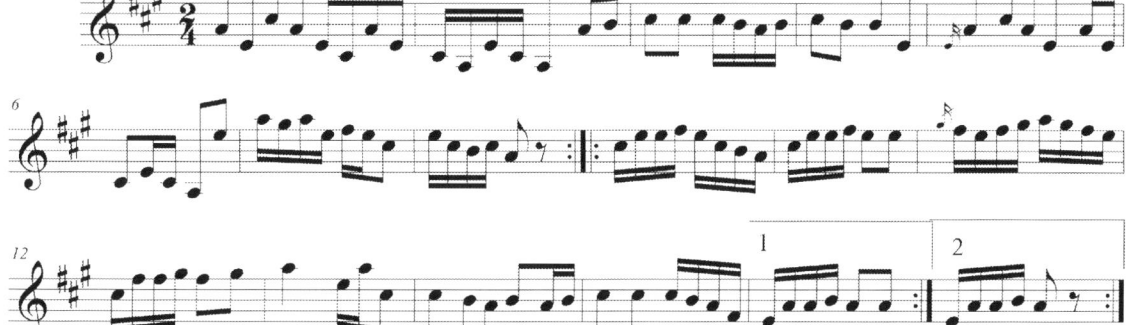

Figure 30. *Virginia Reels* I, #1–#3.

Figure 30. *Virginia Reels I*, #3.1–#5.

Slighted Jenny
VR I, #6

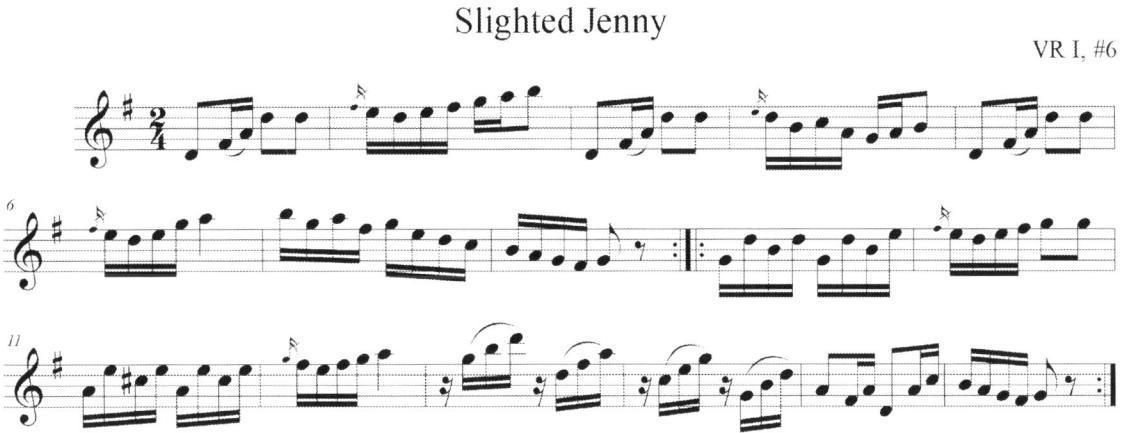

Mississippi Sawyer
VR I, #7

Forked Deer
VR I, #8

Figure 30. *Virginia Reels I,* #6–#8.

Whiskey Barrel

VR I, #9

Love in the Village

VR I, #10

Figure 30. *Virginia Reels I,* #9–#10.

The Ridge

VR I, #10.1 (added by Benteen)

Old Virginia

VR II, #1

Richmond Hill

VR II, #2

Figure 30. *Virginia Reels I*, #10.1–II, #2.

Figure 30. *Virginia Reels II*, #3–#4.

The Hero

VR II, #5

Peter Francisco

VR II, #6

Twenty Second of February

VR II, #7

Figure 30. *Virginia Reels II*, #5–#7.

Island
VR II, #8

The Richmond Blues
VR II, #9

Figure 30. *Virginia Reels II*, #8–#9.

George Booker

VR III, #1

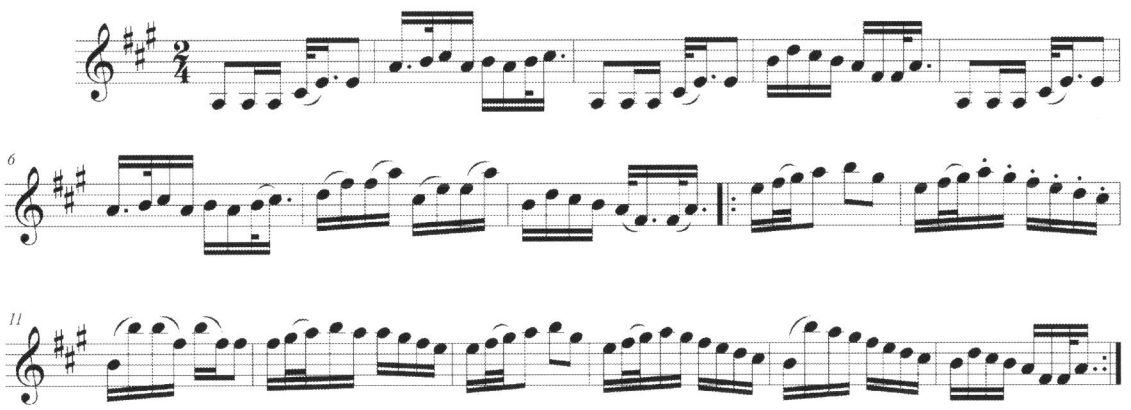

Oh Where Did You Come From

VR III, #2

Colonel Crocket

VR III, #3

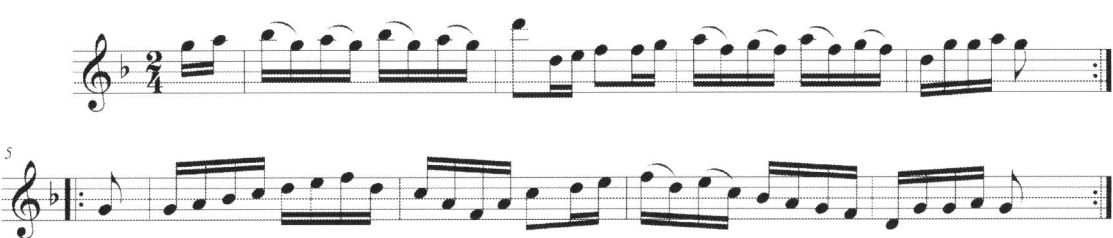

Figure 30. *Virginia Reels III*, #1–#3.

Colonel Crockett

VR III, #3.1 (from Benteen; replaces #3 of Willig edition)

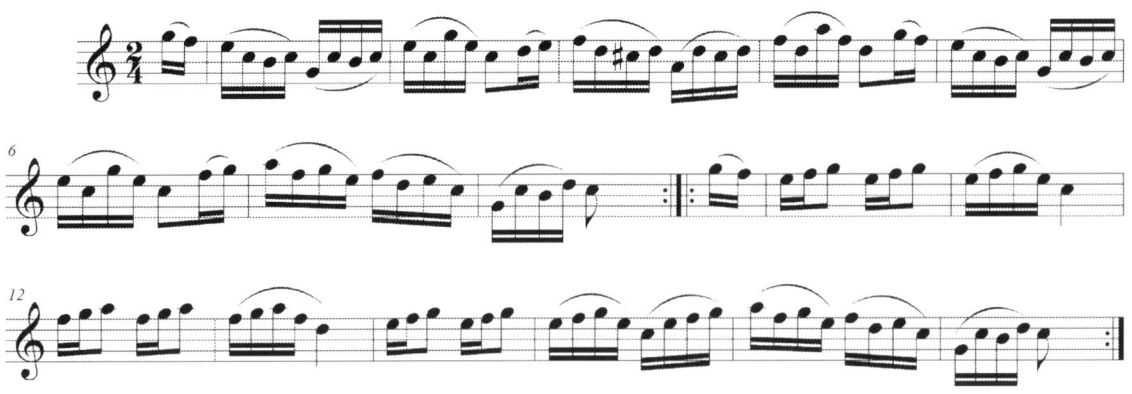

Rose on the Mountain

VR III, #4

Billy in the Low Grounds

VR III, #5

Figure 30. *Virginia Reels III*, #3.1–#5.

Billy in the Woods

VR III, #5.1 (from Benteen; replaces #5 of Willig edition)

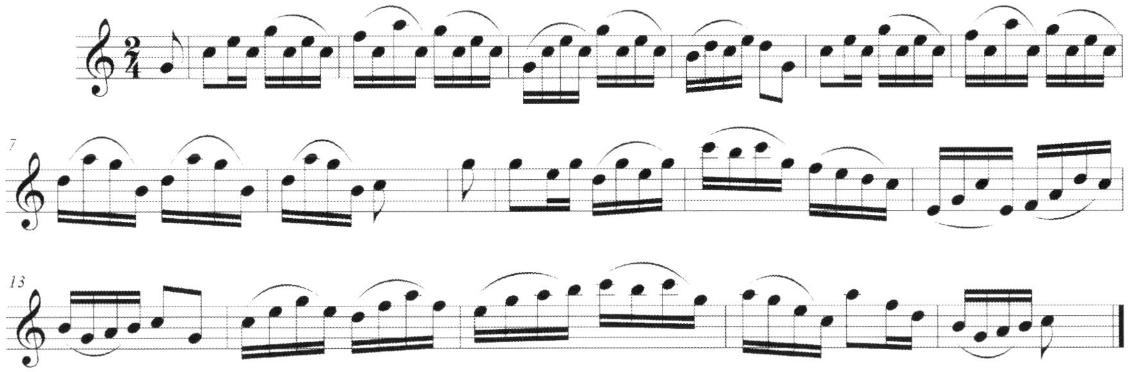

Lockwell

VR III, #6

Juniper Hall

VR III, #6.1 (from Benteen; replaces #6 of Willig edition)

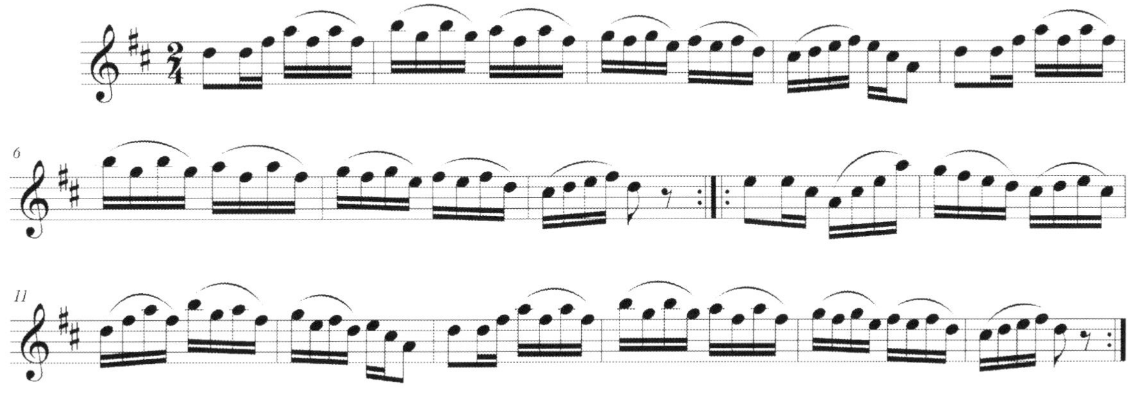

Figure 30. *Virginia Reels III*, #5.1–#6.1.

Figure 30. *Virginia Reels III*, #7–#8.1.

Old Dominion Reel

VR III, #8.2, added by Benteen)

The Fox Hunt

VR III, #8.3 (added by Benteen)

James River Reel

VR III, #8.4 (added by Benteen)

Figure 30. *Virginia Reels III,* #8.2–#8.4.

Figure 30. *Virginia Reels IV,* #1–#2.

Indian Whoop

VR IV, #3

Love from the Heart

VR IV, #4

Ohio River

VR IV, #5

Figure 30. *Virginia Reels IV,* #3–#5.

The Flying Indian

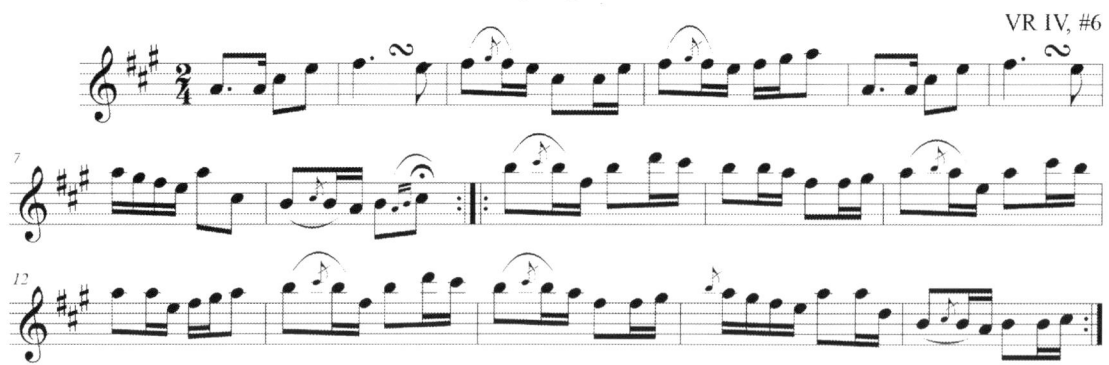

Nancy Anderson

Midnight Serenade, Varied

Figure 30. *Virginia Reels IV*, #6–#8.

GIDEON LINCECUM AND A TEXAS PICNIC IN 1835: THE INTRIGUING EVIDENCE OF SHORT TUNE LISTS

We know so very little about the music making of antebellum fiddlers of the West or the Deep South, whether or not they were music literate. But now and then a descriptive anecdote is helpful, and may even contain a tune list. For instance, Cauthen, in her history of fiddling in Alabama, noted that Alfred Benners (in his *Slavery and Its Results*) "described life at Arcola, a plantation on the Warrior River, six miles above Demopolis [thus about sixty-five miles south of Tuscaloosa]: 'Hospitality ruled supreme at the Big House, and kin, friends and strangers found constant welcome and lavish entertainment. At night Jim Pritchett and his fiddle, Mingo with his triangle, and Mose with his banjo came from the quarters and made music for the happy belles and beaux. They danced cotillions and the Lancers [a subset of the quadrille, related to cotillions], winding up with the Virginia Reel. Sundry drams livened old Jim's fiddle, as the "Forked Deer," "Arkansas Traveller" and other old tunes of a like lilt and swing, quickened their flying feet. Jim was a noted mimic, as well as fiddler, and usually wound up with an improvisation of his own, which he called "The Dying Coon," in which his voice added to the witchery of his bow the shouts of the hunters, the baying of the dogs and the snarls and dying wail of the fighting coon'" (2001, 10–11). Regarding these citations of titles, we can note that "Forked Deer" was first printed in Knauff's *Virginia Reels* (see Figure 30, I, #8), and that "Arkansas Traveller" was ubiquitous back then (see Figure 22). "The Dying Coon" can be placed in context by looking at narrative descriptive compositions like Kotzwara's *The Battle of Prague* and other "battle" suites that flourished at the intersection of art music and pop music, more rustic, traditional story tunes like "Fox Chase," and by studying Howe's imitations of animal sounds (see Figure 24). "The Dying Coon" seems closest to "Fox Chase," but featuring an especially generous complement of animal sounds.

On rare occasions, anecdotes yield even more information. I learned about a fiddler and Texas pioneer named Gideon Lincecum (1793–1874) because one of my English professors at Austin College had been Jerry Lincecum, a descendant of Gideon. Jerry discovered that this ancestor, a conveniently loquacious polymath, left behind letters and serial journal publications. This prose output lets us witness his activity as a dedicated practitioner of botanic medicine, as an informal scholar of Choctaw language and lore, and, above all, as a naturalist with a special interest in ants (he corresponded with Darwin about this topic!). He also fiddled regularly throughout his long life, and left behind a few passing references and a pair of page-long narratives about this, writings that cite several tune titles and several performance venues.

Gideon Lincecum's great-grandfather was a Huguenot who immigrated to the United States when his son was an infant. The son (named Gideon) grew up in Maryland and fell in love with a Scottish immigrant girl, Miriam Bowie. Neither family approved, so the couple eloped. They carved out a farm in the western mountains of North Carolina. This Gideon and several sons fell in the

Revolutionary War. His youngest son, Hezekiah, survived, and was father to our Gideon. Hezekiah's family moved west every year or two between frontier locations in South Carolina, Georgia, and Tennessee while Gideon was young. Hezekiah, said to have had a fine singing voice, bequeathed his affection for music and his enduring restlessness to this son.

While living near the Mississippi Choctaw as a young adult, Gideon learned homeopathic remedies from the Indians, and in turn arranged a social affair for his new friends at which he fiddled. He averred that it must have been quite a treat for his audience (Lincecum and Phillips 1994, 89–90). His richest anecdote concerning music originally appeared in "Personal Reminiscences of an Octogenarian," which came out serially in *The American Sportsman*. This selection, from November 21, 1874, describes a serendipitous picnic in 1835 near Eagle Lake, about thirty miles west of Houston. Lincecum, then living in Monroe County, Missouri, had traveled with friends to see if Texas would be a suitable place for a restless fraction of his community to relocate. He stayed on after the party disbanded, and explored on his own, basing a series of small trips at Burnham's Ferry on Texas's Colorado River. He stated that this was "the most desirable part of Texas," with ample timber and good grass for stock, yet plenty of wildlife, though he harbored reservations concerning "unsettled" government and "predaceous" Indians (Burkhalter 1965, 316). Indeed, the county where the picnic took place had been devastated by floods and cholera in 1833, and would be overrun during the Texas Revolution soon after Gideon left (Shatto 1986, 45–46). He would wait until 1848 to move his family to Texas, settling just a few dozen miles north of the picnic site by Eagle Lake.

On this day in 1835, Lincecum was traveling alone. With the aid of two Indians serendipitously (and warily) encountered, he gathered venison and honey. A Mr. Heard, with whose family Gideon had recently stayed for a few days, happened along with two neighbor families. His host must have been William Jones Eliot Heard, who had recently founded the nearby settlement of Egypt, who would fight in the upcoming war establishing an independent Texas, and who became a prominent figure in the young temporary country (Shatto 1986, 54, 63–65). This group had a picnic planned. Gideon joined forces with them, and invited the families to camp overnight with him:

> The carriages were immediately unloaded, and the negroes started back for a supply of blankets, more bread, coffee and so on. One of the younger men told the negro to bring his violin,—which was as much as to say invite the neighborhood to come.... Seeing the violin case thrown out amongst their pots and blankets, and not having had one in my hands for months, I was hungry for music. I opened the case and found a splendid violin, in excellent condition. I took it out, and going near to two or three ladies, said, "some of you were telling a new comer what the wild man could do. With this good violin, I will furnish you with a little story that will bear telling as long as you live." I performed "Washington's Grand March" so loud that I could distinctly

hear the tune repeated as it returned from the echo on the opposite lake shore. I could feel that my very soul mingled with the sound of the instrument, and, at the time I was about to become so entranced as to be unfit for such jovial company; the handsome lady ran up and, slapping me on the shoulder, exclaimed, "Good heavens, Doctor! Where are you going?" I was startled, and training up [tuning? positioning?] the violin, performed Gen. Harrison's march, then Hail Columbia and then the No. 1 cotillion in the beggar set. They all went to dancing. I quit [playing].

Everything being in readiness Mrs. Heard beat a tumbler with the handle of a knife, and the *fiesta* commenced. They ate, and bragged, and laughed, until the darkness came, and they had waked all the echoes of the old lake. Then they called up the Negro fiddler and tried to dance awhile, but the grass was too much for them; when one of the ladies proposed that all should be seated and get the Doctor to treat them to a few pieces of his good music.

While they were fixing the seats, Oka-noo-ah was expressing to me the delight he had experienced, and how glad he was that he had accidentally found me in his journey. These people had treated him so politely, he should never forget it. When the company were all seated, I inquired, "What style of music would you prefer; the lively, or the grave?" "Oh, give us your own musical taste; we don't want to hear anything we are accustomed to."

I was in high tune myself; and on that clear-sounding instrument, before that gleeful company, I poured forth the wild, ringing, unwritten harmony, that is only heard and learned by the student of nature from her sweetest songsters, in the deep unhacked forest of Florida, and the jungle enveloped coast lands of Mexico. I continued before that silent audience for at least an hour. "Is it enough," I said? "Oh no; go on, go on," they all cried. I played on, till my musical appetite was satiated. When the music ceased preparations for sleep were made, and all lay down for the night . . . (1874–75, 10–12).

The last excerpt, centering on Gideon's regular performance of one tune, "Killie Krankie," comes down to us through the interpretation of Gideon's first biographer, Lois Burkhalter. She interwove description of this with an account of Gideon's last days.

When Gideon was seventeen years old and clerking in an Indian trading post in Eatonton, Georgia, his employer, Ichabod Thompson, brought him from Savannah a black English violin as a Christmas present. It was the treasure of his life. Not being acquisitive of worldly goods, he made it the only possession he cherished throughout his life.

It was at dawn on Christmas of 1810 when young Gideon answered a knock at his door and found the kindly Ichabod Thompson standing outside with the violin in his hands. Gideon, barefooted and in his nightgown, stepped outside the door to accept the wonderful instrument, the dearest Christmas present of his life. He placed the violin against his shoulder and, disregarding the cold wind, played a Mississippi popular tune, "Killiecrankie" [Burkhalter adds in a footnote that Gideon spelled this tune title "Gillie Crackie"].

To commemorate this momentous occasion, every Christmas dawn thereafter, for sixty-three years, Gideon arose from bed wherever the day found him, and, as he was, in nightclothes and barefooted, played his Christmas tune three times . . .

[He took as good care of the violin as circumstances allowed, taking pains to restring it whenever possible.]

In his younger days, when his house was full of visiting relatives and friends and all his musical children lived under his roof, the violin was a source of conviviality. In his old age it was a solace, a link with the happy days of his youth . . . The violin—Gideon seldom belittled it by referring to it as a fiddle—soothed the aches and pains of his tired old body after a day's hard work in his Tuxpan fields: "I retire to my room, get out my old violin and the stimulus of half a dozen merry tunes sets up a healthy action in all the electric currents belonging to my old machine and all pains and aches are gone." . . . When he returned to Texas the old black violin was one of his few possessions which Gideon took with him. . . .

[Finally, as he lay on his deathbed in November 1874, suffering from paralysis] he remembered all of the sixty-three Christmases he had played his happy Christmas tune on that old black violin. . . . Gideon chuckled as he recalled that he had camped near Willbourn's place on Chocolate Bayou. Mr. Willbourn, a very religious man, came to camp later that day to inquire about the weird daybreak music. Gideon explained he belonged to a new religious sect, and that playing the tune three times at daybreak was part of the devotional. "He thought it very strange and left."

Gideon remembered his sixty-third playing of the Christmas tune, in Long Point in 1873, which was to be his last . . . In the doorway, the night-shirted old man, barefooted, stood on his weary old legs and played his violin:

O Killiecrankie is my song;
I sing and play it all day long,
From the heel unto the toe
Hurrah for Killiecrankie O!
And ye had been where I hae been
Ye wad na be so cantie O!
And ye hae seen what I hae seen
On braes of Killiekrankie O! (Burkhalter 1965, 290–99; reproduced, partly in
    paraphrase, in Lincecum and Phillips 1994, xxxi–xxxii)

When Gideon was given his "English fiddle," in 1810, he was seventeen, about as old as Arthur McArthur and Philander Seward had been when they began to fiddle just a few years earlier, but living in a less settled area. He already knew enough about fiddling to be able to immediately whip off a tune. At the time of marriage, many young gentlemen of that day retired their flutes, fifes, and fiddles, and young ladies their pianos, guitars, and harps. Philander Seward may have left music at this point, but Arthur McArthur still performed as an adult, as did Lincecum, Cobb, and Mount. In general, musical training was intended to foster appreciation of the finer things, and that is what cultured adults were supposed to do: appreciate. The reason many slaves were trained to fiddle was to allow upper-class fiddlers to be gentlemen first and fiddlers a distant second. At a dance, they wished to dance and to socialize, not sweat in the corner for others' benefit. At the picnic in question, Gideon Lincecum played to entertain, but did so in a brief informal concert. When it was time to dance, the Heard family's slave fiddlers took over.

Was this interaction with black fiddlers an isolated occasion in Gideon's life? His parents owned several slaves. He would own slaves, too, and would defend the institution of slavery, though now and again spoke of a slave as a friend. We don't know if any of his own slaves fiddled, but he must have regularly encountered black fiddlers. And he clearly was open to learning music from outside of his own culture. During his lengthy sojourns among the Choctaw, he absorbed songs and dances some of which he later taught to Alabama-Coushatta Indians (Burkhalter 1965, 47). His remarkable openness to influence and his opportunities to hear black fiddling add up to the likelihood of mutual influence. Other researchers have remarked on the ubiquity of black fiddlers in Texas later in that century and into the next (Sanders 1941, 83; Angle 1975, 62). Sanders also mentioned a white fiddler (born in 1846) who had "learned to fiddle . . . from a Negro slave belonging to [his] grandfather" (1941, 86). Gideon's citing of black fiddlers at his 1835 picnic extends such evidence back in time, and cannot have described a unique occasion.

Lincecum's fiddle was from England. Most instruments sold in the United States during the eighteenth and early nineteenth centuries came from—or through—there, simply because England was then the United States' main mercantile connection (though German-born musical merchants, including Knauff, looked home for their merchandise). Second, fiddling and religion have frequently been at odds—hence Gideon's rascally pleasure on informing the pious Mr. Willbourn, who had overheard Gideon's playing one Christmas morning, that this was part of his own sect's ritual observance of the day. Third, when Gideon performed "Washington's Grand March" so loudly that he could hear it echo from the opposite lake shore, he was following the same desideratum as Pushee, Mount, and other fiddlers who played alone for dances, and needed to be heard over "squeaking floors, shuffling feet, crying babies, and the sonorous voice of the caller" (Sanders 1941, 82). That Gideon felt his "soul mingled with the sound of the instrument" plugs into general romantic thought, as does his description: "I poured forth the wild, ringing, unwritten harmony that is only heard and learned by the student of nature from her sweetest songsters in the deep unhacked forest of Florida and the jungle-enveloped coast lands of Mexico."

Now to Gideon's tunes: We get a hint of his repertoire from his writings: "Killie Krankie" plus, from the picnic, "Hail Columbia," "Washington's Grand

Figure 31. Marches that Gideon Lincecum may have played at a picnic in rural Texas in 1835.

March," "General Harrison's March," and the "No. 1 Cotillion in the Beggar Set." The "cotillion" is dance fare by definition, and "Killie Krankie" was both a song and a solo tune appropriate for dancing. Lincecum's five tune titles run a gamut from commonplace through elusive. "Hail Columbia," which began life as a bold melody entitled "President's March," was anthologized under one or the other name by McArthur, Seward, Cobb, and hundreds of other fiddlers, and is the one of the tunes that Gideon Lincecum mentioned that most Americans alive today have heard (the reader may return to Philander Seward's version of "President's March" given as Figure 12, #5).

All three marches Lincecum cited appear over and over in Elias Howe's collections of instrumental music. Gideon claimed that no member of his family ever had "the advantage of a lesson in music" (Burkhalter 1965, 159), but this should not be taken to indicate that he didn't read music. It was his habit to be extravagantly self-taught in each area to which he turned his energy. He probably could puzzle out melodies from print, and likely had seen some of the Howe publications. I take this illustration of "Washington's Grand March" from Howe's *Musician's Companion* (1844), and note that Charles Cobb must have copied Howe's version—his matches it precisely.

Gideon mentioned a "General Harrison's March." I haven't found any tunes bearing exactly that title. If he really remembered the precise names of the tunes he played at the 1835 picnic, his "General Harrison's March" may have been first published as "The Battle of the Wabash" (1814), which honored Harrison's victory over the Indians at Tippecanoe (Spaeth 1948, 41). If, on the other hand, Gideon was recalling representative tunes from that period of his life rather than exactly which ones he played on that occasion, this reference may be to a casual retitling of a not-too-common tune called "Harrison's Grand March," which was written between 1825 and 1835, and which can be traced in print back to 1843 (Howe 1843, I, 106). It is generic, yet has survived in oral tradition (see Bayard 1982, 217).

But if Lincecum may have omitted the "grand" in "Harrison's Grand March," might it be just as plausible that he inserted the "grand" in "Washington's Grand March?" Might he have played "Washington's March" rather than "Washington's Grand March" at that Texas picnic? "Washington's Grand March" was first published under the title "New President's March" in 1796. It was soon reprinted as "President's New March," "General Washington's March," "Washington's New March," "Washington's March," and finally the title it settled into, "Washington's Grand March." It shared each of these titles with other pieces. Two tunes called "Washington's March" were especially popular; this was the second to arrive, and so it became "grand" when titles started to stabilize a few decades into the nineteenth century—the "grand" may mark the march as serving as a ballroom piece. This tune remained popular well into the century, but wasn't particularly distinctive, and fell out of use. But we certainly know the type of tune Lincecum was referring to, and can narrow it down to a few similar tunes. But which tune he played, and whether his style was as straightforward as Howe's versions of tunes, may have been in performance—Cobb seems to have played them that simply—we can't know.

Next we have Lincecum's nostalgic "Christmas tune," a melody well known in Scotland but uncommon in the United States, "Killie Krankie." Its title commemorates a battle in Perthshire in 1689. The King's forces lost, but, on the Cavalier side, two important generals fell, John Claverhouse and Haliburton of Pitcur (specified in many versions of the lyrics). Their deaths constituted a serious setback; the decline of the cause of James VII is said to date from the battle of Killiekrankie.

If Lincecum sang this song as part of his Christmas ritual, then maybe when he also fiddled it he copied the simple style of the sung melody. But perhaps he played it in a more elaborate way. The example at the top of Figure 32 is from the most famous nineteenth-century Scottish fiddler, Niel Gow ([1784], 6). Robert Burns added a text to the tune in 1790 as one of many contributions he made to the *Scots Musical Museum*, a widely distributed national—and nationalist—song book compiled by James Johnson (1790, I, 302). This is in the middle of the figure. Below I present a fancier "Original Sett of Killiecrankie" that Gow and his sons put out later, but here in a version that William Sidney Mount anthologized. Mount's "Original Sett" is elaborately ornamented, but Gow's fancier still. Gow's version has absolutely all of the decorations and articulations that Mount marked, plus a few more, which I place in parentheses in this two-for-one transcription. Lincecum did not shrink from boasting or from putting on airs in general, so perhaps he played a tricky version of the tune, like these. On the other hand, playing this tune was part of his personal Christmas dawn ritual, so he may have opted for something simpler. Or, adding another factor, since he was not accompanying a dance, but rather concertizing for himself, he may have leaned in the direction of complexity.

The last tune Lincecum named in the picnic description was "No. 1 Cotillion in the Beggar Sett." I have never encountered a cotillion bearing that title, despite watching for it for decades. This suggests that if the "Sett" was published, any source in which it appeared is lost. This would not be surprising: the vast majority of surviving American sheets and anthologies from this period are unica. Print runs were so very short, too abbreviated to ensure an exemplar's survival. The Sett title must refer to Christopher Pepusch and John Gay's *Beggar's Opera* of 1728, the first ballad opera, which was performed many times over many decades in the colonies and young United States. It was said to have been the favorite musical play of George Washington (Gay 1966, xi). Perhaps we should be skeptical of such claims, since innumerable legends grow around our presidents, particularly Washington (Smith 2009 throughout, but especially 1–81). However, we do know that *Darby's Return*, the sequel to another extremely popular ballad opera, *Poor Soldier*, was performed at his inaugural celebrations (O'Keefe 1978, vii). Ballad operas, starting with and still including *The Beggar's Opera*, were standard, much-loved theatrical fare in the British colonies and the young United States.

What might a cotillion called "Beggar's Sett" have been like? When considering this question, we must keep the essential characteristics of cotillions in mind. To review: they were dances in sets of five or six tunes that individually look like jigs or reels on the page, each of the associated dances consisting of a few simple

Kilecrankie

Gow [1784], 26

Whare hae ye been sae braw, lad! Whare hae ye been sae brankie O?
Whare hae ye been sae braw, lad? Can ye by Killiecrankie O?

An ye had been whare I hae been, ye wad na been sae cantie O:
An ye had seen what I hae seen, I' th' braes o' Killiecrankie O.

[Johnson gives two more verses, which concern the battle and the narrator's experience there.]

The Original Sett of Killiecrankie

Mount, Sept. 1843*

*The grace notes, trills and slurs in parentheses are not in the Mount version, but are added to the same tune in Gow and Sons [1799], 7, a version in C Major which has detailed dynamic markings.

Figure 32. Gideon Lincecum's "Christmas tune," "Killiecrankie," as published in Scotland as a fiddle tune and as the later song, and, finally, also as played by Mount (combined with yet another Scottish fiddle tune version).

FIDDLERS MOVING SOUTH AND WEST, AWAY FROM NOTATION

Over the hills and far away
Air XVI from The Beggar's Opera

Were I laid on Greenland's coast, and in my arms em- brac'd my lass Warm a- midst e- -ternal frost, too soon the half year's night would pass. Were I sold on Indian soil, soon as the burning day was clos'd, I would mock the sultry toil When on my charmer's beast repos'd. And I would love you all the day, Every night would kiss and play, If with me you'd fondly stray, Over the hills and far away.

Over the Hills and Far Away
(Eames MS, 178)

O'er the Hills and Far Away
1806
(McArthur, 96)

Figure 33. Lincecum said that he played "No. 1 in the Beggar Sett" at the 1835 Texas picnic. The most likely candidate to be that tune is a Scottish oral tradition melody, "Over the Hills and Far Away," shown here as popularized in The Beggar's Opera in 1728 and in three versions penned in American music commonplace books early in the nineteenth century.

Over the Hills and Far Away

(Tallmadge MS, 22)

Jockey was with Jenny fair by this dawning of the day Jockey now is fu' of care, since Jenny staw his heart awa'

[d# is probably not correct.]

Altho she promised to be true, she's proven she's, alak, unkind that gave poor Jockey aften rue that he e'er lov'd a fickle mind and its over the hills and far away, over the hills and far away, over the hills and far away, the wind has blown my plaid awa'.

Now Jockey was a bonny lad
And e'er was born in Scotland fair;
But now poor man he's e'er gone mad,
For Jenny caused him to despair;
Jockey was a Piper's son
And fell in love when he was young
But aw the springs that he could play
Was over the hills and far away &c.

He sung,"When first my Jenny's face
I saw, she seem'd so fu' of grace
Wi' mickle joy my heart was fill'd
That's now alas wi' sorrows kill'd.
O were she but as true as fair
I would put an end to all my care.
Instead of that she is unkind
And wavers like the winter wind &c.

Hard was my fate to all in love
With one was has so faithless proved
Hard was my had to court a maid
Who has my constant heart betrayed
A thousand times to me she swore
She would be true forever more
But to my grief alas I say
She sta' my heart and run away &c.

Figure 34. If there ever was a "Beggar's Cotillion," it might have resembled this.

figures. Most of the tunes in a set of cotillions were in one key, though one tune might be in a closely related key instead. Many of the tunes were in 6/8, while a substantial minority were in simple duple time.

There are many catchy, durable tunes in *The Beggar's Opera*. While I couldn't find a "Beggar Sett," as an exercise in imagining how a "Beggar Sett" might have been put together, I chose melodies from the ballad opera and put them in a logical order, with the best known ones first and last in the cotillion. "Over the Hills and Far Away," the *Beggar's Opera* tune most frequently included in antebellum music commonplace books, leads off, conforming to normal practice for how to start a cotillion named for any kind of opera. Then I chose the second most common *Beggar's Opera* tune to be found in those manuscripts, "Greensleeves," to close out the cotillion, and finally filled the middle with other reasonably familiar tunes in appropriate meters. I revised the melodies to be a little bit more rhythmically dense, as was customary when songs were arranged for instruments. To illustrate how that process worked, I give several versions of "Over the Hills and Far Away" in Figure 33, then complete my hypothetical version of "The Beggar Sett" as Figure 34. If Gideon Lincecum did play "No. 1 in the Beggar Sett" at the 1835 Texas picnic, the tune was indeed probably "Over the Hills and Far Away," in a version much like the one starting this "Sett."

Decades after the picnic at Eagle Lake, in 1868, Gideon visited his youngest daughter's home in Richmond, Texas (just west of Houston). She owned a cabinet organ, and borrowed a violin for her father to play. They performed for an audience that Gideon thought "not as fascinated by their music as it was amazed at a seventy-five-year-old man with a long white beard nimbly playing waltzes, cotillions, reels and marches on a violin" (Burkhalter 1965, 251). Our five tune titles include no waltzes, but do invoke the other three genres that formed the enduring core of Gideon's repertoire. In short, the sample of tune titles deeded us in Gideon's writings comes remarkably close to being representative of this nineteenth-century Texas fiddler's repertoire as he himself defined it.

Gideon was one-fourth Scottish: one of his grandmothers was also one of Jim Bowie's aunts. Enough Scots were important in the early settlement of Texas that many county names are Scottish family names. Scots were known for individualism, and often also for interest in preserving Scottish folkways such as versions of the Highland Games, first held in their modern form in the mid-eighteenth century in order to "preserve the colorful culture and traditions of the Scottish people" (Gordon 1975, 169, 172). Scottish tunes, which tend to have been relatively complex in the context of America's legacy of British fiddle tunes, may have come by their ear-rewarding intricacy because of the remarkably early Scottish practice of *listening* to dance tunes in order to wax nostalgic. It would be natural for early Texas fiddlers to latch onto such tunes during the long hours they played solely for their own enjoyment, and for later Texas fiddlers to revive such tunes as fodder for contests. A long tradition of fiddle and bagpipe contests in Scotland (see, e.g., Collinson 1966, 214) may have followed Scots and Scottish tunes around America, and the variation common in Scottish performance joined naturally with that intrinsic to jazz and blues, and to Texas's special contribution to the black-white musical mix, Western swing.

Gideon played mainstream American tunes on mainstream British models for dancing at the 1835 picnic at Eagle Lake, but it is no accident that he chose an uncommon and uncommonly graceful Scottish tune, "Killie Krankie," for his solitary annual Christmas ritual. I will close this section by referring to the list of Texas fiddle favorites given by Sanders in 1941 (88–89). After a short dozen tunes he classified as "from the British Isles, but more or less naturalized by now," he listed over a hundred as "American favorites, most of which originated in the South." Among the best known of the many "American favorites" that actually came from Scotland are "Turkey in the Straw" (a descendant of the eighteenth-century Scottish "Rose Tree"; Goertzen and Jabbour 1987, 126), "Leather Britches" (previously "Lord Macdonald's Reel"), and "Billy in the Low Ground" (the Texas—and now national—version of which hearkens back to Scotland's "The Braes of Auchtertyre").

Music occupied only a tiny corner of Gideon Lincecum's prose, but clearly was important in his life, and was enhanced in the lives that he and his fiddle touched. The little he tells us about fiddling in early Texas is immediately much of what we know on the subject. His ancestry, temperament, and even his repertoire all fit well into the hazy picture of the roots of Texas contest fiddling, the most widespread and influential of modern American fiddle styles. He was a charismatic and influential traveler, who transferred styles and tunes—many of which antedated him by many years, and would survive him by even longer—to a new frontier in the United States.

THE HAMBLEN COLLECTION:
THE GRANDSON OF AN ANTEBELLUM FIDDLER AS
AMATEUR ETHNOMUSICOLOGIST

One collection of transcribed fiddle tunes on deposit at the Library of Congress has been known to generations of fiddle scholars, but has remained something of a research hot potato due to intractable problems with the musical notation. This mixed typescript and manuscript bears an explanatory title: "A COLLECTION of violin tunes, popular during the early 1800s as played by David Russell Hamblen (1809–1893) and his son Williamson (1848–1920) arranged and copied by A[rmeanous] Porter Hamblen (1875–1958) son of Williamson." Steve Green studied the collection closely and recorded his own playing of the tunes privately; these recordings then inspired more widely available recordings. The most numerous and intriguing of these interpretations are by fiddler Christian Wig (see especially his CD *Chadwell's Station*, available as of this writing through his website: chriswig.com). The collection itself has circulated in photographed form for decades through the informal fiddle scholar network. Garry Harrison placed it on his website, along with speculative recordings (computer generated from his transcriptions of the tunes; http://www.pickaway.press/doi/hamblen_fidtunes.

html), and Christian Wig put a beautifully reproduced and easily downloadable copy on his website (a few penciled-in tune attributions on that copy come from Steve Green, from an early stage in the distribution of a well-traveled photographed copy).

The oldest fiddler whose playing is purportedly represented in the Hamblen collection, David R. Hamblen, lived and made music in Lee County, Virginia, before the Civil War. The main transcriber of the tunes, his grandson, Armeanous Porter Hamblen, learned tunes from David Hamblen both in person and through intermediate sources including his father, David's son Williamson Hamblen. A. P. Hamblen, like legions of fiddlers past and present, was intelligent, was hard-working, and had some acquaintance with musical notation, but lacked formal musical training. His transcriptions of fiddle tunes from his grandfather's and father's playing can be perplexing. Nevertheless, his collection offers the best evidence we have concerning antebellum fiddling that flourished far, far away from the influence of print. I decided to present the complete collection here, along with my recommendations for how to deal with the questions that Mr. Hamblen's tune transcriptions provoke.

Armeanous Porter Hamblen seems to have been a little like Charles Cobb, very intelligent but awkward in conversation—indeed, often avoiding social interaction—and bordering on obsessive in collecting and labeling things. For instance, he gathered up stones from most states and organized them in a cabinet made for that purpose. His application of energy, organizational skills, and sheer doggedness culminated in his creating two books, the smaller of which is this manuscript/typescript collection of fiddle tunes. The other is a massive, detailed published genealogy, *A History of the Hamblen and Allied Families*, first published in 1940, then reprinted in 1985 with an added preface by a distant cousin, John W. Hamblen. This book yields generous information about the grandfather whose fiddling A. P. Hamblen memorialized and about the lives (and, incidentally, the musical activities) of numerous other relatives.

A. P. Hamblen could not have been more ambitious in the scope of this family history. The first forty-eight pages describe the emergence of the name Hamblen (variously spelled) and the large populations in which the name appeared over the centuries, tracing these peoples back to Noah and the Deluge. In the nascent United States, the direct lineage began with an emigrant from England, a George Hamblen, first documented as a resident of Maryland, but living in Charlotte County, Virginia, by 1776, when a son enlisted in the Continental army. He and his family relocated thirty-five miles west, to Pittsylvania County (Hamblen 1984, 50–51). George's son, Job (1762–1833), treated by A. P. Hamblen as the family patriarch, followed an overlapping pattern of moves, traveling with his father's family from the two Virginia locations already mentioned to Lee County in the far west of the state (about eighteen miles from the Cumberland Gap), then moving on to Brown County, Indiana, by 1818. Job was a farmer, expert carpenter, and jack-of-many-trades. His son John Mullins Hamelin (1783–1864) also farmed in Lee County, Virginia, and then in Indiana, as would John's son David R. Hamblen

(1809–1893). John and then David added the skill of shoemaker to those commanded by Job.

Job Hamblen and his family's repeated moves kept them on the edge of the frontier, where they repeatedly cleared land, planted it in Indian corn, raised pigs, hunted deer and other game, and gathered berries and other wild bounty. In almost every way, this was life reduced to essentials. They shaped most of their belongings from raw materials. Clothing came from buckskin and the spinning and weaving of flax and later wool, while cabins and items of furniture started out as trees felled on the Hamblen properties. However, certain important items such as pots and firearms couldn't be manufactured on the spot, and so were purchased from the East. A. P. Hamblen notes that "Another accomplishment that this ancestor possessed, and one that has been handed down to many individuals through all branches of his descendants, was the fact that he made music on the VIOLIN" (1985, 75; his use of capital letters). Where did Job get a violin? Did he craft some sort of proto-violin or, more likely, did he make room in a far-from-robust budget to buy one from the East when he was acquiring guns and kettles?

A. P. Hamblen supported his broad statement asserting that skill on the violin was widespread in the Hamblen family in dozens of the hundreds of short individual biographies making up his family history. He routinely mentioned this skill right before reporting how the individual in question voted, almost always for Democrats—those who voted Republican were mentioned tersely. A given Democrat usually "played the violin well," while each musical Republican merely "played the violin" (see, e.g., 1985, 266 and 270). Several of Job's sons played violin (A. P. Hamblen never used the word "fiddle"), including John Mullins Hamelin. Multiple male descendants in each line of the next generation played, too, and so on. In a sample entry, A. P. closed his brief discussion of distant cousin John Franklin Hamblen (a livestock dealer born in 1869; no death date given) with this description: "Plays the violin, is an ardent Democrat, belongs to Woodlawn Lodge, #522, I.O.O.F. [Independent Order of Odd Fellows], and is a genuine all around fellow" (236).

The violin would remain the instrument of choice for most of the Hamblen family members whose musical skills were mentioned, most of whom were men. The rare exceptions to either generalization came during or after the Civil War. For instance, Job Hamblen's great-granddaughter Sarah Bell Goforth married one "Adam Forest Small, from Pennsylvania who, while in the Union Army 1861–64, was principal musician 132nd Illinois Volunteer Infantry" (248). Mr. Small was probably a wind player; this individual, since he both married into the Hamblen clan and voted Republican, was not really part of the picture of Hamblen musicianship. An exception in the area of gender, Martha Evaline Gillaspy (a descendant of Job born in 1872) "played violin and piano some, but preferred to give her energy to church work" (291). In a more typical path for the Hamblen family women musicians, Florence Amanda Mead, another great-granddaughter of Job and thus a member of A. P.'s generation, was a "beautiful singer" (257). The men (and violinists) in the Hamblen line from Job through John to David, on to his son Williamson and to Williamson's son Armeanous Porter Hamblen, all lived long lives, and resided most years with or near parts of their extended families. There was plenty of opportunity to transmit musical techniques and tunes between generations.

David Russell Hamblen (1809–1893), the second of ten children, was born near Hamblen Creek, Lee County, Virginia, and lived there until 1857, when he joined his parents and many other members of the extended family who had already moved to Brown County, Indiana. He and they initially planned to move on to Kansas as a group, but his wife became too ill to make that final part of the trip, so Indiana was as far as David and some other members of the family got. He revisited Lee County, Virginia, several times, but resided in the Midwest for most of the rest of his life. In his declining years, he lived with his son Williamson's family, so that three generations of fiddlers shared a home. His grandson A. P. learned enough from him directly (plus indirectly through his father) to assemble the written collection transcribed as the last tune anthology in the present book.

Armeanous Porter Hamblen praised his grandfather at considerable length. According to A. P., David Russell Hamblen had just a few months of formal schooling, but read avidly, wrote with a fine hand, and calculated well in the ways needed in his professions. David farmed and matched his own father's expertise making shoes, had a combination grist and sawmill for a time, then returned to farming with considerable success. In the best of his years in Indiana, he had a good log home with several rooms, a barn, and a variety of stock animals. He was known for an active sense of humor, and certainly was musical (he was one of three of Job's sons who fiddled). Armeanous reported that his grandfather:

> learned to play the violin as a small boy. At the age of seventeen, he sent by his home merchant, Robert M. Bales, to Baltimore and purchased a violin which he named "Betty." This instrument continued to be almost his daily companion the remainder of his life. It, yet, [in] 1934 remains in [the] possession of his descendants (the writer [A. P. Hamblen]) and is pronounced by experts to have exceptional quality of tone, and to be of considerable value.
>
> His performance on this instrument brought high compliments from the professional, as well as joy to the amateur, admirer of violin music. He could not read the written scale, but possessed a vocabulary in memory that, it was claimed by some of his friends, he could recite some seven or eight hundred compositions in his playing" (124).

Armeanous described the middle generation, Williamson—his father, who was one of several of David's sons who fiddled—more briefly but in much the same way: he had little formal schooling of any kind, but great talent on the violin, which he started playing at the age of six, accumulating an enormous repertoire learned entirely by ear. "It was conceded by experts that his playing was of the highest order." In addition, Williamson crafted some twenty-five violins beginning at the age of thirty-seven (1985, 199); his father, David, helped with this on

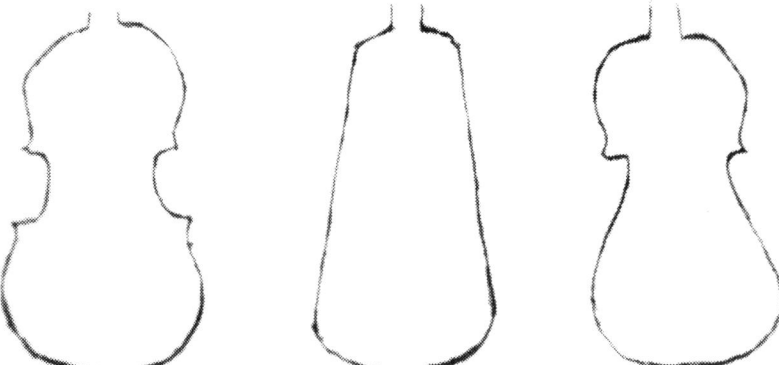

Figure 35. Shapes of fiddles: conventional violin, Mount's "Cradle of Harmony," and Williamson Hamblen's "two-point" shape; David Hamblen was involved in building at least one of these.

occasion (1985, 201). Williamson did not regard the normal shape of the violin as sacred. He had his father's violin "Betty" as a model, but was also influenced by one that he purchased, "Tilda," which had an unconventional shape. Its "corners" in the upper bout were smoothed out, then erased on the lower bout, which now featured uninterrupted curves.

Armeanous placed a photograph of the dozen violins Williamson owned at his death in the genealogy, and commented on them (1985, 200–201). In a few of the violins he built, Williamson tried replicating the upper half of "Betty"—thus, the conventional violin shape—but then adopting the graceful uninterrupted curve of "Tilda" for the lower bout. Armeanous noted that one violin his father crafted in that shape was "'fully breasted,' or deeper through, with the result of a very pleasing tone for the performer's own enjoyment, but not so loud" (201).

In Williamson's later instruments, including those that A. P. considered his best, he returned to the normal violin shape. Williamson's experiments, like those done by Mount (the "Cradle of Harmony") and witnessed by Cobb (Abram Pushee's violin with a stick running through it lengthwise) did not catch fire. Williamson Hamblen pursued better tone, but found he could not spare the volume that, according to his son, was lost in that construction. Conversely, the seeking of increased volume to help with the function of dance accompaniment in the cases of Mount and of Cobb's associates upset the balance of good tone and sufficient volume in the other direction. In the end, after these and other experiments, the partnership of tone and volume offered by the conventionally made violin has been judged best over and over.[1] Another great-grandson of Job Hamblen, Charles Caswell Lock, a mechanic, invented "and patented, in 1925, an eight-stringed violin, said to be a musical marvel" (1985, 265).

Charles Cobb's search for volume led to his often playing in bands rather than as a solo fiddler; Williamson Hamblen did this in a small way, too. David Hamblen Curry, a cousin of Williamson, "played the violin well, was a warm friend and companion, and the two played the violin much for public entertainments" (1985, 252). Williamson also played the fife.

Now we can shift from Armeanous Porter Hamblen the family historian to him as transcriber. In his own entry in his family history he notes that he was always academically inclined, taught school while still a teenager, and attended college. He practiced numerous professions, including carpenter, post office functionary, worker in a general store, manager of a telephone system, and finally grocer. He wrote short historical articles and poems for local newspapers. He "composed several songs, sacred, sentimental and comic, as well as some instrumental numbers for violin." He, like two of his brothers and at least two of his nephews, played the violin (1985, 280–84). John Marshall Gillaspy (1877–1952), who transcribed three of the first four items in the Hamblen fiddle collection, belonged to an even more musically inclined branch of the family (he was a grandson of Job's son Reverend William Hamblen).

The Hamblen collection consists of thirty-eight tunes, which Armeanous Hamblen numbered (I follow his numbering; his #1 is his prose introduction and index of the tunes, so that entry #39 is the 38th melody). He annotated almost every tune in one of these ways: "as played by David R. (or Russell) Hamblen," or "as played by Williamson Hamblen." A few aren't labeled that way separately, but each of those doubtless inherits the attribution given for the previous piece. And there is one tune composed by A. P. Hamblen, a melody that he dedicated to his grandfather. About half of the melodies are well known, and bear their usual titles, while most of the remaining half are truly obscure, resulting in proportions of ubiquity versus rarity reminiscent of Knauff's *Virginia Reels*. I will focus on the antebellum part of Hamblen's collection, the tunes that A. P. Hamblen remembered as being played during that era by his grandfather. However, I have transcribed the whole collection as the final tune anthology in this book.

What are we to make of Armeanous as a recorder of his grandfather's and father's fiddling? In my transcriptions of his always legible music writing, I reproduce what A. P. Hamblen wrote, then mark where pitches seem mistakenly recorded (rarely), and where the key signatures seem simply wrong, containing too many sharps. What caused what I believe to have been his errors with key signatures? A clue comes from his notation of a hymn that he composed and inserted within the published family history. This hymn, entitled "Book Divine," Armeanous said was inspired by a sermon given late in life by his uncle, the Reverend William Hamblen (David's brother), a sermon ecstatically celebrating the infinite sweep and absolute authority of the Bible. Just below the title on the left we see the words "Words and Melody by A. Porter Hamblen," with the addendum on the right "Harmony by John Marshall Gillaspy" (1985, 144). This cousin was indeed a skilled violinist, but also a pianist, piano tuner, and music store owner, in short, someone with much more musical training than Armeanous claimed for himself (1985, 292). While Gillaspy is credited with helping notate the first few numbers in Armeanous's collection of his grandfather's and father's playing (see the descriptions that accompanied those specific tunes), the remainder represent A. P. Hamblen's more limited training.

Regarding the assignment of key signatures, my sense is that Armeanous looked at the last pitch in a tune, identified that automatically as the tonic, then almost always mechanically wrote down the appropriate key signature for the major key having that tonic. This strategy goes awry if a tune is not in major (several of these tunes are in dorian mode) and also leads to error if the tune has a circular ending, that is, if the last note is not in fact the tonic. For the "not in a major key" problem, see numbers 12, 13, and 37 among David Hamblen's tunes, and numbers 7, 8, and 39 among Williamson Hamblen's tunes. For key signature problems linked with circular endings, see numbers 9, 19, and 38. Number 9 offers an especially transparent illustration: the tune is the well-known "White Cockade," which usually (and here) is in G Major. The last note of each section is e, the sixth degree of the scale, so Armeanous Hamblen, taking that to be the tonic, gave a key signature representing E Major, which bears three sharps too many.

While the key signature errors are troublesome but easily solved, the "crookedness" of many tunes is more intriguing (modern fiddlers call tunes with unusual strain lengths "crooked"). Most fiddle tunes in most fiddlers' performances consist of two strains, each of which is eight measures long, with those eight measures dividing nicely into two 4-measure phrases. Many of the Hamblen tunes fit that norm, but many do not. When they don't, that might result from David Hamblen's conception of a given tune, or instead might be an artifact of Armeanous Hamblen's inexpert transcribing. First, I must mention that there is reason to lack unalloyed confidence in Armeanous's own sense of form. He added his own "variations" to "Queen of France" (#23, which has the contour and key of the "Braes of Auchtertyre" / "Billy in the Low Ground" tune group). The last line, meant to be a variation of the A strain, falls out of regular phrasing, instead becoming one 3-measure phrase and one of five measures (or the reverse, or 3 + 2 + 3, at any rate not 4 + 4). This raises the possibility that A. P. Hamblen may have taken more than the usual oral-tradition liberties with some of his grandfather's tunes in terms of form, erring either during the process of transcription or earlier, through possessing a memory unusually flexible in the area of phrasing.

We can be more confident in the transcription skills of Gillaspy, the cousin who was a professional musician, who A. P. Hamblen reported to have worked directly from his own memories of the playing of David Hamblen. The first two tunes in the collection, the only two David Hamblen tunes transcribed by Gillaspy, do illustrate two kinds of phrase lengthening common in contemporary old-time fiddling. "Three Forks of Cumberland" has a regularly shaped A strain: 4 + 4. But the B strain illustrates David Hamblen doing something common today, that is, extending cadences. Instead of a single measure wrapping up the first phrase in that strain, he uses the two-measure opening of the A strain as the conclusion of the phrase, resulting in a five-measure phrase. In the B strain, he does that again, then, at the end of that strain, also appends the two-measure cadence of the A strain. The total form of B becomes (3 + 2) + (3 + 2) +2. The B strain works musically both as a complement to the A strain and as an expansion of that strain; this is a musically unified and quite satisfying "crooked" tune.

The following tune, "Big Tennessee," is less compelling. The A strain, although the conventional eight measures long, seems loosely woven. Then, in the nine-measure B strain, measures 6–7 seem to me to be one measure stretched into two in order to accommodate a sequence that covers the large range between the high b ending the fifth measure of the strain and the much lower e commencing the penultimate measure. Plausible sounding or not, this is a good example of the second most-common way phrases become extended in current old-time fiddling, by a measure's contour suggesting extending that contour in sequence, and thus justifying the insertion of an "extra" measure. In short, the phrase extensions in this pair of tunes transcribed by Gillaspy were likely truly part of David Hamblen's playing. At a minimum, these extensions make sense in terms of patterns of "crooked" phrasing in current American fiddling.

Yet another way that phrases stretch longer than the conventional four bars in this collection may reflect a very different factor. I believe that David Hamblen inserted "dwells" in performance (meaning notes held longer than regular phrasing would lead the listener to expect, doing so for emphasis, as was common in the singing of ballads). I further believe that Armeanous Hamblen tried to cope with his memory of that practice while transcribing, but wasn't sure how to do so. A convincing example of this sequence of events can be found in unnamed tune #16. The A strain is currently laid out in notation as filling five measures that divide 2 ½ + 2 ½, a layout not just unusual, but highly unlikely. I imagine a very different solution: perhaps David Hamblen landed firmly on the open string e in measure 2. He may have emphasized this arrival with a characteristic fiddlers' double stop combining playing on an open string with that same pitch slid up to on the next lowest string, and getting louder while maintaining the note for longer than it is notated here—perhaps for the rest of the measure, but for as long as the dramatic moment allowed. (This is cumbersome to explain in prose, but is straightforward in the transcription.) This would build suspense, and add to the impact of closure in the subsequent cadential measure. All of this would happen again as the phrase repeated, and would occur on the same pitch in the B strain. The A strain in Armeanous's transcription counts out 2 ½ + 2 ½ measures (then the five measures repeat), and the B strain stretches to 4 ½ + 4 ½ in his interpretation. A simpler and more rational alternative reading would result from letting what seem to be dwells last longer than notated, but a predictable amount, with each dwell filling out the measure in which it commenced. The A strain would then count out as 3 + 3 measures, then the B strain 5 + 5 measures, still audibly irregular, but making more musical sense than in Armeanous Hamblen's interpretation (see Figure 36a).

Hamblen's version of a famous tune, "The Flowers of Edinburgh," surprises in several ways. The A strain spans nine measures. Perhaps the functions of measures four and five are similar enough that one could be considered an extension. More likely, the strain as transcribed could be understood as having a dwell at the beginning and at the end; removing those arguably "extra" pitches (the second halves of the first and sixth measures) would leave a more conventional A strain.

Unnamed tune, #16, Strain A only, as transcribed by A. P. Hamblen

Same section of same tune, with dwells and a characteristic double stop incorporated

"Flowers of Edinburgh as transcribed by A. P. Hamblen, but with dwells suggested (in brackets)

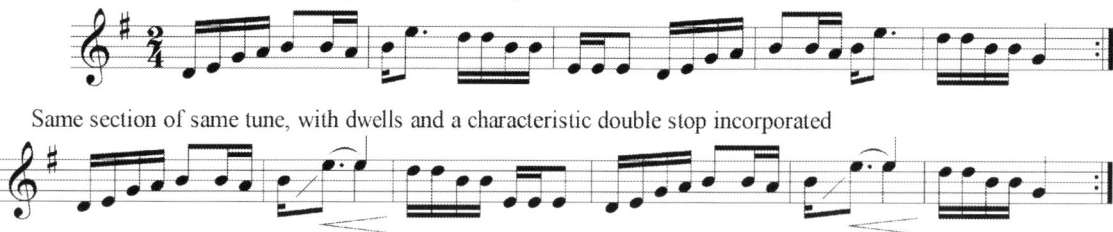

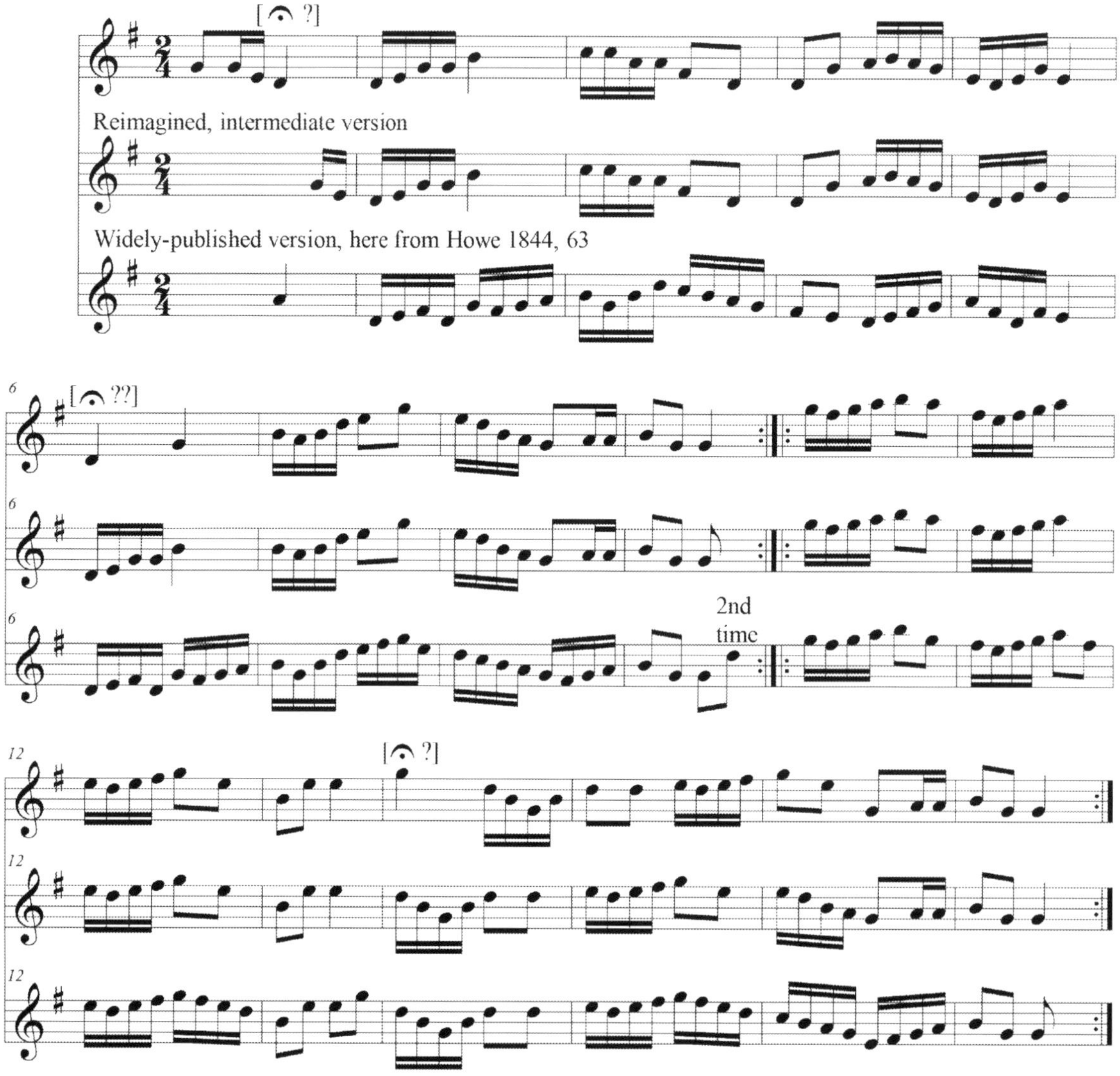

David Hamblen's version of "Flowers of Edinburgh," and some possible "corrections," that is, ways that this might become a more regularly phrased tune (or, perhaps, a suggestion for a more conventionally constructed source tune.

Figure 36. Some possible corrections of Armeanous Hamblen's transcriptions of his grandfather David Hamblen's playing, these highly speculative repairs based on the theory that A. P. Hamblen didn't know how to transcribe notes that were held for emphasis ("dwells").

The B strain is even trickier. On the face of it, it is eight measures long, but this breaks down into awkward phrases of 4 ½ and 3 ½ measures. However, the g in measure 14 is an expendable dwell. If that note were removed, and the last two measures were repaired to match the corresponding measures ending the first strain, then the whole strain would parse more conventionally. In Figure 36b, I give Armeanous Hamblen's transcription of David Hamblen's version on the top line, and place the most frequently printed antebellum version of "The Flowers of Edinburgh" on the lowest of the three lines (as published in Howe's *Musician's Companion*, 1844, I, 63). I then insert my *very* hypothetical "regularized" revision of the Hamblen version in between.

"The Flowers of Edinburgh" has been especially prone to growing into "crooked" forms. Most versions of it collected by Bayard in Pennsylvania were irregular (1982, 326–28), and Art Galbraith's Missouri performance of it is one of the all-time most lovely and convincing crooked versions of any tune (1980, and see Marshall 2012, 104, and Goertzen 2017, 108). We do know that many music-literate fiddlers like Cobb and Mount owned and surely sometimes played directly from the Howe publications, and so probably reproduced the regular phrasing of the tune, even if they changed a few pitches or added ornaments. At the same time, we expect that David Hamblen's version may have been very similar to what his grandson wrote down. The version that I made up might actually be closer to what David Hamblen played than is Armeanous's transcription. Or, if my doubts concerning A. P.'s transcribing skills are misguided, my version still might represent the approximate shape of some oral-tradition performances resting between the "straight" and the very crooked forms represented in the figure. In my opinion, versions exactly like or at least very similar to each of the three versions must have been heard in the antebellum era.

A COLLECTION

of violin tunes, popular during the early 1800s as played by David Russell Hamblen (1809-1893) and his son Williamson (1848-1920) arranged and copied by A[rmeanous] Porter Hamblen (1875-195-) son of Williamson.

INDEX.

Introduction [These are item numbers, not a pagination; this list was originally in two columns. I added the column of tune attributions; D = David, and W = Williamson.]

Three Forks of Cumberland	D
Big Tennessee	D
Chadwell's Station	D
Lost Indian	D
Calahan	W
Roving Sailor	W
Shelbyville	W
White Cockade	D
The Cuckoo	W
The Mocking Bird	W
Tune (Name not known)	D
Speckled Apron	D
Hankins' Raid	W
Spirit Of David R.	Armeanous
Tune (Name not known)	D
Turkey In The Straw	W
Sally Goodin	D
Cotton Eyed Joe	D
Tune (Name not known)	D
Mountain Hornpipe	W
Bonapart [sic] Crossing The Rhine	D
Queen Of France	D
Drummer Boy Of Waterloo	D
Bonapart's [sic] Retreat	not marked; probably D, since part of five-tune series
Isle Of St. Helena	D
Flowers Of Edinburgh	D
The Campbells Are Coming	D
Indian Eat The Woodchuck	D
Forked Ear	W

Haste To The Wedding	W
Tune (Name not known)	D
Girl I Left Behind Me	W
Jay Bird	W
Knock At The Door Till The Cook Comes In	D
Cold Rain	W
Pride Of America	D
Blue Bonnets Over The Border	D
Jolly Blacksmith	W

[new page in this typescript portion of the Hamblen Collection]

THREE GOOD OLD TIME TUNES PROBABLY NEVER PUBLISHED, WITH OTHERS

The following three tunes, "Three Forks of Cumberland," "Big Tennessee" and "Chadwell's Station," were played by David R. Hamblen (1809-1893) of Cumberland Gap, Lee County, Virginia. It is believed they were never published except as they were passed by ear from one local player to another and were composed by some local musician of the region. Mr. Hamblen moved to Brown County, Indiana, 1857. No one outside the Hamblen families ever knew or played them there.

John Marshall Gillaspy was a professional musician as was also his brother Richard J. Gillaspy. They both traveled and played extensively over Indiana and Illinois. Both asserted that they never heard any one play these tunes except as stated above. John Marshall Gillaspy (1877-1952) composed a number of excellent compositions Among them were the marches, "With Flag and Fleet and "Culver Black Horse Troop" which were published, copyrighted and played by military bands extensively. The later [sic] was adjudged by some very competant [sic] band masters as, "The greatest march ever written."

Mr. Gillaspy was a grandson of the Reverend William Hamblen, a brother of David R. Hamblen. A. Porter Hamblen who arranged these melodies in this booklet in co-operation with Mr. Gillaspy was a grandson of David Russell Hamblen and played the violin and composed a number of songs and instrumental numbers.

Referring to "Three Forks of Cumberland" Mr. Gillaspy wrote: "This tune was my favorite of all dear Uncle David's library and I believe it is the hardest tune to put on paper I have ever tackled. This haunting melody will come to you as you play it. Tune your violin with D and G strings up (to E & A). David called it "Italian Key." I am mailing you as perfect a photograph of Uncle David's playing this tune as it would be possible for me to make. You know it has been a long time since I sat at his knee to record it and he pronounced it perfectly. Let us hope that nothing has slipped.

Figure 37. A. P. Hamblen's "Collection of Violin Tunes," following Hamblen's numbering.

Three Forks of Cumberland

(H #2)

A Virginia violin melody as played by David Russell Hamblen, 1840s. Translated by John Marshall Gillaspy, Anderson, Indiana 1949. Copied by A. Porter Hamblen, Del Rio, Texas.

Big Tennessee

(H #3)

A Virginia violin melody. As played by David Russell Hamblen. 1840s. Translated by John Marshall Gillaspy and A. Porter Hamblen, Del Rio, Texas.

Figure 37. A. P. Hamblen's "Collection of Violin Tunes," #2–#3.

Chadwell's Station

(H #4)

A Virginia melody. As played by David Russell Hamblen, 1840s. Translated and copied by A. Porter Hamblen, Del Rio, Texas.

Chadwell's Station is a small village located on Highway 58 about six miles east of Cumberland Gap, Lee County, Virginia. A prominent family by name of Chadwell were pioneer settlers near the place which later took their name.

Lost Indian

(H #5)

As played by David R. Hamblen. Accompaniment by Hanly Cartwright. Translated by A. Porter Hamblen.

Figure 37. A. P. Hamblen's "Collection of Violin Tunes," #4–#5.

Calahan

(H #6)

A violin melody. As played by Williamson Hamblen, 1890s. Piano arr. by Hanly A. Cartwright. Translated by John Marshall Gillaspy and A. Porter Hamblen.

Calahan was convicted of murdering a Jewish peddler and legally hanged at Barbourville, Kentucky, May 15, 1835. At the hour of his execution he requested to be allowed to play a farewell on his violin. While seated on his coffin he played this tune which since has borne his name. He then handed the violin to the sheriff, was load[ed] onto the gallows and the trap sprung, sending Calahan to his maker.

Roving Sailor

(H #7)

As played by Williamson Hamblen. Arranged by A. Porter Hamblen.

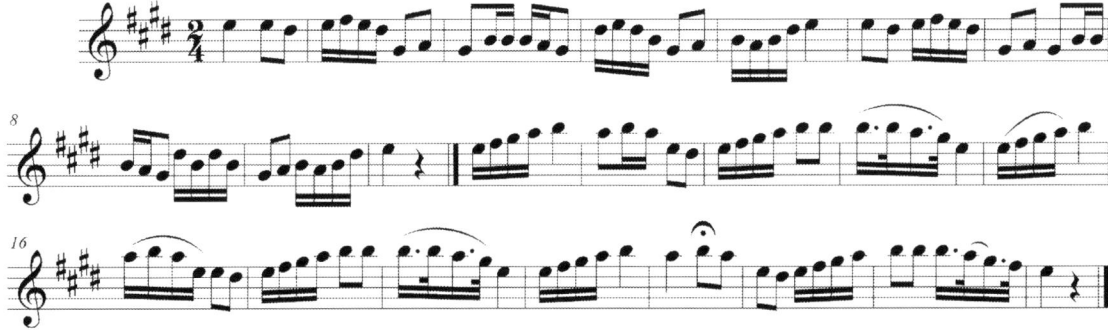

[Key signature should probably be one sharp, for E Dorian.]

Figure 37. A. P. Hamblen's "Collection of Violin Tunes," #6–#7.

Shelbyville

(H #8)

As played by Williamson Hamblen. Arranged by A. Porter Hamblen.

[Key signature should probably have just one sharp, for A Dorian.]

White Cockade

(H #9)

As played by David R. Hamblen. Arranged by A. Porter Hamblen.

Along came a Yankee and his knapsack, and a great big pumpkin on his back, An Indian pone and

three pounds of pork, On his way down to New York.

[Again, the key signature seems to be wrong. The tune is usually in G Major, thus with just one sharp.]

Figure 37. A. P. Hamblen's "Collection of Violin Tunes," #8–#9.

The Cuckoo

(H #10)

As played by Williamson Hamblen. Arranged by A. Porter Hamblen.

|Another case in which A. P. Hamblen mechanically assigned the wrong key signature. Sharps may be ignored.|

Mocking Bird

(H #11)

As played by Williamson Hamblen. Arranged by A. Porter Hamblen.

Figure 37. A. P. Hamblen's "Collection of Violin Tunes," #10–#11.

Tune (Name not known). A Virginia Violin Melody

(H #12)

As played by David R. Hamblen (1809-1893). Composer not known. Arranged by A Porter Hamblen.

[I would delete both sharps; other scholar/fiddlers are not so sure, particularly concerning how to treat each c/c#.]

Speckled Apron

(H #13)

As played by David R. Hamblen. Arranged by A. Porter Hamblen.

[*Probably repeat to here, not to beginning.]   [Probably neither C nor G should be sharped.]

Figure 37. A. P. Hamblen's "Collection of Violin Tunes," #12–#13.

Hankin's Raid

(H #14)

As played by Williamson Hamblen. Arranged by A. Porter Hamblen.

Spirit of David R.

(H #15)

Dedicated to David R. Hamblen (1809-1893). Composed by A. Porter Hamblen, his grandson. Attempting to record the melodious tones he brought forth from his violin.

Figure 37. A. P. Hamblen's "Collection of Violin Tunes," #14–#15.

Tune (Name not known). A Virginia Violin Melody

(H #16)

As played by David R. Hamblen (1809-1893). Composer not known. Arranged by A. Porter Hamblen.

Turkey in the Straw

(H #17)

As played by Williamson Hamblen. Arranged by A. Porter Hamblen

Figure 37. A. P. Hamblen's "Collection of Violin Tunes," #16–#17.

Sally Goodin

(H #18)

As played by David R. Hamblen. Arranged by A. Porter Hamblen.

I had a piece of pie and I had a piece of puddin'. I gave it all away to kiss Sally Goodin.
The old blue hen, the speckled hen's mother, laid three eggs and she never laid another.

Cotton Eyed Joe

(H #19)

As played by David R. Hamblen. Arranged by A. Porter Hamblen.

I'd a been married some forty years ago if it had not been for Cotton Eyed Joe.
Oh, my little girl if you don't do better I'll build me a boat and send you down the river.

[Wrong key signature. Should be in G Major; doesn't matter, since neither f# nor c# used.]

Tune (name not known). A Virginia Violin Melody

(H #20)

As played by David R. Hamblen (1809-1893). Composer not known. Arranged by A. Porter Hamblen.

Figure 37. A. P. Hamblen's "Collection of Violin Tunes," #18–#20.

Mountain Hornpipe

(H # 21)

As played by Williamson Hamblen. Arranged by A. Porter Hamblen.

Bonaparte Crossing the Rhine (Bonaparte's March)

(H #22)

As played by David R. Hamblen. Arranged by A. Porter Hamblen.

Figure 37. A. P. Hamblen's "Collection of Violin Tunes," #21–#22.

Queen of France

(H #23)

As played by Williamson and David R. Hamblen. Arranged with variations by A. Porter Hamblen.

Drummer Boy of Waterloo

(H #24)

As played by David R. Hamblen. Arranged by A. Porter Hamblen.

Bonapart[e]'s Retreat

(H #25)

Figure 37. A. P. Hamblen's "Collection of Violin Tunes," #23–#25.

Isle of Saint Helena

(H #26)

As played by David R. Hamblen. Arranged by A. Porter Hamblen.

Flowers of Edinburgh

(H #27)

As played by David R. Hamblen. Arranged by A. Porter Hamblen.

The Campbell's Are Coming. Ancient Scotch Air.

(H #28)

As played by David R. Hamblen. Arranged by A. Porter Hamblen.

The Campbell's were a powerful warlike clan of ancient Scotland. When they marched a battle was to be expected.

[Note lengthened first three measures of second strain.]

Figure 37. A. P. Hamblen's "Collection of Violin Tunes," #26–#28.

Indian Eat the Woodchuck

(H #29)

As played by David R. Hamblen. Arranged by A. Porter Hamblen.

Forked Ear

(H #30)

As played by Williamson Hamblen. Arranged by A. Porter Hamblen.

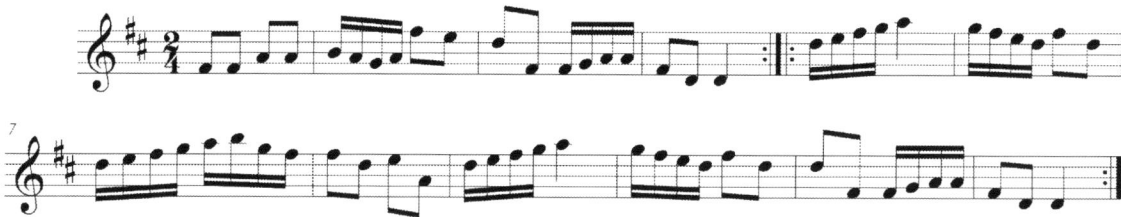

Haste to the Wedding

(H #31)

As played by Williamson Hamblen. Arranged by A. Porter Hamblen.

[I changed the 16th notes with which A. P. Hamblen started and ended each section to eighth notes.]

Figure 37. A. P. Hamblen's "Collection of Violin Tunes," #29–#31.

Tune (Name not known). A Virginia Melody.

(H #32)

As played by David R. Hamblen (1809-1893). Composer not known. Arranged by A. Porter Hamblen.

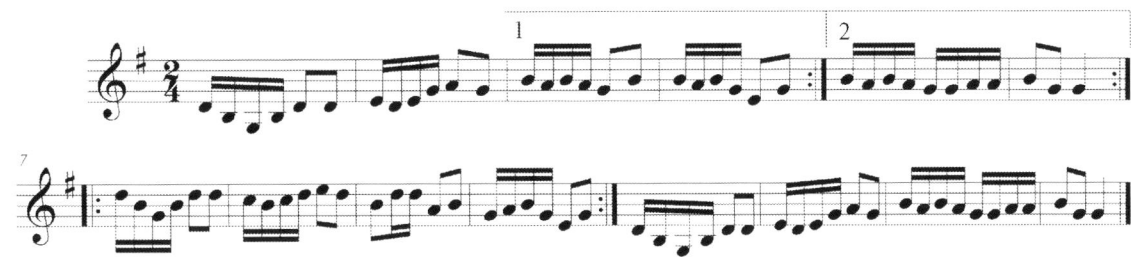

Girl I Left Behind Me

(H #33)

As played by Williamson Hamblen. Arranged by A. Porter Hamblen.

Jay Bird

(H #34)

Played by Williamson Hamblen. Arranged by A. Porter Hamblen.

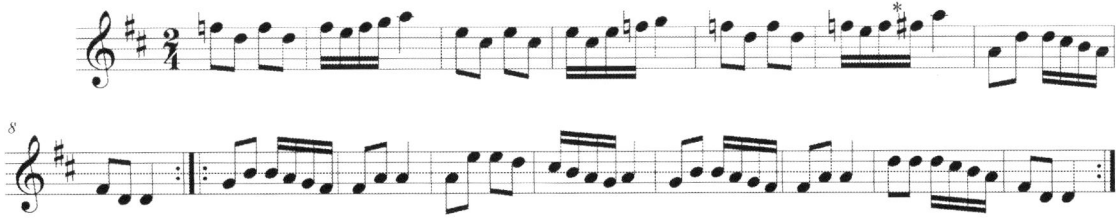

*[Dubious. Might this actually be a slide?]

Figure 37. A. P. Hamblen's "Collection of Violin Tunes," #32–#34.

Knock at the Door Till the Cook Comes In

(H #35)

As played by David R. Hamblen. Arranged by A. Porter Hamblen.

Cold Rain

(H #36)

As played by Williamson Hamblen. Arranged by A. Porter Hamblen.

Pride of America

(H #37)

As played by David R. Hamblen. Arranged by A. Porter Hamblen.

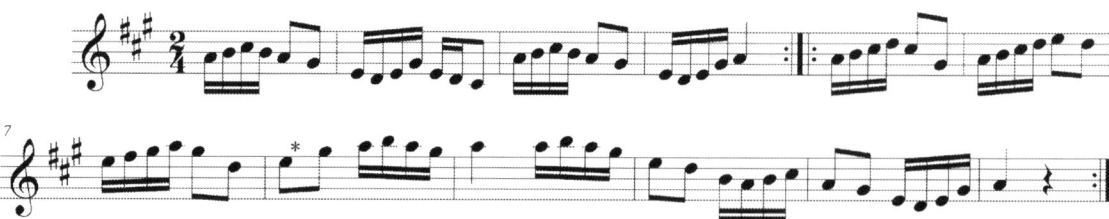

[Key signature: Doubtless just one sharp.]

[*I suggest a dwell here, turning this eighth note into a dotted quarter, then omitting the final rest. The strain will still be eight measures long, but now with balanced phrases.]

Figure 37. A. P. Hamblen's "Collection of Violin Tunes," #35–#37.

FIDDLERS MOVING SOUTH AND WEST, AWAY FROM NOTATION

Blue Bonnets over the Border

(H #38)

As played by David R. Hamblen. Arranged by A. Porter Hamblen.

Ancient Scotch clansmen wore blue head dress as part of their army uniform. When they marched over the border of a neighboring clan war was imminent.

[In D Major: should have just two sharps in key signature.]

Jolly Blacksmith (She Wouldn't Come At All)

(H #39)

As played by Williamson Hamblen. Arranged by A. Porter Hamblen.

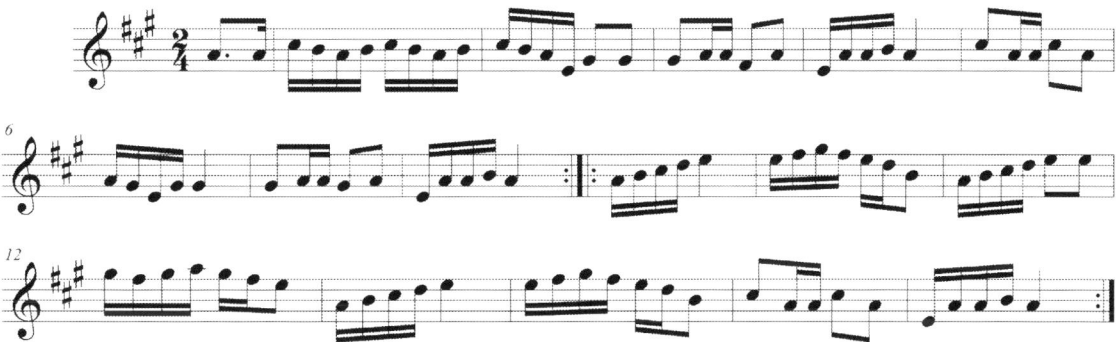

[It's in G Major; sharp only the f.]

Figure 37. A. P. Hamblen's "Collection of Violin Tunes," #38–#39.

- 211 -

A. P. Hamblen summarized his own sense of what his grandfather David Hamblen's repertoire and playing were like in the composition that Armeanous wrote as an explicit homage, which he named "Spirit of David R" (tune #15). First, it is in G Major. If we count pentatonic tunes with a tonic of G and including a major third above the tonic as being in G Major, then G Major was David Hamblen's favorite key (followed by D Major, then A Major, then by the few Dorian tunes). Second, this tune stays in first position, as do all in the collection—no shifting required. Third, there is about the same level of syncopation in "Spirit of David R." as is typical in the collection, with sixteenth-note runs nestled between eighth notes in measures 7–11. The longer notes that create suspense in the second and sixth measures also illustrate syncopation, and simultaneously remind us subtly of the dwells that I believe punctuate a number of David Hamblen's pieces.

Also, A. P. employed a rhythmic texture and motto that David used in a majority of his pieces. Overall, he devoted roughly equal space to the shortest note value and the next longer one. The patterns of lengths are either two eighths followed by four sixteenths or the reverse, yielding a family of rhythmic mottos. Perhaps that was part of regional style, or perhaps it was personal. Either way, that element is as pervasive in this little repertoire as the melodic element permeating the playing of George Knauff's source fiddler, that is, cascades of arpeggios. I think that it is possible that it was Knauff's fiddler's affection for arpeggios that led him to play "Old Virginia" rather than a more orthodox "Flowers of Edinburgh," and "Natchez on the Hill" rather than the more common "Old Zip Coon"; both "Old Virginia" and "Natchez on the Hill" commence with arpeggios. Knauff's fiddler's preferences place him closer to Mount and Cobb than to David Hamblen in several other ways, notably extending the keys chosen from the fiddle core (D, G, and A Major) to C Major and F Major. Like Mount and Cobb, Knauff's source fiddler ventures into third position regularly, and, for many of the "reels," opts for a rhythmic texture dominating by constant sixteenth notes.

Some of Knauff's source fiddler's proclivity for tunes with local or regional titles marks the Hamblen collection too, as well as an affection for tune titles celebrating heroes, and titles with a general rural flavor. The physical Chadwell's Station, also called Chadwell's Fort, is in Powell Valley, Lee County. It was founded by Captain David Chadwell, a Revolutionary War veteran, and served as a waystation for people traveling the Wilderness Road. It was also important during times of tension with local Indians (Hannings 2006). "Three Forks of Cumberland" celebrates the Cumberland River, which arises not far from Lee County, Virginia, and the Cumberland Gap in Leitchfield County, Kentucky. "Big Tennessee," if describing the Tennessee River, doesn't refer to a place quite so near to Lee County, but remains a somewhat local reference. Conflicts and local heroes—so important in the *Virginia Reels*—have an odd position in the Hamblen Collection. Williamson Hamblen played a tune called "Hankin's Raid," which is doubtless named for Jonathan Hankin, a Civil War captain in the Sixteenth Virginia Cavalry, which drew primarily on communities no more than a hundred miles from Cumberland Gap. And there are a few very common titles associated with war: "White Cockade," "The Campbells Are Coming," and "Blue Bonnets Over the Border" (both white cockades and blue bonnets have to do with Scottish war history). But the most remarkable cluster of titles in the Hamblen collection honors Napoleon, an enduringly evocative figure, followed in the collection from his early "crossing the Rhine" to his exile on the "Isle of St. Helena." I picture David Hamblen telling the story of Napoleon to a rapt audience, pausing to illustrate high points in his narrative with fiddling.

But let us return to the three tunes just mentioned that refer to Scotland, and supplement them with Hamblen's "Flowers of Edinburgh" and even one of the Bonaparte-titled tunes, "Queen of France," which seems related to the Scottish "Braes of Auchtertyre" (see Figure 27, #17 and #18). In the Hamblen collection, David Hamblen is cited as the source of twenty-three tunes, four of which have no name. Of the nineteen tunes left, five have Scottish connections, so just over a quarter of them. Turning again to the *Virginia Reels* tunes published by Willig in 1839, that is, the twenty-eight tunes in the first three pamphlets, these are of Scottish origin: "Killie Krankie" (mistaken Scottish title; this is a version of "Money Musk," which, however, is also Scottish), "Whiskey Barrel" (more commonly "Madam Parisott's Hornpipe"), "Old Virginia" ("Flowers of Edinburgh"), "Richmond Hill" ("Perthshire Hunt"), "George Booker" ("Marquis of Huntley's Farewell"), "Billy in the Low Grounds" ("Johnny in the Nether Mains"), and "Scott's Favorite" ("Duke of Gordon's Rant"), thus seven of twenty-eight, again a fourth. This is a relatively big Scottish component in comparison with that part of the collections of McArthur, Seward, Cobb, and Mount (who copied a handful of tunes from the Gow collections), and certainly in comparison with Howe's published collections.

The relatively large Scottish presence in the Knauff and Hamblen arrays of tunes is understandable. In addition to the sizeable body of Scottish tunes that traveled to the colonies and young United States through sources in England, we should take into account the implications for oral-tradition music of the immigration of highland Scots to eastern North Carolina (and to parts of contiguous states) early in the history of that state, and also the cultural impact of the Scots-Irish mass immigrations. This composite demographic factor didn't directly affect music publishing, but touched all aspects of rural culture in the Upper South. The results become complicated even on the level of the individual tune. "The Flowers of Edinburgh" traveled to America in English publications, and also in the hands of fiddlers in each stream of Scottish immigration, and through individuals like Mount, who carefully sought out fiddle collections published in late eighteenth- and early nineteenth-century Scotland. "Rose Tree" started in Ireland or Scotland, then hitched a ride on an Ireland-associated British ballad opera to the United States on its way to being fleshed out as "Old Zip Coon," this last transformation symptomizing the complex Scottish/African American musical interface. And "Savourna Delish" followed a complementary winding path, starting in Ireland, traveling to Scotland, and then joining the many streams of Scottish songs and fiddle tunes coming to the New World.

The underdocumented Scottish factor is just one symptom of a larger truth: the picture of antebellum American fiddling that can be assembled by evaluating surviving notation plus bits of contemporary testimony is incomplete, like a jigsaw puzzle with only a fraction of the pieces available. What parts of the picture are most conspicuously missing? It is easy to chart a "glass half empty" view. Part 1 of this book concerned relatively affluent, literate, and at least somewhat music literate young men learning to play the violin/fiddle as an avocation. Their custom of keeping music commonplace books left valuable evidence concerning what music they played and how they played it. That practice was made possible by the blossoming of music publishing in the United States during the first decades of the nineteenth century, but which waned when such an arduous undertaking became unnecessary; that is, when printed collections of instrumental melodies became significantly bigger and cheaper. The population of young amateur music makers like McArthur and Seward didn't go away, but the evidence concerning which tunes they favored became much less precise. Our speculation has to shift back a step in the transmission process, to the contents of the big collections; that is, to music professionals' choices based on their own hypotheses about what these young violinists/fiddlers could be convinced to purchase. Perhaps we could have recovered evidence that directly continued the hints provided in the earlier music commonplace books if enough of those customers had identified which pieces they actually played in another way, by marking fingerings in their copies of, for example, volumes of Howe's *Musician's Companion*, but I haven't seen much of such evidence.

Part 2 of the current book concerns the generous body of manuscript evidence left just after the heyday of music commonplace books by two fiddlers/violinists of professional caliber. Charles M. Cobb, although eventually a bandmaster by trade, was primarily a fiddler during his first years of musical activity, and never stopped. William Sidney Mount, although earning his living as a painter, seems to have been at least as thoughtful and learned a fiddler as was his brother Nelson, the professional fiddler and dance master. In part 1, I focused my exploration of young gentlemen's music commonplace books that were made very early in the nineteenth century on just two collections because these two particular collections aptly represented a widespread and well-documented practice. But in part 2, dealing with fiddling several decades later, I look at just two men's massive manuscript collections because that is all I have located. Cobb's sometime teacher Abram Pushee must have had a substantial collection of handwritten tunes, and the same goes for several of Mount's fiddler acquaintances, particularly the Pfeiffers. If and when these or similar collections surface, we will be able to learn much more about the traditional/art musical interface immediately before the Civil War.

The materials discussed in part 3, the most immediate edges of oral tradition, proved to be not just the most tantalizing but the most elusive. What can we do with the surviving brief anecdotes about fiddling? Take Gideon Lincecum—was his flowery verbal self-expression matched with elaborate musical performance?

Also, when he stopped playing during the 1835 picnic next to Eagle Lake in Texas that he described, and he turned over the violin that he had borrowed to his host's slave fiddlers, how did their repertoire and style contrast with what he had been doing? Indeed, how little information survives concerning fiddling of African Americans is especially aggravating. Knauff's source fiddler, whom I have inferred was black, would represent African American fiddling at one end of a spectrum—he likely performed a fairly faithful imitation of white fiddling suitable for dances among the white farm/plantation owners. The other end of the spectrum would have been fiddling thoroughly infused with African-derived tastes and musical traits (from a variety of African traditions!), fiddling that slaves did for their own communities' enjoyment. Last, the Hamblen collection yields one glimpse of fiddling among frontiersmen who loved to make music, men who entertained their neighbors and accompanied dances, but who were musically illiterate. How sad it is that this body of evidence concerning oral-tradition processes is small and unique.

In the end, I wrote this book because I believe it is worthwhile to explore as much of the mosaic of antebellum American fiddling as we can. It is valuable both for its intrinsic interest and because we can better savor many features of modern fiddling through witnessing how long a tenure those factors hold. This begins with repertoire, with a core of tunes already old when they crossed the Atlantic Ocean, this core buffeted by, regularly interacting with, and replenished by fresh additions adjusted to suit fiddle tune aesthetics. It continues with the persistence of the appeal of the fiddle regardless of evolving accompaniments and despite legions of new competitors in performance media, and the partnership of dance tempos and rhythms with an ever-changing roster of alternatives. The Hamblen collection anticipates current old-time fiddling of the Upper South (and thus also urban revivalist fiddling). Mount and his friends Mathewson and the Alabama Pfeiffers and to a degree Knauff's source fiddler, with the expanded roster of keys they used, their bold and frequent use of third position, and their affection for variation set the scene for modern contest fiddling.

Moving from music to people, we witness fiddling's multigenerational appeal then and now, and the enduring identity of the fiddler—a self-reliant individual who learns best in informal environments, who is willing to work hard to imbue performances of deceptively simple two-strain tunes with energy, beauty, and fun, and who has enough personal and cultural self-confidence to bridge the differences between violin and fiddle over and over. That was American fiddling before the Civil War, and that is fiddling now.

NOTES

PART TWO

1. Cobb's journals form the raw material for Leslie Askwith's *Thunderstruck Fiddle: The Remarkable True Story of Charles Morris Cobb and His Hill Farm Community in 1850s Vermont* (2017). Askwith turned Cobb's journal entries into more of a narrative, and adjusted many small facts in the interest of grace and continuity. For instance, "thunderstruck fiddle" has a nice ring to it, but the instrument Cobb called "thunderstruck" was a broken one, never Cobb's favorite violin. This self-published volume is part meticulous scholarly work and part historical fiction, and is very entertaining.

2. While Cobb's father was an inveterate tinkerer with fiddles and then with wind instruments, Cobb himself abstained. The closest he reported himself coming to passing beyond routine maintenance to changing the nature of an instrument was minor: he said that when he was waiting for his father to do some grafting in their orchard, "I essayed to make a butternut whistle but found I hadn't mechanical skill enough" (*Journal* May 15, 1853).

3. For an oral-tradition version of "Fest March," see Williams 2008, 25. This is a use of that tune within a quadrille; Charles Cobb noted such an employment also, when listing a quadrille by fellow New England band musician Alonzo Bond (see above, in Figure 26).

4. See, for instance, variations on the tune "Yell, Yell" as set by Gow ([1784], 27–28) and by Alexander McGlashan ([1780], 11) and variations on "Sow's Tail" by these same fiddlers/composers (Gow [1788], 32–33, and McGlashan [1781], 39–41).

The closest parallel in American music manuscripts that I have seen is in a problematic music commonplace on deposit at the Center for Popular Music. This manuscript, labeled "Hornpipes" on its cover, is inscribed as follows on the flyleaf: "Clinton W. Bisbee's book/ West-Sumner, Me./ Aug. 1904/ copied from Frank Richardson's book/ formerly Mt. Vernon/ Maine/ now Canton/ Dec. 25, 1864." My sense is that Bisbee did copy quite a few tunes from Richardson's book, but inserted other tunes also, so that parts but not all of this book date from 1864, from Mount's lifetime. The version of variations on "Money Musk" ([4]) does look like Mount and friends' variations on that tune in its general character and is marked "F. R." by Bisbee, so likely is in fact from Richardson's playing, and from 1864. According to Paul F. Wells, Richardson, a violin maker, was Bisbee's fiddle teacher (2015, 9–10).

BIBLIOGRAPHY

American Vernacular Music Manuscripts ca. 1730–1910. Digital Collections from the American Antiquarian Society and the Center for Popular Music. http://popmusic.mtsu.edu/manuscriptmusic/.

Anderson, William F., Jr., Abstractor and Indexer. 1999. *1850 Census of Prince Edward County, Virginia, Including Slave Schedules*. Farmville, VA: Southside Historical Press.

Angle, Joe. 1975. "Fiddlers: A Texas Tradition." In *Some Still Do: Essays on Texas Customs*, edited by Francis Edward Abernethy, 85–73. Publications of the Texas Folklore Society Number XXXIX. Austin: Encino Press.

Askwith, Leslie. 2017. *Thunderstruck Fiddle: The Remarkable True Story of Charles Morris Cobb and His Hill Farm Community in 1850s Vermont*. N.p.: Blurb (a self-publishing company).

Barlow, Milton. 18??. "Manuscript Music B Belonging to Milton Barlow." On deposit at The Center for Popular Music, Middle Tennessee State University. Accessed through website *American Vernacular Music Manuscripts ca. 1730–1910*.

Bayard, Samuel P. 1950. "Prolegomena to a Study of the Principal Melodic Families of British-American Folk Song." *Journal of American Folklore* 63: 1–44.

Bayard, Samuel P. 1982. *Dance to the Fiddle, March to the Fife: Instrumental Folk Tunes in Pennsylvania*. Urbana. University of Illinois Press.

Bisbee, Clinton W. ca. 1904. "Hornpipes." Manuscript on Deposit at the Center for Popular Music, Middle Tennessee State University. Available through website *American Vernacular Music Manuscripts ca. 1730–1910*.

Bronson, Bertrand. 1959. *The Traditional Tunes of the Child Ballads, Vol. 4*. Princeton, NJ: Princeton University Press.

Buckley, J[ames] and Sons. 1855. *Buckley's Violin Tunes; A Collection of Beautiful Marches, Waltzes, Quadrilles, Polkas, Schottisches, Operatic Melodies, Hornpipes, Reels, Jigs, etc. etc. and Many Other Melodies Never Before Published, Including Buckley's Celebrated Imitations of the Farm-Yard, and Briggs Power of Music. The Whole Selected, Arranged and Composed for the Violin by J. Buckley and & Sons of Buckley's Serenaders*. New York: Firth, Pond, & Co.

Burkhalter, Lois Wood. 1965. *Gideon Lincecum 1793–1874: A Biography*. Austin: University of Texas Press.

Burney, Charles. 1957. *A General History of Music from the Earliest Ages to the Present Period (1789)*. New York: Dover. 2-vol. reprint of 4-vol. original.

Case, Mose. [n.d.]. "Arkansas Traveller." Buffalo, NY: J. R. Blodgett.

Cauthen, Joyce. 2001. *With Fiddle and Well-Rosined Bow: Old Time Fiddling in Alabama*. Tuscaloosa: University of Alabama Press.

Chaff, Gumbo [pseudonym of Elias Howe]. 1848. *The Ethiopian Violin Instructor, Containing Full and Complete Instruction with All the Popular Negro Melodies of the Day, Including Those of the Christy Minstrels. By Gumbo Chaff, A.M. A., Author of the Ethiopian Glee Book, Ethiopian Accordeon Instructor, Ethiopian Flute Instructor, &c, &c.* Boston: Elias Howe.

Clark, William H. (of Hudson, New York). [1820–30?]. "Manuscript Music Book Belonging to William H. Clark." On deposit at the Center for Popular Music, Middle Tennessee State University. Accessed through website *American Vernacular Music Manuscripts ca. 1730–1910.*

Cleaveland, Nehemiah. 1882. *History of Bowdoin College, with Biographical Sketches of its Graduates.* Boston: James Ripley Osgood & Co.

Cobb, Charles Morris. "Diaries, 1850–1862." Manuscript (thirteen very small bound books), MSA Box 480, Leahy Library, Vermont Historical Society.

Cobb, Charles Morris. "Diaries, 1850–1862." As copied by Michael McKernan, with an index by Kathryn D. Wending. Typed transcript, on deposit at Leahy Library, Vermont Historical Society.

Cobb, Charles Morris. *Song-Verses, Legends, Ballads and Other Sketches in Rhyme.* n.p. 190?

Cobb, Charles Morris. *The Universal Musician.* Music Manuscript, written in Woodstock, Vermont, in the 1840s through perhaps 1870s. On deposit as MS 780.8, C633, Leahy Library, Vermont Historical Society.

Cockrell, Dale. 1997. *Demons of Disorder: Early Blackface Minstrels and Their World.* Cambridge: Cambridge University Press.

Coes, George H. 1876. *Coes Album of Jigs and Reels. Something New for Professional and Amateur Violinists, Leaders of Orchestras, Quadrille Bands, and Clog, Reel, and Jig Dancers; Consisting of a Grand Collection of Entirely New and Original Clog-Hornpipes, Reels, Jigs, Scotch Reels, Irish Reels and Jigs, Waltzes, Walk-Arounds, Etc., for the Violin.* New York: T. B. Harms & Co.

Cohen, Norman. 1981. *Long Steel Rail: The Railroad in American Folksong.* Urbana: University of Illinois Press.

The Cradle of Harmony: William Sidney Mount's Violin and Fiddle Music. 1976. Folkways Records FTS 32379 (with violinist Gilbert Ross; notes by Albert Frankenstein).

Cumming, William. 1847. "The Arkansas Traveller and Rackinsac Waltz." New York: W. C. Peters.

Deisler, Cheri Wolfe. 1984. "Two Generations in the Texas Fiddling Tradition: An Analysis of Interlocking Symbolic Systems, 1900–1940." MA thesis (folklore), University of Texas, Austin.

Dickinson, Silas. 180-?. Music Manuscript entitled *Silas Dickinson's Book.* On deposit at New York Public Library.

Dixon, William. [ca. 1790]. *Psalmodia Christiana. A Collection of Sacred Music in Four Parts Designed for Public Worship. Containing 200 Plain Psalm Tunes, 50 Fugues, & a Few Pieces in the Hymn Stile for the Three Great Festivals, Christmas Day, Easter Day, and Whit-Sunday.*

Dulles, Foster Rhea. [1965]. *A History of Recreation.* 2nd edition. New York: Appleton-Century-Crofts.

Ely, Melvin Patrick. 2004. *Israel on the Appomattox: A Southern Experiment in Black Freedom from the 1790s through the Civil War.* New York: Knopf.

Epstein, Dena. 1983. *Sinful Tunes and Spirituals: Black Folk Music to the Civil War.* Urbana: University of Illinois Press.

Farnham, Christie Anne. 1994. *The Education of the Southern Belle: Higher Education and Student Socialization in the Antebellum South.* New York: New York University Press.

Fischer, David Hackett, and James C. Kelly. 2000. *Bound Away: Virginia and the Westward Movement.* Charlottesville: University of Virginia Press.

Fithian, Philip Vickers. 1957. *Journal and Letters of Philip Vickers Fithian, 1773–1774: A Plantation Tutor of the Old Dominion.* Edited by Hunter Dickinson Farish. Williamsburg, VA: Colonial Williamsburg.

Ford, Ira W. 1940. *Traditional Music of America.* New York: E. P. Dutton.

Frankenstein, Alfred. 1975. *William Sidney Mount.* New York: Harry N. Abrams.

Frankenstein, Alfred. 1976. Notes to *The Cradle of Harmony: William Sidney Mount's Violin and Fiddle Music.* Folkways Records FTS 32379 (with violinist Gilbert Ross).

Fuld, James J. 1971. *The Book of World-Famous Music*. New York: Crown Publishers.

Galbraith, Art. 1980. *Dixie Blossoms*. Rounder Records LP 0133.

Gay, John. 1966. *The Beggar's Opera and Companion Pieces*. Edited by C. F. Burgess. Northbrook, IL: AHM.

Goertzen, Chris. 1982. "Philander Seward's 'Musical Deposit' and the History of American Instrumental Folk Music." *Ethnomusicology* 26(1): 1–10.

Goertzen, Chris. 1995. "Mrs. Joe Person's *Popular Airs*: Early Blackface Minstrel Tunes in Oral Tradition." *Ethnomusicology* 35(1): 31–53.

Goertzen, Chris. 2008. *Southern Fiddlers and Fiddle Contests*. Jackson: University Press of Mississippi.

Goertzen, Chris. 2014. "Southern American Fiddling through the Mid-Nineteenth Century: Three Snapshots." In *Theory and Method in Historical Ethnomusicology*, edited by Jonathan McCollum and David G. Hebert, 257–77. New York: Lexington Books.

Goertzen, Chris. 2017. *George P. Knauff's Virginia Reels and the History of American Fiddling*. Jackson: University Press of Mississippi.

Goertzen, Chris, and Alan Jabbour. 1987. "George P. Knauff's *Virginia Reels* and Fiddling in the Antebellum South." *American Music* 5(2): 121–44.

Gordon, Harry. 1975. "Scottish Texans and the Highland Games." In *Some Still Do: Essays on Texas Customs*, edited by Francis Edward Abernethy, 166–73. Publications of the Texas Folklore Society Number XXXIX. Austin: Encino Press.

Gow, Nathaniel. 1809. *Fifth Collection of Strathspey Reels*. Edinburgh: Gow and Shepherd.

Gow, Niel. [1784]. *A Collection of Strathspey Reels*. Edinburgh: author.

Gow, Niel. [1788]. *A Second Collection of Strathspey Reels*. Edinburgh: Corri and Sutherland.

Gow, Niel. [1800]. *A Fourth Collection of Strathspey Reels*. London: Gow and Shepherd.

Gow, Niel, and Sons. [1799]. *Part First of the Complete Repository of Original Scots Slow Strathspeys and Dances*. Edinburgh: Rob't Purdue.

Gow, Niel, and Sons. [1802]. *Part Second of the Complete Repository of Original Scots Slow Strathspeys and Dances*. Edinburgh: Gow and Shepherd.

Hamblen, Armeanous Porter. [194-?]. A COLLECTION of violin tunes, popular during the early 1800s as played by David Russell Hamblen (1809–1893) and his son Williamson (1848–1920) arranged and copied by A[rmeanous] Porter Hamblen (1875–195-?) son of Williamson. Mixed manuscript and typescript on deposit at the Library of Congress, Music Division.

Hamblen, Armeanous Porter. 1985. *A History of the Hamblen and Allied Families* (1940). 2nd edition. J. H. Hamblen.

Hamm, Charles. 1983. *Yesterdays: Popular Song in America*. New York: Norton.

Hannings, Bud. 2006. *Forts of the United States: An Historical Dictionary, 16th Through 19th Centuries*. Jefferson, NC: McFarland.

Hawkins, Micah. 1794. Music manuscript entitled *Micah Hawkins Book*, on deposit at New York Public Library.

Hessler, M. Hunt. [1984]a. "Long Island Documentation for the 'Catching the Tune' Exhibition, The Museums at Stony Brook." Unpublished typescript.

Hessler, M. Hunt. [1984]b. "'Rusticity and Refinement': Long Island Music and Dance, 1800–1870. Prepared for the "Catching the Tune" Exhibition, The Museums at Stony Brook. Unpublished typescript.

Howe, Elias, Jr., compiler. 1843. *Instrumental Musician*. 3 vols. Boston: Howe.

Howe, Elias, Jr., compiler. 1844. *First Part of the Musician's Companion: Containing 18 Setts of Cotillions Arranged with Figures, and a Large Number of Popular Marches, Quick-Steps, Waltzes, Hornpipes, Contra Dances, Songs, &c. &c., Several of Which are in Three Parts—First Second,* and Bass for the Flute, Violin, Clarionett, Bass-Viol, &c. . . .* Boston: Howe. The *Second Part . . .* advertises *36 Setts of Cotillions.* The *Third Part . . .* has 40 sets, and is still published by Howe. All three volumes reissued 1850.

Howe, Elias, Jr., compiler. 1848. See under pseud., Gumbo Chaff.

Howe, Elias, Jr., compiler. 1851 [first printed 1843]. *Howe's School for the Violin: Containing New and Complete Instructions for the Violin, with a Large Collection of Favorite Marches, Quick-Steps, Waltzes, Hornpipes, Contra Dances, Songs, and Six Setts of Cotillions, Arranged with Figures. Containing Over 150 Pieces of Music.* Boston: Ditson.

Howe, Elias, Jr., compiler. 1851. *Self-Instructor for the Violin . . .* Boston: Ditson.

Howe, Elias, Jr., compiler. 1864. *Musician's Omnibus: Containing the Whole Camp Duty, Calls and Signals used in the Army and Navy, Forty Setts of Quadrilles (Including Waltz Polka and Schottische with Calls [ ]); and an Immense Collection of Polkas, Schottisches, Waltzes, Marches, Quicksteps, Hornpipes, Contra & Fancy Dances, Songs, &c. For the Violin, Flute, Cornet, Clarionett, &c. Containing Over 700 Pieces of Music.* Boston: Howe.

Howe, Elias, Jr., compiler. 1869. *Quadruple Musician's Omnibus, Containing 3300 Pieces . . .* Boston: Howe.

Hursh, David, and Chris Goertzen. 2009. *Good Medicine and Good Music: A Biography of Mrs. Joe Person, Patent Remedy Entrepreneur and Musician, Including the Complete Text of Her 1903 Autobiography.* Jefferson, NC: McFarland.

Johnson, James. 1790. *The Scots Musical Museum* (reprinted 1853). 3 vols. Consulted: Rpt. Hatboro, PA: Folklore Associates, 1962.

Kaplan, Elizabeth Kahn. 1999. "Ties of Family, Friendship and Music: William Sidney Mount and Shepard Smith Jones." In *William Sidney Mount: Family Friends and Ideas; Essays by Members of the William Sidney Mount Project*, edited by Elizabeth Kahn Kaplan, Robert W. Kenny, and Roger Wunderlich. Setauket, NY: Three Village Historical Society.

Knauff, George P. *Virginia Reels* (4 vol.). Baltimore: Willig,1839 and 1850?; Benteen, 1852.

Kotzwara, Frantisek. 1788. "The Battle of Prague, Sonata in F Major with [optional] accompaniments for Violin, Cello, and Drum." Boston: Graupner.

Kotzwara, Frantisek. n.d. "As Pendant O'er the Limpid Stream." New York: G[eorge] Gilfert.

Kotzwara, Frantisek. n.d. "Ah Seek to Know." New York: G[eorge] Gilfert.

Kuntz, Andrew. *The Fiddler's Companion, 1996–2009.* http://www.ibiblio.org/fiddlers/RI_RJ.htm1.

Lincecum, Dr. Gideon. 1874–75. *Personal Reminiscences of an Octogenarian.* Published serially in *The American Sportsman*; quotes used from the episode printed in the November 21, 1874, issue, 10–13.

Lincecum, Jerry Bryan, and Edward Hake Phillips, eds. 1994. *Adventures of a Frontier Naturalist: The Life and Times of Dr. Gideon Lincecum.* College Station: Texas A and M University Press.

McArthur, Arthur. [181-?]. Untitled manuscript music commonplace on deposit at the New York Public Library.

McArthur Family (of Limington, ME). n.d. "McArthur Family Papers M116." George J. Mitchell Department of Special Collections & Archives, Hawthorne-Longfellow Library, Bowdoin College.

McFarlane, Thomas. [181-?]. Untitled manuscript music commonplace on deposit at the New York Public Library.

McGlashan, Alexander. [1780]. *A Collection of Strathspey Reels.* Edinburgh: Neil Stewart.

McGlashan, Alexander. [1781]. *A Collection of Scots Measures, Hornpipes, Jigs, Allenmands, Cotillions.* Edinburgh: Neil Stewart.

Marshall, Howard Wight. 2012. *Play Me Something Quick and Devilish: Old-Time Fiddlers in Missouri.* Columbia: University of Missouri Press.

Martin, Susan F. 2011. *A Nation of Immigrants.* New York: Cambridge University Press.

Merrow, J[ames] M. (almost certainly American; precise location unknown). 1806. *Manuscript Music Book Belonging to J.M. Merrow.* On deposit at the Center for Popular Music, Middle Tennessee State University. Accessed through website *American Vernacular Music Manuscripts ca. 1730–1910.*

Moore, Thomas. 2000. *Thomas Moore's Irish Melodies [1808–1834]: The Illustrated 1846 Edition.* New York: Dover.

Mount, William Sidney. [1850s–1860s]. Manuscript music collection, on deposit at the Long Island Museum of American Art, History and Carriages.

Pichierri, Louis. 1960. *Music in New Hampshire, 1623–1800.* New York: Columbia University Press.

Rice, Edw. LeRoy. 1911. *Monarchs of Minstrelsy, from "Daddy" Rice to Date.* New York: Kenny Publishing Co.

Riggs, Robert, ed. 2016. *The Violin.* Rochester, NY: University of Rochester Press.

Riley, Edward. Volumes from 1814, 1817, 1820, and 1827. *Riley's Flute Melodies.* 4 vols. New York: Riley.

Ring, Elizabeth. 1991. *The McArthurs of Limington, Maine 1783–1917: The Family in America a Century Ago.* Maine: Kennebec River Publishing.

Ritchie, Fiona, and Doug Orr. 2014. *Wayfaring Strangers: The Musical Voyage from Scotland and Ulster to Appalachia.* Chapel Hill: University of North Carolina Press.

Russell, Henry. Lyrics by Eliza Cook. 1861. "I'm Afloat, I'm Afloat." Boston: Geo. P. Reed.

Sacks, Howard. 2015. Personal communication August 2.

Sacks, Howard, and Judith Rose Sacks. 1993. *Way Up North in Dixie: A Black Family's Claim to the Confederate Anthem.* Washington, DC: Smithsonian Institution Press.

Sanders, J. Olcutt. 1941. "Honor the Fiddler!" In *Texian Stomping Grounds*, edited by J. Frank Dobie and Harry H. Ransom, 78–90. Texas Folklore Society Publication Number XVII. Austin: Texas Folklore Society.

Seward, Philander. [1807 or soon thereafter]. *Philander Seward's "Musical Deposit."* Manuscript music commonplace book largely for unspecified treble instrument (probably violin) compiled in Fishkill, New York, on deposit in the Music Library of the University of Illinois.

Shatto, Janice. 1986. "Early Settlement." In *Colorado County Chronicles: From the Beginning to 1923*, compiled by Colorado County Historical Commission. 2 vols. Austin: Nortex Press. 30–57.

Shepard, William. 1940. "Buckingham Female Collegiate Institute." *The William and Mary Quarterly. Second Series* 20/2 (Apr.): 167–93. Concluded in Vol. 20/3 (July): 345–66.

Slobin, Mark, James Kimball, Katherine K. Preston, and Deane Root, eds. 2011. *Emily's Songbook: Music in 1850s Albany.* Middleton, WI: A-R Editions.

Smith, Christopher J. 2013. *The Creolization of American Culture: William Sidney Mount and the Roots of Blackface Minstrelsy.* Urbana: University of Illinois Press.

Smith, Jeff. 2009. *The Presidents We Imagine: Two Centuries of White House Fictions on the Page, on the Stage, Onscreen, and Online.* Madison: University of Wisconsin Press.

Sonneck, Oscar. 1911, July 1. "Ciampi's 'Bertoldo, Bertoldino, e Cacasenno' and Favart's 'Ninette ála Cour,' a Contribution to the History of Pasticcio." *Sammelbände der Internationalen Musikgesellschaft* 12(4): 525–64.

Sonneck, Oscar G. 1916. "Benjamin Franklin's Musical Side." *Suum Cuique: Essays in Music.* New York: Schirmer. 59–84.

Sonneck, Oscar, and William Treat Upton. 1945. *A Bibliography of Early American Music.* Washington, DC: Library of Congress. Rpt. Da Capo, 1964.

Spaeth, Sigmund. 1948. *A History of Popular Music in America.* New York: Random House.

Stoutamire, Albert. 1972. *Music of the Old South: Colony to Confederacy*. Madison, WI: Fairleigh Dickinson University Press.

Twain, Mark. 1917. *Life on the Mississippi* (1874). New York: P. F. Collier & Son Company.

Valentine, Harriet G. 1981. *The Window to the Street: A Mid-Nineteenth-Century View of Cold Spring Harbor, New York, Based on the Diary of Helen Rogers*. New York: Exposition Press.

Waldon, Carolynn Knauff. [n.d.]. "Timeline of George P. Knauff's Life." Unpublished typescript.

Walls, Peter. 2016. "The Violin in Italy During the Baroque Period." In *The Violin*, edited by Robert Riggs, 63–94. Rochester, NY: University of Rochester Press.

Watkins, Samuel. 1815. Unpublished manuscript music commonplace book, on deposit at the University of Colorado Library.

Wells, Paul F. 1978. "New England Traditional Fiddling." Liner Notes to *New England Traditional Fiddling: An Anthology of Recordings 1926–1975*. One LP. Los Angeles: John Edwards Memorial Foundation JEMF-105.

Wells, Paul F. 2003a. "Fiddling as an Avenue of Black-White Interchange." *Black Music Research Review* 23 (1–2): 135–47.

Wells, Paul F. 2003b. "The Music of The Poor Soldier." In *Irish Drama of the Seventeenth and Eighteenth Centuries, II*, edited by Christopher Wheatly and Kevin Donovan, 472–531. Bristol, UK: Thoemmes Press and Edition Synapse.

Wells, Paul F. 2015. "Wicked Good Fiddling: Two Tune Manuscripts from Nineteenth-Century Maine." Paper read at Society for American Music, 41st Annual Conference.

West, Sue Roberson. 1990. *Buckingham Female Collegiate Institute: First Chartered College for Women in Virginia, 1837–1843; 1848–1863*. Charlotte, NC: Delmar Printing.

Wheatly, Christopher, and Kevin Donovan, eds. 2003. *Irish Drama of the Seventeenth and Eighteenth Centuries, II*. Bristol, UK: Thoemmes Press and Edition Synapse.

Williams, Vivian, ed. 2008. *The Peter Beemer Manuscript: Dance Music Collected in the Gold Mining Camp of Warren's Diggins, Idaho in the 1860's*. Seattle, WA: Voyager Publications.

Winans, Robert. 1990. "Black Instrumental Music Traditions in the Ex-Slave Narratives." *Black Music Research Journal* 10(1): 43–53.

Winner, Septimus. 1853. *Winner's Collection of Music for the Violin, Consisting of Marches, Waltzes, Polkas, Cotillions, Hornpipes, Reels, Jigs, Fancy Dances, Mazourkas, Schottisches, Polka Quadrilles, and all other Fashionable Airs, Arranged in an Easy Manner, in the First Position* (1853). Philadelphia: Charles H. Davis, and Philadelphia: Winner & Shuster.

Winner, Septimus (under the pseudonym of Alice Hawthorne), lyrics, and Richard Milburn, music. 1855. "Listen to the Mockingbird, Sentimental Ethiopian Ballad." Philadelphia: Winner & Shuster.

Wolfe, Richard J. 1964. *Secular Music in America: 1801–1825*. 3 vols. New York: New York Public Library.

INDEX

Page numbers in **bold** indicate that the melodies cited appear on those pages, either transcribed or photographed.

"Adam and Eve," 7
"Adeste Fideles," 16, **17**
Adkins, Phebe L., 22
"Alpha" (hymn), 7, 9
"America Quadrille," 102
American Vernacular Music Manuscripts ca. 1730–1910, 18, 33
"Andante, the Surprise, by Haydn," 8
"Anna Polka," **120**
"Annie Laurie Sett," 102–3
"Anthem," 7
"Appollo Turn'd Shepherd," 8
"Arkansas Traveller," 92, 94–95, **126–27**, 151, 171
"Arlington" (hymn), 7
Arne, Dr., 7
"Arundel" (hymn), 7
"Auld Robin Gray," 8
"Aurora Waltz" (Joseph Labitsky), **81**, 83, 91, **119**
"Austria Grand Imperial March," 8
"Austrian Waltz by Haydn," 8
"Away with Melancholy," 24, 32–33, **45**

"Bailey's Waltz," 91, **117**
Ballad operas, 10, 32
"Baltimore," 7
"Bangor Castle," 7
banjo, 150
"Barbara Allen," 32
Barnum's Museum and Menagerie, 73
"Basses Comic Tune," 25, **58**
Battle of Prague, The (Franticek Kotzwara), 75, 98, 171
Bayard, Samuel, 88

"Beaus of Albany," 90, **111**
Beemer, Peter, 92
Beethoven, Ludwig van, 8
"Beethoven Sett," 99–102, **130–31**
"Beggar Sett," 173, 177–78, 180, 183
"Beggar's Cotillion" (Goertzen), **182**
Beggars Opera, The (John Gay and Christopher Pepusch), 178, 180, 182–83
"Belisle's March," 24, 30, **35**
"Belknap's March," 7
"Belles of America," 102
"Bells [Belles?] of New York," 8
"Ben Bolt Sett," 102–3
Benners, Alfred, 171
Benteen, F. D., 142–47
Bertold (Vincenzo Ciampi), 77
"Big Tennessee," 191, 195, **196**, 212
"Billy in the Low Grounds," **164**, 184, 190, 213
"Billy in the Woods," **165**
binder's volumes of sheet music, 61–62
Bisbee, Clinton W., 217
"Black Sloven," 24, **44**
"Black Toney's Juber," 94, **125**
"Black Walnut," 92, **123**
blackface minstrelsy, 62–63, 73, 93–97, 125, 141–43, 149–54
"Blue Bells of Scotland," 7
Blue Beard (Michael Kelly), 32
"Blue Bird, The," 25, **58**
"Blue Bonnets Over the Border," **211**, 213
"Blue-Eyed Mary," 8
"Boatman Dance," 92, 149, 151–52
"Bob Ridley Quadrille," 102–3
"Bobtail Horse," 94

Bolick, Harry, vii
"Bonaparte Crossing the Rhine," **205**
"Bonaparte's Grand March," 7
"Bonaparte's March," 25, **49**, **205**
"Bonaparte's Retreat," **206**
Bond, Alonzo, 101–3, 217
"Bond's Grand March," 102
Bondurant, Ann S. C., 140
"Bonny Jean of Aberdeen," 7
"Book Divine," 189
Bousquet, Narcisse, 102–3
"Bostonian, The," 102
Bowdoin College, 2–4, 16
Bowie, Miriam, 171
"Boyne Waters," 8, 24, 32, **39**
"Braes of Auchtertyre," 90, 99, **111**, 184, 190, 213
"Braes of Tullymet, The," **115**
Brainard, Catherine, 22
"Bridgewater" (hymn), 7
Buckingham Female Collegiate Institute, 141–42, 150
Buckley, James, 98
"Buffalo Gals," 153
Burney, Charles, 77
Burns, Robert, 60, 178
"Butterfly Polka," 102

"Cabbage Duett," 92, **124**
cabinet organ, 183
"Cachuca, The, Waltz," 91
"Cackling Hen," 93, **124**
"Caledonia," 25, 60 (text)
"Caledonian March," 24, **42**
"Callahan," **198**
"Camp-Meeting Hornpipe," **107**
"Campbells Are Coming, The," **207**, 213
"Camptown Races," 94
Cape Elizabeth, Maine, 3
"Carolyn Bowen's Music Book," 18
Cartwright, Hanly A., 197–98
Case, Mose, 95
"Catching the Tune" conference, 104
"Cathleen McChree," 7
Cauthen, Joyce, 171
Chadwell, Captain David, 212
"Chadwell's Station," 195, **197**, 212
Chaff, Gumbo (Elias Howe), 93

"Chargoggagoagomanchagogg," 8
"Chester Castle," 8
child ballads, 10, 32
"Chorus Jigg," 8, 102
"Christmas" (hymn), 7
Ciampi, Vincenzo, 76
circus, 150
Clapp, Anthony Hannibal, 77, 93–94, 149
"Clara Polka Sett," 102
"Clare de Kitchen," 150
"Clark manuscript," 13–14
Cleaveland, Nehemiah, 3
Cobb, Charles Morris, x, 61–74, 77–78, 84–92, 94–95, 98–112, 116–18, 121–24, 126, 130–31, 134–35, 139, 149, 175, 177, 185, 188, 193, 212–14, 217; appearance of head, 66; family belongings, 67–69; learning process, 69; musical training, 70; prose, 74; "The Universal Musician," x, 69, 71–72 (photographs)
Cobb, Gains P., 64, 66, 70, 84, 217
Cobb, Lucia, 66
Cockrell, Dale, 149
"Cold Rain," **210**
"College Hornpipe," 8, 19, 80, 102
"Colonel Crockett," **163**, **164** (not same tune)
"Come, All Ye Faithful," 16, **17**
"Come Fill the Glass," 77
"Comin' Through the Rye," 102
commonplace books, x, 1
Complete Repository (Niel Gow), 11, 13
Cook, T. J., 95, 126
"Coral Schottisch," 102
cornet, 73
cotillions, 8, 98–99, 130, 171, 173, 177–78; forms, 100–101
"Cotton-Eyed Joe," **204**
"Courland Quadrille by Haydn," 8
Crow Quadrilles, The, 150
"Cuckoo, The," 92, 95–96, 98, **122**, **128** (not same tune), 154, **200**
"Culver Black Horse Troop," 195
Cumming, William, 94
Curry, David Hamblen, 188

"Danish Waltz," 8
Darby's Return, 178

"Das klinget so herrlich" (Mozart), 32
"Democratic Rage [Hornpipe]," 102
"Den Ant de las Silas," 8
"Devil's Dream, The," 24, 27, **43**
"Dexter's Sett," 102
"Diamond Schottisch," 102
Dickinson, Silas, 23, 33, 76
"Dirge by Herrick," 7
"Dixie," 152
Dixon, William, 16
Dixon's College, 7
"Doct. Swazey's Fancy," 8
"Dorothy Draggletail," **116**
"Dorsetshire March," 7
"Dream of Love," 102
"Drink to Me Only with Thine Eyes," 24, **45**
"Drummer Boy of Waterloo," **206**
"Duett in Rosina," 24, 32, **47**
"Duetto by Olmstead," 7
"Duke of Gordon's Fancy, The," **82**, 83, 91, **114**
"Duke of Gordon's Rant, The," 213
"Duke of Holstein's March," 24, **44**
"Duke of York's Cotillion," 24, **46**
"Duke of York's March," 24, 30, **35**, **46**
"Durang's Hornpipe," 4, 90
Dutchess County Historical Society, vii
Duzzek, Jan Ladislav, 32
"Dying Coon, The," 171

Eaton, E. K., 101–2
Ely, Melvin, 150
"Emerald Schottische," 91, **121**
"Emily's Book," 62
Emmett, Daniel Decatur, 152
"Ere Around the Huge Oak," 8
"Ernani Quadrille," 102
"Ethiopian Violin Instructor" (Gumbo Chaff, i. e., Elias Howe), 93
"Exile of Erin," 7

"Fair Margaret," 32
"Fancy by Ignace Pleyel," 8
"Fantasia Sett," 102
"Farmer's Joy," 25, **52**, 92, **124**
"Favorite March in Blue Beard," 32, **55**
Felton, William, 77
"Felton's Gavotte," 77, **78–79**

female seminary, 141
"Fest March," 102, 217
"Festival March," 87
"Few Happy Matches," 7
fiddle: contests, 183, 215; construction and maintenance, 83–84, 188; prices, 67; tone, 84, 188
fiddle tunes, ix-x; "crooked," 190–93, 210; didactic music, 5–7, 9, 26, 63; from Great Britain, x, 1; from Ireland, 11, 14; from Scotland, 11, 14, 151, 183–84, 207, 213–14; pictorial, 95–98, 154, 171, 200; personal repertoires, 5, 187; Scots-Irish, 151, 213
fiddlers: music literacy, ix-x, 29–30, 70, 177, 187, 189, 215; musical taste, x, 1–2; transcribing melodies, x-xi, 184
fiddling: African American, 73, 85, 93, 139, 149–51, 154, 171–72, 175, 215; and emotions, 85; in ensembles, 14, 23–24, 26, 188; on the frontier, x; patriotism, 1; performance technique, ix, 6, 9, 94, 151, 191; playing in positions, x, 18, 20, 63, 80, 212, 215; prose testimony concerning, xi; scordatura (cross-tuning), 85, 92, 123, 195; variations, 153, 178, 206, 217; versus violin, ix, 9
fife, 80, 174
"Firemen's Sett," 102
"First Monday in May," 25, **49**
"Fisher's Hornpipe," 8, 24, 27, **38**, 90, 98, 102
Fishkill, New York, 19, 22
"Flight of Fancy," **116**
"Flowers of Edinburgh," 24, 27, **28**, 29, **38**, 146–47, 191, **192**, 193, **207**, 212–13
flute, 2, 4, 18, 20, 23, 26, 62, 66, 75, 174
"Flying Indian," 153, **170**
"Foots Minuet," 8
"For England When with Favoring Gale," 7
Ford, Ira, 91, 94
"Forked Deer," 146, **157**, 171, **208** ("Forked Ear")
Foster, Stephen F., 94
"Four Times Over," 8, 19
"Fox Chase," 171
"Fox Hunt, The," **167**
Frank Melville Junior Memorial Library, State University of New York at Stony Brook, vii
"French Air," 7–8
"French Dance," 24, **35**

"French Muse," 92, **123**
"French Tune," 8
"Fresh and Strong," 7
Fryeburg Academy, 2–3

Galbraith, Art, 193
"Galley Slave, The," 7
"Gallopade," 104, **136–37**
gapped modes, 10
"Garland of Love, The," 24, 32–33, **41**
"Garry Owen," 29–30
"Gaston," **168**
Gay, John, 178
"General Green's March," 24, 30, **43**
"General Harrison's March," 173, 177
"General McDonald's March," 8
"George Booker," 147, **163**, 213
George J. Mitchell Department of Special Collections and Archives, Hawthorne-Melville Library, Bowdoin College, vii
German immigrants to US, 1
Gilfert, George, 75
Gillaspy, John Marshall, 189–91, 195–96, 198
Gillaspy, Martha Evaline, 186
"Girl I Left Behind Me," 102, **209**
"Glasgow Lasses," 7
"Go to the D____ and Shake Yourself," 24, **45**
"God Save America," 7
"Godfrey's Death March," **122**
Gow, Nathaniel "Niel", 11, 13–14, 91, 104, 148, 179, 213
"Grand March by Alonzo Bond," 102
"Grand March from Enchanted Beauty," 102
"Grand March in Pizzaro," 8
"Grande Entré," 8
Green, Steve, vii, 184–85
"Greensleeves," **182**, 183
"Green's March," 25, **56**
Grout, John William, 88–89
"Grovenor's March," 7
"Gumbo Chaff," 150

Hagen, H. L., 123
"Hail Columbia," 30, 173, 175, 177
Hamblen, Armeanous Porter, xi, 140, 184–213, 215
Hamblen, David, xi, 140, 184–87, 189–97, 199, 201–13

Hamblen family, 185
Hamblen, George, 185
Hamblen, Job, 185–86
Hamblen, John Franklin, 186
Hamblen, John Mullins, 185–86
Hamblen, John W., 185
Hamblen, Reverend William, 189, 195
Hamblen, Williamson, 184–90, 194, 198–200, 202–3, 205–6, 208–11
Hanby, Benjamin, 89
Handel, George Frederick, 77
"Handel's Clarionet," 7
Hankins, Jonathan, 212
"Hankins Raid," **202**
"Hark Away," 8, 19
"Harlington," 8
Harrison, Garry, 184
"Harrison's Grand March," **176**, 177
Hartwell, Mr., 70
Harvey, James, 18
"Haste to the Wedding," **208**
"Haunted Tavern," 8
Hawkins, Micah, 75–77, 83
"Haymakers, The," 24, **37**
Haydn, 8
"Health to all Good Lasses," 7
Heard, William Jones Eliot, 172, 175
"Hen's March," 93, **124**
"Hero, The," **161**
Herrick, [Robert], 7
Hessler, M. Hunt, 104
Hewitt, John Hill, 150
"Heyden's [Haydn's?] March," 8
"High Pretty Martin Toploc," 8
"High Road to Linton," 90, 111
"Highland Reel," 8, 25, **51**, 102
"Hob or Nob," 7
"Holy" (hymn), 7
"Honey Moon, The," 25, **51**
"Horse Races," 7
"Hortesia Quadrille," 102
"House Carpenter," 10
"How Imperfect is Expression," 24, 32, **44**
Howe, Elias, Jr., 62, 75, 85–87, 95, 148, 151, 171, 176–77
Howe's School for the Violin (Elias Howe), 62, 80, 87

"Hull's Victory," 90, 102, **108–9**
"Humours of Boston," 8
"Humours of Glenn [or Glynn]," 7, 25, **56**
Huntington Brass Band, 93
"Hurra, or the Swiss Battle Song," 8
hymns, 5, 9, 16–18, 26; arranging of, 18

"In the Cars on the Long Island Railroad," 95–96, 98, **129**, 154
"In the Dead of the Night," **23**, 25, 32–33, **47**
"Indian Ate the Woodchuck," **208**
"Indian Philosopher, The," 8, 24, **37**
"Indian Whoop," 147, 153–54, **169**
"Instructions for the Violin" (photograph of handwritten), 9
Instrumental Musician (Elias Howe), 63
"Irish," 7
Irish Melodies (Thomas Moore), 10
"Irish Washerwoman, The," 8, 25, 27, **51**
"Irish Wedding," 25, **50**
"Island," **162**
"Isle of Saint Helena," **207**, 213

"Jackson's Bottle of Claret," 7
"James, River Reel," **167**
Janissary music, 100–101
Jawbone Band, 93
"Jay Bird," **209**
"Jefferson and Liberty," 24, 32, **43**
"Jenny Lind Polka," 102
"Jenny Nettles," 8
"Jim Brown," 150
Johnson, James, 178–79
"Jolly Blacksmith (She Wouldn't Come At All)," **211**
Jones, Shepard Smith, 77, 83, 90
"Jones' Favorite," 90, **108**
"Jordan Medley Sett," 102
"Juniper Hall," **165**
"Justice" (hymn), 7

"Katherine Ogre," 8
"Katies Rambles," 25, **56**
Kelly, Michael, 32
"Kendalls Hornpipe," 102
"Killie Krankie," 143, 146–47, **155** (renaming of "Money Musk"), 173–75, 178, **179**, 184, 213

"King of Prussia's March," 7
"Kiss, The," 7
"Kitty of Coleraine," 116
Knabe, William, 141
Knauff, Ann, 141
Knauff, George P., xi, 139–70, 212, 215
"Knock at the Door Till the Cook Comes In," **210**
Knowlton, H., 8
Kotzwara, Franticek, 75, 171
Kuntz, Andy, vii

"La Belle Catherine," 8
"La Fete de Loups," 102
"La Joya Arroyonese," 102
Labitsky, Joseph, 81, 83, 91, 103, 118–19
"Ladies Excuse," 25, **54**
"Lady of the Lake," 146, **166**
"Lady Walpole's Reel," 102
"Lango Lee," 8, 18, **20, 21**
"Lara O'Grath," 102
"Lass of Patie's Mill, The," **182**
"Le Chasse Infernale," 102
"Le Fille de Marbre," 102
"Le Patricien Quadrille," 102
"Le Printemps Quadrille," 102
"Le Salon des Delices," 102
Leahy Library, Vermont Historical Society, vii
"Leander," 7
"Leather Britches," 90, 104, 143, 184
"Lesson by Morelli [or Murillo]," 7, 24, 26, 30, **31, 36**, 87
Lester S. Levy Sheet Music Collection, 11
Library of Congress, Music Division, vii, xi, 11, 27, 75, 184
"Life Let Us Cherish," 7, 24, 32–33, **40**, 92
Life on the Mississippi, 152
Limerick Academy, 3
Limington, Maine, 2–3
"Limington March," 8
Lincecum, Gideon, xi, 86, 139–40, 171–84, 214–15
Lincecum, Jerry, 171
"Listen to the Mockingbird," 98
"Litchfield March," 7
"Little Musgrave," 32
Lock, Charles Caswell, 188

"Lockwell," **165**
"Logan Water," 8, **20, 21**, 92, **122**
Long Island Museum of American Art, History, and Carriages, vii, 80
"Long Time Ago," 150
"Lord Barnett's March," 7
"Lord McDonald's Reel," 8, 19, 90, 104, **112**, **137**, 143, 184
"Lord Nelson's Hornpipe," 24, **42**
"Lost Indian," **197**
"Love from the Heart," 146, **169** (i. e., "Mississippi Sawyer")
"Love in the Village," 146, **158**
"Low Down in the Broom," 7
"Lucrezia Borgia [Waltz]," 102
Lull, Leverett, 70

"Mackintosh's March," 87, **105**
"Madam Parisott's Hornpipe," 213
Magic Flute (Mozart), 32
"Major Minor," 7, 25–26, **57**
"March in Bellini's Grand Opera of La Norma," 87–88, 92, **105**
"March in the Battle of Prague," 25, **48**
"March in the Blue Beard," 7, 25, 32
marches, 5, 14–16, 30, 63, 86–87; forms, 87; in operas, 86; within dances, 14
"Margaretta Polka," 102
"Marquis of Huntley's Farewell," 147, 213. See "Duke of Gordon's Fancy"
"Marquis of Pombal's March," 8
"Mary's Dream," 7
"Masonic Air," 7
"Masonic Hymn," 7
masonry, 3, 10
"Mason's Daughter, The," 7, 9–10
"Massachusetts March," 7
Matthewson, Nelson, 77–80, 82, 91, 94, 99–101, 107, 114, 133–34, 215
"Mazurka," **121**
McArthur, Arthur, 2–22, 26–27, 33, 61, 70, 75, 139, 174–75, 177, 180, 213, 215; as fiddler, 4; as flutist, 4
McArthur, Arthur, Jr., 4
McArthur, Catherine, 4–5
McArthur, John, 2–3, 10–11
McArthur, Mary, 4

McArthur, Mary Miller, 2
McArthur, Sarah Miltimore, 3
McArthur, William, 4
"McDaniel's Reel," 90, **112**
"McDonald's Reel," 8
McKissick, Emily Esperanza, 62
Mead, Florence Amanda, 186
medicine shows, 153
Meditations and Contemplations (James Harvey), 18
"Medley Sett," 102
"Megan Oh! Oh Megan Ee," 7
"Meig's March," 25, **50**
melodeon, 66–67
Merrow manuscript, 13–14, 21, 23, 33
Merrow, James. M., 14, 23, 33
"Midnight Hours," 25, **53**
"Midnight Serenade," 153, **170** (a version of "Buffalo Gals")
Military service, 3–4
Miltimore, Rev. William, 3
Miltimore, Sarah Prince, 3
"Mill, the Mill O, The," 32
"Minerva [Polka Quadrille]," 101–2
"Minuetto," 8
"Miss Brown's Reel," 143
"Miss Clark's Hornpipe," **166**
"Miss Johnson of Houston Hill," 104, **137**
"Miss Johnston's," 104
"Mississippi Sawyer," 146, **157** (not usual tune)
"Mockingbird," **200**
modes, 11, 14, 92, 122, 190, 198–99, 201; gapped, 10–11
"Money in Both Pockets," 8
"Money Musk," 8, 24, 27, **43**, 90, 102, **113**, 143, 146–47, 213
Moore, Thomas, 10
"Morepang," 8
"Motion of the Boat," **96**, 97
Mount, Robert Nelson, 75, 77–80, 84–85, 92, 95, 99
Mount, William Sidney, x, 61, 63–64, 74–100, 104–8, 111–15, 117, 119–21, 123, 125–29, 131–34, 136–37, 139, 149, 152, 154, 175, 179, 188, 193, 212–15; "Cradle of Harmony," 83–84, 86, 188
Mount Holyoke Academy, 4

"Mountain Echoes Quadrille," 102
"Mountain Hornpipe," 92, **205**
Mozart, Wolfgang Amadeus, 8, 32
"Mozart's Favorite Waltz," 8
"Mrs. McLeod's Reel," **82**, 147, **148**, **156**
"Mrs. Wright of Salons [Laton] Strathspey," 115
"Mulberry Tree," 8
Music and Performing Arts Library, University of Illinois, vii
music commonplace books, x, 1–19, 61–63, 75–76, 214, 217
Musician's Companion, The (Elias Howe), 63, 64 (photograph), 67, 75–76, 87–88, 98, 148, 176–77, 192–93, 214
Musician's Omnibus (Elias Howe), 75–76, 88, 97, 143
"My Long Tail Blue," 150

"Nae Luck About the House," 7
Nägeli, Hans Georg, 32
"Nancy Anderson," **170**
"Natchez on [under] the Hill," 146, **155**, 212
Native Americans, 153, 172, 174–75, 212; music, 175
"Negro jigs," 63
"Nelly Gray," 89, **106**
"Nelson's Victory," 25, **52**
"New Haven Green," 25, 29, **48**
"New Jersey," 24, **44**
"New Music from C. M. Cobb" (cotillion ingredients), **134–35**
"New Orleans Waltz," 91, **119**
New York Public Library at Lincoln Center, vii, 2, 27
"Newell" (hymn), 7
"Nightengale by Haydn, The," 8
"Nong Tong Paw," 8
nostalgia, 11, 89, 149
notation, 10, 14

"O Dear Mama," 7
"Oh, Dear, What Can the Matter Be," 25, **54**
"Oh, Say, Simple Maid," 25, 59 (text)
"Oh Susanna," 92, 94, **126** ("Old Sussanna . . .")
"Oh Where Did You Come From," **163**
"Ohio River," 149, 151, 153–54, **169**
O'Keefe, John, 32

"Old Beethoven Sett," 102
"Old Dominion Reel," **167**
"Old Molly Hare," 154
"Old Opera Sett," 102
"Old Virginia," 146, 149, **159**, 212–13
"Old Zip Coon," 32, 102, 150, 212–13
"One, Two, and Begin," 7, 25, **52**
"Opera Sett," 102
oral tradition: evidence found in written tradition, ix-x; interaction with popular music, 10, 27, 32, 151; marketable, 146; variation in, 27, 29, 32
"Orange Blossom Special," 98
"Original Sett of Killie Krankie." *See* "Killie Krankie"
"Oscar's Ghost," 7
"Over [or O'er] the Hills and Far Away," 8, **115**, **180**, **181**, 183
"Owen," 7
"Oxford Camp," 7

"Paddy O'Rafferty," 8
"Pantheon Cotillion," 8
patent medicine trade, 153
"Pauvre Madelon," 7
"Pennsylvania Sett," 102
"People's Quadrille," 102
"Pepperell March," 7
Pepusch, Christopher, 178
"Perthshire Hunt," 213
"Peter Francisco," 147, **161**
"Petersburg Ladies," **160**
Pfeiffer, A., 80
Pfeiffer, Fred, 80
Pfeiffer, S. L., 80–81, 83, 91, 95, 103, 108, 111, 119, 126, 139, 154, 215
"Philadelphia March," 24, 30, **40**
"Philander Seward's Musical Deposit," 2, 19, 22–26, 34–60
Pleyel, Ignace, 7–8
"Pleyel's Hymn," 7
Plimpton, J., 7–8
"Polka Redowa," 102
"Polka Sett," 102
Poor Soldier, The (William Shield and John O'Keefe), 10–11, 32, 178
"Pop Goes the Weasel," 102, **136**

"Port Gordon," 24, **39**
"Portland Fancy," 102
"Portugal" (hymn), 7, 9, 18
"Portuguese Hymn," 7, 16, **17**, 18
"Possum Hunt," 92, **123**
"Possum Up a Gum Tree," 75, 92
"Pray, Fair One, Be Kind," **182**
"Prelude in G Major," 25–26, **51**
Preót, Arnaud, 142
"President's March," 24, 25, 30, **36**, **55**, 177
"Pride of America," **210**
"Primrose Hill," 24, **38**
"Prince Eugene's March," 7
Pritchett, Jim, 171
Psalmodia Christiana (William Dixon), 16
Pushee, Abram, 70, 72–73, 84, 90, 107, 111, 188, 214
"Pushee's Hornpipe," 90, **107**, 108

quadrilles, 91–92, 98–99, 171, 217; polka quadrille, 101; waltz quadrille, 101
"Quarrel and Reconciliation," **116**
"Queen of France," 190, **206**, 213
"Quibilano," 7
"Quick Step [by] Haydn," 8
"Quito S. M." (hymn), 18

"Rahlau's Polonaise," **121**
"Rainbow Schottische," 91, **121**
Rawsom, R. W., 110
"Reed's March," 7
"Republican Spirit," **155**
"Richmond Blues," 147, **162**
"Richmond Hill," **159**, 213
"Ricket's Ride," 8
"Rickett's Hornpipe," 24, 27, **41**, 90, 92
"Ridge, The," **159**
"Rifle Waltz," 91, **117**
Riley, Edward, 23
Riley's Flute Melodies (Edward Riley), 23, 25, 27, 33
"Riney [Ranz] des Vaches," 5, 7
Ring, Elizabeth, 3
"Rise Columbia," 7
Rogers, Helen, 93
"Rondo," 25, **57**
Root, George F., 88

"Rose, The," 25, 32, **48**, 99, 213
"Rose on the Mountain," **164**
"Rose Tree, The," 8, 10, **20**, **21**, 184
Rosina (William Shield), 32
"Roslin Castle," 7, 24–25, **37**, **57**
Ross, Gilbert, 84
"Roving Sailor," **198**
"Rustin Reel," **136**

Sacchini, 7
Sacks, Howard and Judith Rose, 152
"Sailor's Hornpipe," 80
"Sally Goodin," **204**
"Savourna Delish," 7, 10–11, **12**, **13**, 14; lyrics, 10–11, 32, 213
"Saw Ye My Father," 8
Sawmill, or the Yankee Trick (Micah Hawkins), 75
Scales, George, 67, 70, 72, 84–85
Schubert, Franz, 102
Scots-Irish, 151
Scots Musical Museum (James Johnson), 178
"Scotts Favorite," **166**, 213
"Seasons, The," 8
Self-Instructor for the Violin (Elias Howe), 62–63, 87
"Serenade," 8
"Sett of Cotillions in the Key of C from Nelson Matthewson," **134–35**
Seward, Philander, 2, 19, 22–61, 70, 75, 87, 139, 174–75, 177, 213–14; family, 22
Seward, Thankful Parmalee, 19
Seward, William III, 19
Shannon, Thomas W., 4
"Shawl Dance," 8
"Shelbyville," **199**
Shield, William, 32
"Shoe Strings," 25, **53**
"Sich a Gittin' Upstairs." *See* "Such a Getting Up Stairs"
"Silver Moon," 8
"Silver Star," 7
singing schools, 4, 9, 14
"Sittin' on a Rail," 150
"Slighted Jenny," **157**
Small, Adam Forest, 186
Smith, Christopher, 93, 152

Smith, J. C., 88
Smith, O. C., 121
Snowden family, 152
"Soldier's Joy," 75, **76**
"Soldier's Return, The," 24, 32, **42**, 87
"Sontag Polka," 62, 92, 102
"Sontag Polka Medley," 91, **120**
"Southegan Bridge by Herrick," 7
"Sow's Tail," 217
"Speckled Apron," **201**
"Speed the Plough," 102, 143, 146–47, 149, **156**
"Spirit of David R. [Hamblen]," **202**, 212
"Spirit of Ireland," 8
"Spring Waltz," 91, **118**
"Sta Cecilia," 8
"Star-Spangled Banner, The," 82
"Sterne's Maria," 7
Stony Brook and Smithtown Fusiliers, 80
"Stony Brook Hornpipe," **107**
"Stop Jig," 94–95
"Streamlet that Flow'd Round her Cot," 7
"Such a Getting Up Stairs," 92, 150, 153–54, **168**
Surprise Symphony (Haydn), 8
Suvorov, Alexander Vasilyevich, 87
"Suwarrow's Grand March," 87
"Sweeney, Joel," 150, 154
"Sweet Ellen," 8
"Swiss Battle Song," 8
"Swiss Guard's March," 7, 14, **15**

"Their Groves of Sweet Myrtle," 25
"There's Three Good Fellows Down in Yon Glens," 7
"Thomas, I Cannot," **182**
Thomas Moore's *Irish Melodies*, 10, 89
Thompson, Ichabod, 173
"Three Forks of Cumberland," 190, 195, **196**, 212
"Through the Green Fields," 24, 26, **37**
"Thunder Hornpipe," 90, **110**
"Tid Re I," 24, **39**
Tilton, Wm. B., violin modification, 84
"Tink a Tink," 8
"'Tis the Last Rose of Summer," 89, **106**
Titus, Mr., 126
"To an Early Bee," 25, 60 (text)
"Trumpet March," 8
"Tullochgorum," 92, **122**

"Turkey in the Straw," 32, 184, **203**
"Turkish Quick Step," 8
Twain, Mark, 152
"Twenty-Second of February," 147, **161**
"Two Sisters, The," **156**

untitled tunes (transcribed by A. P. Hamblen), **201, 203, 204, 209**

"Vacant Chair, The," 88–89, **106**
"Valencienn's March," 24, **36, 41**
Vermont Historical Society, vii
"Vicar and Moses," 8, **20, 21**
"Vice President's March," 7
"Village Festival," 102
"Villalave," **160**
"Vinton's Hornpipe," 90, **110**
Virginia Cotillions, 145
Virginia Minstrels, 150, 152
Virginia Reels, xi, 139–70, 212; dance steps, 143
"Von Weber's Favorite Waltz," 82

"Wake, Dinah, Wake," 102
"Waltz," 7–8
"Waltz by Beethoven," 8
"Waltz Quadrille," 102
Wappinger tribe of Native Americans, 19
"Wareham" (hymn), 7
Washburn, H. S., 88
Washington, George, 11, 178
"Washington's Grand March," 172, **176**, 177
"Washington's March," 1, **176**, 177
"Washington's New March," 177
"Washington's Ode," 25, **29, 50**
Watts, Isaac, 7, 16
Wells, Paul F., vii, 217
"Wheeler's Polka," **120**
"When the Hollow Drum," 8
"Whiskey Barrel," 158, 213
"Whistle O'er the Lave O't," 29
"White Cockade," 190, **199**, 213
Whitmore, O. A., 91, 118
Wig, Christian, 184–85
Willbourn, Mr., 174–75
Williams College, 7
Williams, Vivian, 92
Willig, George, Jr., 142–47

Willig, George Sr., 147
"Willis Grand March," 8
"Willis Quick Step," 8
Winans, Robert, 152
wind bands, 73
Winner, Septimus, 95
"Winter" (hymn), 7, 9
"Winter Beauties, Waltz Quadrille, The," 102
"With Flag and Fleet," 195
Wittman, A., 102
"Woodpecker Tapping the Hollow Beach [sic] Tree," 96
Woodstock, Windsor County, Vermont, 63–64, 65 (map)

"X Hornpipe," 90, **107**

"Yankee Doodle," 75
"Ye Lads of True Spirit," 7
"Yell, Yell," 217
"Young Widow," 8

ABOUT THE AUTHOR

Chris Goertzen is professor of music history at the University of Southern Mississippi. His earlier books are *Fiddling for Norway: Revival and Identity*; *Southern Fiddlers and Fiddle Contests*; *Made in Mexico: Tradition, Tourism, and Political Ferment in Oaxaca*; and *George P. Knauff's* Virginia Reels *and the History of American Fiddling,* the latter three published by University Press of Mississippi.

Printed in the United States
By Bookmasters